ISSUES IN POLITICAL THEORY

Political Theory has undergone a remarkable development in recent years. From a state in which it was once declared dead, it has come to occupy a central place in the study of Politics. Both political ideas and the wide-ranging arguments to which they give rise are now treated in a rigorous, analytical fashion, and political theorists have contributed to disciplines as diverse as economics, sociology and law. These developments have made the subject more challenging and exciting, but they have also added to the difficulties of students and others coming to the subject for the first time. Much of the burgeoning literature in specialist books and journals is readily intelligible only to those who are already well-versed in the subject.

Issues in Political Theory is a series conceived in response to this situation. It consists of a number of detailed and comprehensive studies of issues central to Political Theory which take account of the latest developments in scholarly debate. While making original contributions to the subject, books in the series are written especially for those who are new to Political Theory. Each volume aims to introduce its readers to the intricacies of a fundamental political issue and to help them find their way through the detailed, and often complicated, argument that that issue has attracted.

PETER JONES
ALBERT WEALE

ISSUES IN POLITICAL THEORY

Series editors: PETER JONES and ALBERT WEALE

Published
David Beetham: **The Legitimation of Power**
Tom Campbell: **Justice** (2nd edition)
John Horton: **Political Obligation**
Peter Jones: **Rights**
Albert Weale: **Democracy** (2nd edition)

Forthcoming
Raymond Plant: **Equality**

Issues in Political Theory series
Series Standing Order

ISBN 978-0-230-54393-5 hardback
ISBN 978-0-230-54394-2 paperback
(outside North America only)

You can receive future titles in this series as they are published by a placing a stand-ing order. Please contact your bookseller or, in the case of difficulty, write to us at the address below with your name and address, the title of the series and an ISBN quoted above.

Customer Services Department, Palgrave Macmillan Ltd,
Houndmills, Basingstoke, Hampshire RG21 6XS, England

Democracy

Second Edition

Albert Weale

First edition 1999
Second edition 2007

Published by
PALGRAVE MACMILLAN
Houndmills, Basingstoke, Hampshire RG21 6XS and
175 Fifth Avenue, New York, N.Y. 10010
Companies and representatives throughout the world

PALGRAVE MACMILLAN is the global academic imprint of the Palgrave Macmillan division of St. Martin's Press, LLC and of Palgrave Macmillan Ltd. Macmillan® is a registered trademark in the United States, United Kingdom and other countries. Palgrave is a registered trademark in the European Union and other countries.

ISBN-13: 978-0-333-94876-7   hardback
ISBN-10: 0-333-94876-9   hardback
ISBN-13: 978-0-333-94875-0   paperback
ISBN-10: 0-333-94875-0   paperback

This book is printed on paper suitable for recycling and made from fully managed and sustained forest sources.

A catalogue record for this book is available from the British Library.

A catalog record for this book is available from the Library of Congress.

10   9   8   7   6   5   4   3   2   1
16   15   14   13   12   11   10   09   08   07

Printed and bound in China

321.8
L 58696 k

For Jan – again

Contents

List of Tables

Acknowledgements

Someone must have said that it would be a good idea to produce a second edition of *Democracy*. I cannot now remember who it was, or why I agreed. But agree I did, and here is the result.

Perhaps it was Steven Kennedy at Palgrave Macmillan, in which case I am sure that he will have regretted the thought on many occasions as my other responsibilities delayed production. Peter Jones was certainly encouraging, and I thank him, as always, for his intellectual stimulus and personal support.

One theme of this book is that we should not separate the normative study of political ideas from the empirical study of political systems. I suppose this is natural for someone working at Essex, where theorists and empirical political scientists rub shoulders regularly. I thank Sarah Birch, Tony King, David Sanders and Hugh Ward for illuminating conversations on the topic of this book. I also thank my colleagues in the Political Theory Workshop for their constant stimulus. They include Michael Freeman, Jason Glynos, David Howarth, Sheldon Leader and Aletta Norval. Ian O'Flynn, who spent some time at Essex, was instrumental in getting me to take deliberative democracy seriously. Ian Budge will also see more than a passing influence. I am sorry that Richard Bellamy is no longer at Essex to continue our stimulating exchanges.

Ron Johnston was encouraging about the first edition (always something that authors value), as was John Street. Two anonymous reviewers for the publisher were helpful. One gave some useful advice on the proposed revised version; the other highlighted the faults in the penultimate draft, to which I hope I have responded. It was a pleasure once again to work with Keith Povey, with the great help of Sue Dickinson, as the copy-editor. Of course, the remaining faults are all mine.

The dedication records debts greater than I could ever hope to repay – once again.

ALBERT WEALE

Preface

Political theorists are awkward people. They question what everyone else takes for granted. It seems clear that democracy means rule by the people and that it is a better form of government than all others. More democracy would mean more responsive governments, more socially representative politicians and policies for the many rather than the few, as decided by majority rule. Where political authority is not accountable to the people through elections, it should be made such, otherwise it is illegitimate. Democracy is government of the people, by the people and for the people. These at least are the commonplaces of democratic societies.

It is these commonplaces that political theorists question. They wonder how a people is constituted. They are puzzled by the thought that a section of the people, even if it a majority section, should be able to rule the whole. They ask whether democracy really is a better form of government than all others and how someone might make such a claim. They dissect the different senses of representation and contend for varying rules of decision. They ask how political authority can be divided territorially or among different political institutions. In good times such questions have only theoretical interest. In hard times, the answers that different people give may come to have practical consequences.

This is a second attempt to deal systematically with a range of these questions on my part. Although it takes the form of a second edition of a work that was first published in 1999, I have made so many changes and added so much material that it is in many ways a quite different book. For those familiar with the earlier edition, it may be helpful if I set out some of the principal changes that I have introduced, as well as state some points of continuity. New readers may wish to move straight to the first chapter, although the Preface is a convenient summary of the principal points of the overall argument.

There were two main theses advanced in the first edition, both of which I have retained in this version. One was substantive, the other methodological. The substantive thesis is that those political systems that we know of as democracies can best be understood in normative terms as institutional arrangements embodying the values of common interests, political equality and a recognition of human fallibility. Other values commonly associated with democracies – including consent, autonomy and popular sovereignty – are either at odds with democracy or should play only a subordinate role in our normative understanding. In effect, these notions need to be explicated in terms of the central values of interests, equality and fallibility, rather than contributing an independent understanding of democracy.

One ambition of the first edition was to bring together the normative and empirical studies of democracy. That ambition was related to the methodological thesis, which was that we could see the centrality of the substantive values if we used a version of the comparative method. In particular, we needed to compare an ideal-type non-democracy with democracies considered as a class in order to identify what distinctive values were to be found in the latter. I called this method 'derivation', seeing it as an extension of Feinberg's (1970) characterization of a 'world without rights' as a device for understanding the nature and value of rights. I was also influenced by Sidgwick's (1891) discussion in *The Elements of Politics* of the individualistic minimum as a way of setting a benchmark standard for arguments about the role of the state in society. It was an important part of the methodological thesis that we could make an intellectual connection between the concerns of normative political theory and the approach of comparative empirical political science.

The values of democracy need to be understood in the context of the circumstances of politics. In the first edition of this book, I introduced this idea by analogy with Rawls's (1999a, pp. 109–12) account of the circumstances of justice, a notion that Rawls himself acknowledged as stemming from the work of Hume (1739–40) as well as Hart (1961) and Lucas (1966). In using this term I meant to indicate more than the nature of political predicaments in general. Rather the purpose was to draw attention to the empirical circumstances within which those political predicaments emerged. The idea of the circumstances of politics in a narrower sense has been used by Waldron (1999a, pp. 101–3), defining those circumstances in terms of the fact that members of a group have to make a common decision even in the face of disagreement about what that decision should be. This situation, however, as Sammy Finer (1970, p. 15) pointed out many years ago, is just a definition of politics, which arises from the predicament of a number of actors needing to agree on a common policy when some at least advance as desirable mutually exclusive alternative courses of action. By contrast with this notion I am, when speaking about the circumstances of politics, referring to something more specific, namely the general empirical features of social life such as constrained generosity, bounded rationality and a context of practical decision making.

The circumstances of politics as a general characterization of social life can be set against the understanding that political science gives us of how different democracies function in practice. The normative method of comparison by derivation needs therefore to be complemented by the empirical comparative method as found in writers such as Lijphart (1984, 1999) and Powell (1982, 2000). Empirical political scientists are concerned to understand how observable and measurable variations in institutional arrangements affect government performance. As well as accepting the general distinction between direct and indirect democracies, which is a commonplace of democratic theory, Lijphart and Powell distinguish among representative governments by reference to electoral laws and the variations in the power of the executive over the legislature. Following them, I marked this distinction in the first edition by referring to 'Westminster systems' and 'representational' systems. (Incidentally, I inexcusably forgot to note that the term 'representational' had been used by Powell in his 1982 book, an omission I hereby willingly correct.) I also picked up a suggestion implicit in some of Powell's work that we could distinguish a third variant of representative government, which I termed 'constitutionalist'.

It is one thing to set two comparative methods alongside one another. It is another to show that they have some logical or theoretical connection. Why should those interested in normative theory think that there is anything of relevance in empirical political science, or why should those concerned with empirical analysis bother about questions concerning the values that are embodied in institutional arrangements?

Philosophers have long been used to using the method of isolation tests. They ask questions of the following sort. Is there value in pleasure if the person experiencing the pleasure in not conscious of the fact (Moore, 1903, pp. 93–4)? What would we do if, under the command of a local military or police commander, we had the choice between shooting one person ourselves or allowing ten persons to be shot by the authorities (Williams, 1973, pp. 98–9)? Or would our experiences be as valuable if they were produced by an experience machine, as they would be if they resulted from our own actions (Nozick, 1974, pp. 42–5)?

Non-philosophers are liable to become impatient of such isolation tests, for, as the examples I have cited suggest, they seem so remote from the real world that they hardly seem to have relevance for the pressing moral and political problems that we face. This impatience is too quick, however. When philosophers use isolation tests, they are merely extending Mill's (1843, book 3, chapter viii) method of differences, according to which if two or more instances of a phenomenon have only one circumstance in common, then that circumstance is the cause of the phenomenon. In the normative case, the application of the method of difference is simply a way of seeking to identify what is really of moral or political value in a situation. For example, if we think that wilderness protection is important, is that because we think it important that individuals know that wilderness areas exist or because we think that such areas have intrinsic value? To help us answer this question, we use the isolation test of imagining a world without knowing subjects to explore how far our convictions about the value of nature are human-centred rather than nature-centred. Similarly, we turn to the imaginary experience machine to explore how far our valuation of experience turns on the qualities of the experience (its pleasurability, say) or the way in which the experience arose (as a result of our own efforts or by some other means).

When we are doing normative theory we do not have to use isolation tests. Some theorists think of normative theory as a form of anthropological explication, laying out in a systematic way the values that are implicit in a political culture. They assert that the only thing we can say in defence of our values is that immoral actions are the sort of thing *we* do not do (Rorty, 1989, p. 59). However, if we aspire to a critical morality in addition to a positive morality (that is to say, if we wish to develop principles upon which we can criticize existing cultural practices, such as discrimination and cultural exclusion), then we shall need something more than just the explication of prevailing norms and values. We shall need some way of exploring what really is important in actual or possible practices. Isolation tests are one such method.

Of course, like any other method of inquiry, isolation tests can be well or badly done. Some tests work well for the purpose they are intended to serve and others work poorly. My own view is that, for the purposes of democratic theory (I cannot speak of other normative issues), we should differentiate among types of political system in ways that are recognizable extensions of feasible political practices and institutions. For example, I do not think that there has ever been a minimal state performing only night-watchman functions in the way I suppose in Chapter 3. However, during the eighteenth century, the British state operating under the constitutional constraints on the executive of the Glorious Revolution, as well as under the common law, came close to such a political disposition. So, it is not too great a leap of the imagination to see what might be involved in minimal state arrangements, taking as our cue the actual arrangements that have historically prevailed. Similarly, political theorists have made much of the experience of Athens. Historically, the picture conjured up by theorists is faulty or one-sided. However, the idealization of the Athenian *polis* is a coherent reference point from which to understand the values of participation and political equality.

If this approach has any validity, then it also answers the question that the empirical comparativist sometimes puts to the theorist: why should there be anything of interest empirically in the normative evaluation? Political institutions and practices embody political values. If certain groups are disenfranchised within a political system, then there is a breach of the principle of political equality. If governments continually fall from office only to be replaced by equally short-lived governments, then there is a loss of political stability. The facts are clear in such cases: such a proportion of the population is excluded or governments only occupy so many months in office. The values supervene upon those facts. We characterize the disenfranchisement as a breach of political equality or we evaluate the constant churning of governments as a loss of stability. The conditions under which we can validly assert that something of value is involved include empirical conditions but are not limited to those conditions. Indeed, there would be no point in trying to understand the empirical unless we thought the values involved were important.

Here we come back to the isolation test. We may be clear that excluding people from the vote is a breach of political equality, but what would we say if some citizens are not formally excluded but are so discouraged by poverty or discrimination from using their votes that their political voices are not heard or are muted? Does such a situation constitute a breach of the principle of political equality? We can answer this question only in the way that philosophers approach their own isolation tests: by considering a range of cases and identifying where the distinctions come. Logically, we identify coherent possible political worlds within the range of the circumstances of politics. Statistically, we do sensitivity analyses.

The methodological approach I have set out above was one of the contributions that I hoped the first edition of *Democracy* would make to the literature. Although I have made many detailed amendments and elaborations in respect of these arguments, the material relating to the comparative approach in Chapters 2 and 3 is less changed than much else in the book. By contrast, subsequent chapters develop the argument in ways that are quite distinct from that of the first edition (except Chapter 9 where there is much continuity), although I hope that the new developments are consistent with the original direction of thinking. The main points are as follows.

Deliberation. One omission in the first edition was the absence of an explicit discussion of the role of deliberation in a democracy. This is more or less equivalent to saying that it omitted a discussion of 'deliberative democracy'. There was some discussion of Habermas's work in the discussion of autonomy, and I also made some passing references to deliberative polling. But I did not treat the subject of deliberation with as much care as I should have done. The reason was quite simple: the book was already delayed a great deal, and to discuss the burgeoning arguments in the field would simply have added extensively to those delays.

A new Chapter 4 now rectifies this omission. I have not sought to cover the literature on deliberative democracy extensively, partly because it is so large and diverse and partly because there are good surveys and anthologies already available. Rather, I have sought to relate issues of deliberation to concerns about the central issues of fallibility, political equality and collective interests. In this context, I discuss the approach of Habermas (1996), which, whilst showing Habermas's usual considerable accomplishments, also seems to me to rest upon an overoptimistic view of the relationships between a dialogic method and its upshot in truth or validity. The more modest variant of deliberative democracy in the work of Gutmann and Thompson (1996, 2004) over-stresses to my mind the possibility of agreement through accommodation and its link to political equality.

One theme that runs throughout this chapter is a concern for the relationship between how we understand knowledge to arise and discursive consensus. To my mind, consensus does not stand in a constitutive relation to truth and validity. That is an epistemological claim. A democratic polity needs to leave open the possibilities of dissent and difference to bring about what is in the common interest. That is a claim in political theory. The best way to link these claims is via a currently unfashionable empiricist reading of method. That at least is the general thread running through this chapter.

Autonomy. As I have noted above, the main substantive thesis of the first edition, which I have kept, was that democratic values were best understood in terms of the protection and promotion of common interests constrained by political equality and in conditions of human fallibility. Well-functioning democratic government is rightful government to the common good, as best as fallible human beings can manage.

One value not included is this account was autonomy, despite its being a value regularly associated with democratic theory. Strictly speaking, what was excluded was a strong version of autonomy, and not just the principle that persons are generally the best judges of their own welfare. I still maintain this position. A strong conception of individual autonomy is incompatible, I argue, with a sense of the common purposes that a political association needs if it is to act on democratically determined principles. Another way of looking at the same point is to say that Robert Paul Wolff (1970) was right to say that a strong notion of autonomy more obviously implies anarchy rather than democracy. Despite some ripostes to Wolff, from intelligent and able theorists, the anarchist reading still seems to me to have the better of the case.

However, I have now located this discussion in a broader discussion of political participation. One serious omission in the first edition was a failure to discuss the classical view that a democratic polity embodied a form of freedom and self-government for its citizens. The claim in Chapter 5 is that this classical view, despite its considerable pedigree among political theorists, can only be maintained by relying upon either or both of two fallacies. The first is a fallacy of distribution, according to which what is true of all is true of each, so that if a political community is free, then we can infer that its members are free. This is like saying that if parliament is an august institution, then all members of parliament are august individuals – an obvious error of reasoning. The second fallacy is to assume that there is a spontaneous identification between individuals and the polity to which they belong, as was supposed of Periclean Athens. That is fallacious because even the idealizers of Periclean Athens think that its moment is now passed.

Representation. Despite receiving some positive comments on the chapter on representation in the first edition, I felt unhappy with the discussion for a variety of reasons. Partly to gain some perspective on the issues, I embarked on a thorough rereading of Hanna Pitkin's *The Concept of Representation* some years ago. This edition of *Democracy* will be published in the same year as the fortieth anniversary of

Pitkin's original work, and I hope that my recasting of the chapter on representation more explicitly in the light of Pitkin's discussion will be regarded as a small tribute to that great and scholarly book. I have dared to add to the categories that Pitkin developed but I have also taken up the suggestion, dropped in almost nonchalantly towards the end of the book, that it is the system of representation, rather than the role characterization of representatives, that is important.

Aggregation. The original edition argued for the importance of the median voter, building on foundational work in social choice theory concerning the characterization of the majority principle. Partly as a result of work recently published and partly as a result of some current research in which I am engaged with my colleague Hugh Ward, I now realize that the original argument can no longer stand. It was too quick and did not pay enough attention to the conditions under which the median voter was justifiably decisive when there were more than two alternatives among which a decision had to be made. Fortunately, and very much thanks to the work done by Hugh Ward on the formal side, the argument for the justification of the decisiveness of the median voter still holds, and in Chapter 7 I rely upon that still-unpublished joint work.

Constitutionalism. The original chapter posed the problem of constitutionalism as one involving a choice between the values of limited government and the values of popular government. Although I have kept that original formulation, I now realize that the problem is deeper than I had originally thought. Following a brief but tantalizing discussion in H.L.A. Hart's (1961) *The Concept of Law*, I have developed the problem as one requiring us to formulate a theory of democracy without the mythical idea of popular sovereignty. (Sometime there is an article to be written on political theory before Rawls's *Theory of Justice* in which the work of Pitkin and Hart would feature prominently as unexploited sources of inspiration – this is not to disparage the greatness of *Theory*.) The reformulation has a number of implications. It means, for example, that we cannot interpret constitutional restrictions on majority rule as a form of popular self-binding, and nor can we see supreme courts as acting according to democratically determined regimes of political order. On the other hand, we can no longer identify one part of the system of secondary rules with democracy without considering the full set.

The International Dimension. In his generally favourable review of the first edition in the *American Political Science Review*, Richard

Bellamy challenged me to apply the theory advanced in the first edition to international organizations including the European Union. Since 1999 I have tried to take up this challenge, a task that has proved more difficult than I originally thought. Chapter 10 takes a broader look at the problems for political theory posed by increasing international interdependence. Readers will see that I am sceptical about transposing the institutions and practices of democracy that are suitable for nation-states to the international level. It seems to me to be as mistaken as seeking to transpose to the national level institutions and practices suitable for city-states. However, some account is needed of how political systems can relate democratically to the international order, and Chapter 10 is an attempt to work out the implications for this problem from the general account of democratic values that I set out in the central part of the theory.

These changes have produced a book that is some 25,000 words longer than the original, even after I have dropped one whole chapter. I reckon that little more than a third remains intact given how much has been rewritten. Even where the topics and substance of the argument are the same, I have tried to improve the expression. How far I have achieved a coherent and plausible argument is, of course, for the reader to judge.

1 The Theoretical Challenges of Democracy

In the last twenty years, there has occurred a 'global resurgence of democracy' (Diamond and Plattner, 1996). The breach of the Berlin Wall in 1989 and the subsequent collapse of communism in central and eastern Europe removed one of the major ideological and political challenges to democratic government not only in Europe but throughout the world. The failure of Latin American military dictatorships to resolve economic problems, as well as their appalling human rights records, dealt severe blows to their attempts to establish a non-democratic form of political legitimacy and paved the way to the restoration of civilian democratic government in the 1980s. The ending of apartheid in South Africa and the coming of mass democracy showed the association between democratic government and the ideal of political equality in which members of the same society were not divided into first- and second-class citizens. Political challenges to the 'soft authoritarianism' of east Asian societies in Korea and Taiwan, as well as the persisting strength of the democratic movement in Hong Kong, surprised those who thought that Asian culture was built upon a principle of respect for those in authority. Democratization in places as diverse as South Africa, Argentina, Poland and South Korea occurred with a speed and vigour that surprised informed and knowledgeable observers. Formerly closed, authoritarian political systems became open to new influences and political ideas. These events and trends prompted many observers at the time to claim that 'we are all democrats now', having reached 'the end of history' (Fukuyama, 1989) or, to put the point less poetically but more accurately, the end of political controversy about systems of government. Democracy – it would seem – has ceased to be a matter of contention and has become a matter of convention.

1

Yet this story, attractive as it is to those who favour democracy, needs to be qualified in various ways. The legacy of authoritarian rule is far from extinct in many parts of the world. In the lead-up to the handing over of Hong Kong from the UK to China, the Chinese government installed its own appointed legislative body to replace the democratically elected legislative council. Within China itself, political dissent has been suppressed, most notably in the violent putting down of the democracy demonstrations in Tiananmen Square and the subsequent persecution and imprisonment of political dissidents. The Russian government under Putin has drawn upon the traditional appeal to the strong leader to control economic activity. The once optimistic forecasts of the extent to which South Africa would lead other African nations towards a democratic future have had to be qualified by the failure of democratic competition to take root in many countries. Resurgent populism in parts of Latin America raises the question of how far democratically responsive governments can act in the best interests of their constituents. If democracy comes in waves (Huntington, 1991), the reverse currents can be surprisingly strong.

The beginning of the twenty-first century also marked new challenges for established democracies and raised questions about the extent to which their practices and institutions could meet those challenges. The attack on the World Trade Center in New York, on 11 September 2001, led to not only a confrontation with al Qua'eda and others intent on attacking democracies, but also serious questions as to whether the US government's response, both in its security legislation and the internments in Guantanamo Bay, were consistent with democratic norms. Military activity in Afghanistan and Iraq raises deep and difficult questions about the extent to which democratic government can be imposed upon societies by outsiders. As Fukayama (2006, p. 116) has written, there was an assumption by those in the US administration that democracy was 'a default condition to which societies would revert once liberated from dictators', and consequently an underestimation of the complexity of the conditions that need to be in place for democracy to grow and flourish. Firmness of conviction is not enough to meet the intellectual challenges that democracy poses.

These issues are ones of practical policy, but they also raise important questions about democratic values. If democracy is justified as the best form of government, does it not follow that there is an obligation on democratic governments and peoples to ensure its spread throughout the world? Moreover, if there is a connection between regime type and international relations, so that democracies tend not to fight wars with one another, then the question of political principle is how far democracies have an obligation to promote the conditions for international peace. Yet, well-established principles of self-government and non-intervention, themselves traditionally part of democratic political culture, would counsel caution in the use of measures to ensure that democracy comes to as many people as possible. The challenges posed for democracies are practical and political, but these practical and political choices themselves depend for their resolution upon normative principles and values.

Moreover, even in well-established political systems that pride themselves on being democratic, there are persistent and pertinent questions about the performance of the political system. The US presidential election of 2000, in which the inefficiency of electoral administration in Florida led to a disputed outcome, revealed that the details of democratic practice can raise large issues of principle. Italy's general election of 2006 led to a close result in which it appeared at one time as though Berlusconi would seek to protect himself from corruption charges by clinging on to office. More generally, falling or low rates of voting in general elections have led observers to wonder about the strength of the affective bonds that link citizens to their political systems, and declining rates of party membership and activity have led some to say that post-parliamentary democracy is the form of the future. Increasing calls for the use of referendums to decide important matters of public policy indicate the growth of 'critical citizens' (Norris, 1999) and the desire to supplant traditional institutions of political democracy. Crouch has even characterized the political systems of traditional democracies as one of 'post-democracy' (Crouch, 2004).

Pessimism about the ability of democratic institutions to perform well in their traditional social and economic environments is reinforced for some when considering the extent to which political authority is becoming an increasingly international phenomenon. The most advanced example of international political integration is the European Union, but it is commonplace to talk of a 'democratic deficit' in the decision-making procedures of the Union. Indeed, it has been said that if the European Union itself applied to become a member state, it would be rejected because its political system was insufficiently democratic. Moreover, it is clear that this is not simply an oversight or accident of history, but that executive government by a political elite was integral to the Monnet method of European integration in the post-war years (Featherstone, 1994) and reflects the interests of key political actors at national and international levels. If we turn to other forms of international organization, there have been calls for their democratization so that they institutionalize some form of direct accountability to those on whose behalf they are making decisions (Held, 1995).

It might be said that these examples merely show how political practice can lag behind political theory, and it takes time for policy to adjust to new circumstances and put democratic arrangements in place. According to this argument, we should expect that in time political reforms will create institutions embodying democratic norms. However, it is not so easy to draw this conclusion. Suppose that democracy is not a default condition of human societies, either in terms of social, economic and cultural conditions or in terms of the values and political principles that people find persuasive. After all, democratic principles are neither self-evident nor universally accepted. Authoritarian rule, at least of a soft kind, has been defended by arguments, sometimes advanced in good faith, to the effect that democratic practices are culturally specific and that in some cultures, for example those influenced by Confucianism, authoritarian systems of government are not only politically defensible but morally justifiable (Freeman, 1996). If this is so, a choice for democracy represents a choice for a certain set of values.

Moreover, if we look at influential strands of contemporary political theory within the western tradition, it is clear that some theorists at least express considerable scepticism about democracy as a system of government. One clear example is to be found in Robert Nozick's (1974) libertarian theory of the state. Although he subsequently recanted his earlier views (Nozick, 1989, pp. 286–96), Nozick's 'invisible hand' theory of political legitimacy left no clear room for democratic institutions. According to this theory, the state emerges from a series of bilateral contracts that individuals make with protective associations in a Lockean state of nature. Yet, there is no reason to assume that the contractual relations between individuals and the protective associations that guard them should be democratic. Indeed, according to the logic of contractual arrangements, it would presumably be up to the contracting parties to negotiate how protective associations would make their decisions. So, on Nozick's account, even monopoly suppliers of protective services might be more fully constrained in their actions by the contestability of their market position through the possibility of other suppliers entering the market than by the institution of democratic procedures.

Sceptical doubts about democracy are not confined to the libertarian portion of the political spectrum, however. In many of his essays,

Dworkin (1986, 1996 and 2000) gives primacy of place to the independent judiciary as interpreter of the political morality of a community, rather than to its elected legislators. Although there are some issues left over from constitutional interpretation on which Dworkin thinks that legislators are free to act, many of the most fundamental questions that a political community can face – equality in employment and education, freedom of association and protest, or the imposition of censorship – are off-limits to legislative action, once the judges have interpreted the political constitution by reference to the principle of political equality. To be sure, Dworkin has sought to defend his political theory as offering a particular account of democratic politics. Yet, his critics have seen in his privileging of judicial modes of collective decision making a way of evacuating democratic politics of serious content. Waldron (1999a, 1999b), for example, has argued that not only is Dworkin's position on judicial review unsustainable but also that the account of democratic politics to which it belongs is shared more generally with other constitutional theorists who neglect the 'dignity of legislation', that is the value of elected representatives making choices on behalf of the community.

   In short, despite many celebrations of democracy and democratization, there are serious questions about the legitimate scope and range of the authority of democratic institutions among political activists, observers and theorists. Once we abandon the view that the development of democratic practice is an inevitable consequence of the progress of history or a default condition of human societies and recognize that articulate political theories are often sceptical of democracy as an ideal, we see that certain questions of political principle cannot be avoided if democracy is to be properly understood. Why is democracy valuable, and can it be justified as being better than alternative non-democratic forms of government? What assumptions about the moral standing of persons lie behind democratic practice, and how far are these assumptions justified? How is democratic performance to be evaluated, and what would count as an improvement in performance? Would an increase in the participation of citizens making political decisions be an enhancement or deterioration in the quality of democracy? What can properly be expected of political representatives? Why should certain features of democratic practice, for example rule by the majority, be thought superior to other ways of making political decisions, for example judicial decision making? How do democratic values relate to the values of constitutional government in general, especially personal freedom, human rights and the rule of law?

The most important feature of these questions is that they concern political values and the principles of political morality. Although responding to them in full may require us to understand how democratic institutions function in practice, we cannot answer such questions solely by empirical description and analysis. We also need to engage in normative argument. That is to say, we need to consider the political principles that ought to define the way that institutions are organized. Of course, no account of democracy can ignore empirical evidence, since we need to understand how the elements of democratic practice hang together and what the consequences are of adopting one set of institutions rather than another if we are to comprehend democracy adequately. Equally, however, we cannot rest content with empirical evidence alone, since the evaluation of institutions and practices requires us to have independent standards in terms of which we can judge the value and worth of practice. To say this, however, is to raise the question of how we might determine the content and form of such standards, and this in turn raises questions about the appropriate methods for approaching questions of political morality. What methods are appropriate to help us answer these normative questions?

Democratic principles and normative methods

Political institutions can be understood as embodying certain principles of action and these principles help define collectively valuable ways of life – or at least forms of collective life that are claimed to be valuable. To endorse a set of institutions is then to favour certain political principles. Conversely, the meaning of political principles is expressed through the institutions that they imply. Institutions such as the universal franchise in a democracy embody such principles as the following. In a democracy, citizens should not be unreasonably denied the opportunity to express their interests. No one should be regarded as especially competent to make political decisions but there should be a presumption of political equality in respect of political influence. Each person is to be regarded as the best judge of his or her own interests. Majority decision making is an appropriate way of making collective choices, at least for some issues. A minority should not be deprived of the opportunity to become a majority. These principles, in turn, suggest ways in which political institutions need to be reformed and improved.

To see how principles and practices interrelate, consider, as a simple example, the question of whether voting should be made compulsory in a democracy, a proposal that some (e.g. Lijphart, 1997) have advocated as a means of addressing political inequality. In some societies voting is compulsory, in others it is not. In all societies there is disagreement as to what the right practice should be, with some policy advocates arguing in favour of compulsory voting and others against. Moreover, these arguments are treated not simply as assertions of personal preference but as claims involving considerations of value and principle. That is to say, they are supposed to justify a particular way of organizing the practice of voting. Thus, those in favour of compulsory voting will appeal to an ideal of citizenship and the responsibilities that citizens have to maintain the integrity of democratic practices. Opponents will point to considerations of personal freedom or the extra administrative costs that compulsory voting requires. On both sides of the argument, however, there is a recognition that principles and values are relevant, even though the principles and values invoked may conflict with one another or presuppose very different conceptions of what a political order involves.

This example illustrates the three main elements that are involved in normative theory: conceptual clarification; the location of values or principles in broader understandings of political order and organization; and the evaluation of the extent to which the results of our analysis are in accordance with existing ethical and political commitments. Each of these dimensions has a role to play in a normative analysis.

Conceptual clarification is necessary because political values and principles are inevitably cast in general terms, and their force and implications are not self-evident. For example, even a principle as apparently straightforward as the claim that citizens should be required to vote in elections requires a great deal of clarification before its extent and practical implications can be understood. Thus, it will generally be admitted, even by those who are strongly committed to compulsory voting, that the obligation ought to be voided in circumstances of illness or accident, but then the exact character of those circumstances needs to be further determined. How much effort, for instance, may be reasonably expected of those who are ill or involved in accidents before they can be relieved of the duty to vote? Do political authorities have the responsibility to ensure that those travelling on polling day have facilities that are compatible with their other commitments? Moreover, if voting is to be made a duty, what penalties may be reasonably applied when citizens fail to act on the duty?

Yet conceptual clarification, though necessary, is by no means sufficient, because those urging the merits of different principles typically do so for a variety of reasons. In evaluating principles it is important to understand not only the scope of the principles themselves but how those principles are related to the reasons that are urged in their favour. In many policy contexts, principles may be justified by reference to hypothesized causal relationships. For example, compulsory voting may be urged as a way of increasing turn-out, on the assumption that democracies need high turn-outs to sustain their legitimacy. So, one way of evaluating the principle is to examine the extent to which its implementation in practice would have the effects claimed. Yet, even where principles are valued instrumentally, as defining practices that are thought to lead to valuable results, there is also a normative task involved in understanding what the valuable features of those consequences are. For example, is compulsory voting still valuable as a means of enhancing legitimacy if many voters spoil their ballot papers when they vote at the polling station or does compulsory voting in this case simply confirm voter disillusionment with the political system? Practices may, in addition, be thought to be intrinsically related to certain values. Thus, some people think of compulsory voting as a way of exhibiting an ethic of political responsibility among citizens, so that the consequences of the practice are less important than citizens acting in accordance with the practice.

Political principles are invoked in arguments about particular issues but they also have a more general scope. That is to say, they are used not only to assert solutions to particular issues of policy but also to define a stance, or political position, towards a wide range of questions. For example, when people defend the principle of majority rule as a proper way of making political decisions, they normally think about the principle as applying across a whole range of public policy, and not simply to one set of political issues. To be sure, they may think that there are limits to the scope of majority rule that may properly be imposed within a justifiable political morality – for example they may hold that a majority is not entitled to deprive a minority of its political rights – but here again the limits are defined in terms of classes of issues, and not simply to a one-off decision.

It is an important feature of any political morality, including democratic political morality, that because principles are general in scope they are prone to conflict with one another, at least if we remain at a common-sense level of understanding. Again the example of compulsory voting can be used to illustrate this possibility. Lijphart (1997) notes that those opposed to compulsory voting agree that it supports the democratic values of participation and equality, but they argue that it conflicts with the ideal of individual freedom. Moreover, someone might also claim that compulsory voting could have perverse effects even from the point of view of those concerned with equality. Suppose that if citizens failed to participate in an election, they lost the right to vote, perhaps for a specified period of time. This could lead to a situation in which the poor and socially excluded would be disproportionately disenfranchised contrary to the principle of political equality. We would thus have a potential conflict between the principle of political responsibility on the one hand and the principle of political equality on the other. In order to avoid incoherence, some priority has to be established between such principles.

It is at this point that the third element of normative method enters, namely 'reflective equilibrium'. So far as I am aware, this method was first formally adopted by Sidgwick (1901) and is now widespread in normative theory (compare Feinberg, 1973, p. 3; Rawls, 1999, pp. 18–19 and 4–5; and Scanlon, 1982). The crux of this method is that the body of political principles to which we subscribe and the priorities that we determine in cases of conflict should be consistent with our most deeply held convictions about what is right or wrong. For example, it is a widespread and deeply held conviction that slavery is wrong as an institution. But we only begin to think about the issue in a theoretical way (which is not to say that this is the only, or even most important, way in which we should think about it) when we consider the grounds upon which we regard slavery as being wrong.

Once we have identified these grounds we then consider other cases to which they might apply and see whether we come to the same judgement, or whether we think that some other principle applies in that case. For example, consider the case of whether non-citizens who were permanent residents in a country should be allowed the vote or not. Some people might think that being deprived of the vote in these circumstances was rather like being a slave, since residents without the vote are subject to the political will of others. A different view would hold that, because residents who are not citizens are always free to return to their original society, being deprived of the vote was quite unlike slavery. In order to solve this dispute, we need to become clearer in our minds about the values associated with condemnation of the paradigm case of slavery. We move from a situation in which our first-order moral judgements are clear – the practice of slavery is wrong – and we then seek both to understand the grounds of our condemnation and to extend our reasoning from that case to analogous cases.

The method of reflective equilibrium therefore works by seeking to build out from agreement on particular institutions to more general principles and thereafter to other institutions that may fall within the

compass of the principle. One general problem with the method, however, is that there may be relatively few fixed points that we can use for
reference. The example of slavery is generally a clear and compelling
one. However, even in that case our firm convictions may be altered
by circumstance. Rawls (1999a, p. 218) himself points out that there
may be conditions in which we would regard the institution of slavery
as acceptable, for example as an alternative to the practice of killing
prisoners of war. Leaving aside these sorts of remote counter-examples,
we may still find that there are few practices such as that of slavery
around which clear convictions converge and by reference to which
controversial examples can be judged. It is not difficult to come up
with circumstances in which some of the central elements in the practice of democracy cease to be firm objects of moral commitment. The
mass franchise can be questioned when it leads to the oppression of
minorities or the abolition of democracy itself; political equality can be
questioned if it exacerbates ethnic cleavages; and freedom of speech
and association may properly be restricted by the need to maintain
public order. In short, it is not difficult to see that certain principles
and the practices associated with them have value. It is difficult to weigh
exactly what value they have and how central they are therefore to the
firm convictions of our considered judgements.

The upshot of this, as Joel Feinberg (1973, p. 3) says, is that correct
general principles 'do not reveal themselves spontaneously, nor are they
deduced from self-evident principles'. We have to continue to move
between judgements, principles and institutional applications itera-
tively, in order to establish any conclusions, and to come to the point
of reflective equilibrium where we feel we have a reasonably comprehensive and coherent point of view. There is no such thing as logical
coercion, only the appeal to certain sorts of arguments, which we hope
that others will find convincing, plausible or justifiable. At some point
on this journey we may well lose certain people, whose views about
the judgements we make, the principles we hold or the institutions we
endorse differ from ours. But they, after all, are always free to define
their own reflective equilibrium.

The most serious challenge to the method of reflective equilibrium
comes from proponents of the view that political concepts are 'essentially contested' (Gallie, 1955–6). Consider, once again, the practice
of slavery. The concept of slavery can be stretched from its core use
to describe legally sanctioned property in human beings in classical
Mediterranean societies or the *ante-bellum* South of the USA to many
other cases. For example, some people think that contractual relations

in a market economy for those who do not own the means of production are a form of slavery, since under these circumstances some individuals have to work under the command of others in order to obtain their means of subsistence. Similarly, some feminists would characterize the situation of the traditional housewife as a form of domestic slavery, in which the woman has to work in the household to maintain the interests and privileges of the husband. This sort of conceptual stretching is integral to the development of languages of evaluation and appraisal (Hacking, 1992).

In his original formulation of the idea of essential contestability, Gallie argued that essentially contested concepts were marked out by their having two features. First, there were multiple criteria for their application to particular cases and, secondly, those contesting an application normally stressed the relevance of one criterion relative to others. For example, it may make a considerable difference to our view about the merits of compulsory voting whether we see it as a device by which all citizens can register their own personal interests under circumstances of equal political rights or whether we see it as the expression of a civic duty in which all citizens are supposedly looking towards some common good. In other words, how we resolve any particular case depends upon the way in which we understand the general institution of democracy, but there is no easy way of resolving disagreements about the way in which the overall institution is to be characterized. If this view is correct, it poses a problem for the method of reflective equilibrium. The method of reflective equilibrium requires some reasonably stable fixed points of judgement that are common to competing moral and political evaluations (thus slavery is a wrong for liberals, socialists and conservatives), but in the light of the thesis of essential contestability, there are very few such fixed and common points, because particular judgements are part of a web of interpretation about the overall character of the institution under discussion.

It would follow from this approach that we could never evaluate particular institutions but only compare distinct conceptions of democracy. For example, we might be able to identify the elements of liberal democracy versus republican democracy versus radical democracy versus cosmopolitan democracy, but we should find it difficult to come to any evaluative judgement about a particular practice within democracy. We could say that for a liberal democrat it would not make much sense to make voting compulsory, whereas it would make more sense from a republican point of view. However, we could only make these evaluations from within differing conceptions, and we would have no reason to expect any sort of reflective equilibrium in the absence of agreement on the assumptions of these broader conceptions. Since, so it might be argued, there is no reason to expect there to be any agreement, we cannot evaluate in any strong sense, but merely lay out the logic of competing and incommensurable conceptions.

There is some truth in the claim that the evaluation of particular practices is embedded in wider conceptual schemes and that whole conceptual schemes may be difficult to evaluate with respect to one another. Yet this need not be a reason for abandoning the method of reflective equilibrium. In the next chapter I suggest that there is a wide variety of institutional forms and practices that can be labelled 'democratic' in some sense. To be sure, these different forms of democracy rest upon different assumptions about participation, representation, deliberation, voting and the role of non-elected bodies such as courts, as well as making different claims upon the actions and consciences of individuals. It is, however, an open question, when we work through these issues, as to what conclusions we come to about particular practices. For example, certain participatory forms of democracy presuppose that many people can and will take an active interest in politics under the right circumstances. This is in part a view about what makes for political virtue and in part a view about the extent to which it is possible, empirically, to provide the right context of incentives and political culture to foster the disposition to participate. Empirical evidence, as well as normative argument, bear upon this question, and may well help to narrow down the range of alternatives that are plausible. To say this, however, is to suppose a certain relationship holds between normative argument and empirical analysis, and it is to the discussion of this question that I turn in the next section.

The circumstances of politics

I have so far distinguished normative arguments about the political morality of institutional arrangements from empirical arguments about how institutional arrangements work, what their consequences are and what the conditions are under which they emerge. However, a distinction does not imply an absence of relation, and in this section I suggest an account of this relation.

One argument that can be appealed to in this context is the doctrine that ought implies can. That is to say, if we hold to a principle implying that a certain set of institutions ought to be maintained or brought into being, then we are also committed to saying that such institutions can be feasibly maintained or introduced. For example, if I say that citizens ought legally to be required to vote, then I am implicitly saying that it is feasible or practicable for a society to institute such a practice. Of course, in the particular instance of compulsory voting, this may seem to be a trivial requirement. Since some societies such as Belgium and Australia require compulsory voting, it might seem obvious that such a practice could be adopted elsewhere. Even in this case, however, the assumption of empirical feasibility may be disputed, since there may be circumstances of political tradition or political culture that make compulsory voting feasible in some societies but not in others. When we consider more widespread or ambitious reforms that have been proposed – for example the institutionalization of greater mass public deliberation in the making of public policy or the selection of political representatives whose characteristics reflect more closely those whom they are supposed to be representing – then the grounds of empirical, as well as normative, dispute may widen even further. Nevertheless, to say that there is empirical dispute about the feasibility of a particular institutional arrangement is not to say that the empirical evidence, such as it is, is irrelevant to the evaluation of that arrangement. If we require of any principle that it should be practicably implementable, then we are saying that the only institutional arrangements we should countenance theoretically are those that have at least a *prima facie* claim to be considered feasible from our understanding of how societies work. For this reason we need to ensure that our principles of democratic theory are consistent with what political science currently understands as a feasible and workable set of institutions.

To impose this requirement of consistency between feasibility and moral desirability is often taken to be a purely formal matter, but it should be clear from the preceding argument that it is more than such, and indeed that it has some substantive implications for political theory. One effect, for example, is to rule out of consideration from the start certain sorts of utopian political theorizing. For some, this is a disadvantage, since utopian theorizing, it is argued, has its own purposes and merits, alerting us to possibilities that our lack of imagination, rather than any state of the world, rules out of bounds (see, for example, Goodwin, 1978, pp. 4–6; and Goodwin and Taylor, 1982, chapter 1). Despite this insight, I shall stick to the principle that ought implies can, recognizing its limitations. In part this is simply to make the argument manageable, but in part the decision rests upon the belief that there are no general reasons stemming from the findings of empirical political science to rule out a wide range of institutional democratic forms. There are in practice substantial institutional choices that confront policy makers and citizens in most democracies and selecting an alternative rests ultimately upon arguments of political principle.

However, the openness of this choice does not mean that anything goes, and we should recognize that the set of the ethically desirable is bounded by the set of the feasible. What can we say of relevance about these constraints of feasibility? Modern political theory normally aspires to be relatively modest about the empirical assumptions it makes. Modern analytic political theorists are unlikely, for instance, to go around sounding off with Bentham (1780, p. 11) that nature has placed mankind under two sovereign masters: pain and pleasure. The reason for this modesty largely stems, I suspect, from acknowledging that the social sciences have shown how difficult it is to establish such bold generalizations about how the world works together with an awareness of the great variety of human interaction and social behaviour. That being so, there is a desire not to make conclusions depend upon particular empirical claims that may well turn out to be false or limited in scope.

Despite this understandable modesty, one is unlikely to get very far in thinking about the institutional consequences of political principles unless one makes certain assumptions about how political institutions work. In particular, we need to consider the empirical conditions within which democratic political choices have to be made. These conditions are intended to embody middle-range empirical generalizations about how social and political institutions work. As empirical generalizations they are obviously prone to revision in the light of further experience, but on present understanding they are at least plausible.

A society can be characterized by a mixture of conflict and cooperation (compare Scharpf, 1989). A society is cooperative in so far as broad agreement on the structure of basic social institutions is necessary in order to provide the conditions under which individuals can escape the state of nature described by Hobbes (1651), that is the hypothetical condition in which life is solitary, poor, nasty, brutish and short. By avoiding the state of nature, individuals are free to enjoy the products of their labour and activity. The institutions that are necessary to create this productive surplus over and above what would be achieved in the state of nature involve: a legal system, including a functioning system of property rights; institutions for coordinating behaviour to mutual advantage; means of educating new generations; and institutions to protect people from the vicissitudes of life (ill health, disability, and so on) to which flesh is heir. The existence of this cooperative surplus means that individuals are in a situation of moderate scarcity. Moderate scarcity means that the competition for resources is always present but not so pressing as to drive out the possibilities for cooperation. The conflictual element in a society arises because there is no one form that these institutions have to take in order to perform their function of enabling individuals to avoid the state of nature, and different institutional arrangements will typically bestow various advantages on different types of people. For example, a system of private property will benefit people with entrepreneurial skills, whereas collective property will benefit people with political skills. Moreover, conflict will also arise not just over the choice of institutions but over their functioning. How rights are exercised and how benefits are distributed are seldom matters that are rigidly fixed in any institutional arrangement, and controversy can arise over the basis upon which alternative allocations or distributions can be made.

Within this situation of partial cooperation and partial conflict, individuals have only constrained generosity. Although there will be saints and heroes who are prepared to act selflessly for what is taken to be the common good, most individuals will want to protect what they regard as their legitimate interests from others. This protective motive is not one of predation, as it would be in the Hobbesian state of nature, but it is sufficiently strong to create the basis for organized interest groups, based on class, ethnic, linguistic, religious or regional identities. Limited generosity therefore involves an unwillingness to carry disproportionate burdens or disadvantages relative to one's reference group, but it does not involve a desire to disrupt a satisfactory balance of interests among potentially antagonistic groups if it can be established.

Social cooperation and conflict exists in the context of bounded rationality (Simon, 1983, pp. 17–23). Bounded rationality arises because human beings have limited processing capacity for the information they need to conduct their lives in a satisfactory way and no one agent is able to understand all the issues that relate to a particular society. All individuals are in a situation of imperfect information, in which their knowledge of the future is limited. However, bounded rationality adds to the problems of imperfect information. To say that human rationality is bounded is to say that there are pervasive and ineliminable asymmetries of understanding in a society, so that some individuals will always know more about some particular facet of social life than any other individuals could. This in turn leads to pervasive problems of trust and commitment.

As a result of imperfect information and bounded rationality there are differences of political perspective among different individuals occupying varying positions in society. Because of these varying positions, there are typically a number of bases upon which political organization can be founded, among which the following are the most prominent: an extensive division of labour (so that individuals in one occupational grouping are simply unable to know what is involved in some other occupation); differences of language (limited information processing meaning that few individuals will be functional in non-native languages); differences of religion (where again limited information processing will preclude mutual understanding); or ethnic differences (in which different formative experiences may be effectively unbridgeable for those with a different background). Other possible sources of mutual incomprehension include gender and age.

As a result of these circumstances, political interaction and decision making is needed not only to resolve the conflicts of interests that arise inevitably in institutions, but also to reconcile differences of view about what is in the common interest, such differences arising from diverse positions that individuals occupy in society. Moreover, political choices have to be made in definite and limited periods of time. We should not conceptualize politics as an open-ended conversation stretching indefinitely into the future, but as a practical activity directed towards solving the inevitable problems that emerge continuously as individuals and groups negotiate with one another over the terms of their cooperation and the resolution of their conflicts. If we accept this characterization of the circumstances of politics, there will be clear implications for the evaluation of political institutions.

The first of these implications is that we should think of the political problem as one in which there is limited mutual understanding and constrained generosity, but not as one in which there is an overriding imperative towards selfish behaviour irrespective of the behaviour of others. One can understand the logic of the war of all against all in a Hobbesian state of nature (though even in this case there are reasons for thinking that it rarely exists in pure form; see Taylor, 1976), since in being subject to the predation of others, all individuals have to be ultra-cautious about their interactions. However, within an established and ongoing political community, it is more reasonable to think that the willingness of individuals to cooperate with one another will depend upon their past experience of cooperation, and in that sense will rest upon a principle of reciprocity rather than selfishness.

The second implication is that we should not automatically assume that political institutions have to be designed to deal with the most pessimistic circumstances we can envisage about human political inter-action. In a famous argument, David Hume (1742, pp. 117–26) offered the maxim that in the design of political institutions everyone should be supposed a knave, an argument that has been more recently echoed by Brennan and Buchanan (1985, p. 59). The argument is that in politics knavery should be assumed, not on the grounds that everyone is in fact a knave, but on the grounds that the consequences of knaves holding political power are potentially so serious that any prudent person would want to guard against that eventuality. We will find ourselves returning to this problem when we consider the evaluation of democratic insti-tutions in detail, but I shall simply assert here, in the context of the cir-cumstances of politics, that it would be unreasonable to make the supposition of knavery a general principle of political reasoning.

The final element in the circumstances of politics is the phenom-enon that has come to be known as 'path-dependence' (North, 1990, pp. 94–102; Putnam, 1993, pp. 179–81). In essence what this means is that the changes it is feasible to envisage in a set of institutions will depend upon the history of those institutions. Thus, Latin America has a poorer economic record than North America, despite their similarity in natural resources, because it inherited a political system based upon hierarchy rather than decentralized parliamentarianism, and once boxed in to these institutions, it was difficult to escape their consequences. Similarly, we can ascribe the higher level of crime in the US, compared with Canada, to the fact that in the latter the Royal Mounted Police in the nineteenth century were able to establish law and order before new settlers arrived in the western territories, whereas no equivalent institu-tion existed in the US. Path-dependence thus suggests that the changes it is sensible to introduce into a political system will depend upon what has happened before, and that fundamental constitutional changes are rare, seismic events.

Taking these features – constrained generosity, bounded rationality and path-dependence – together, it might be thought that we are severely limited in the extent to which we can subscribe to general principles of institutional evaluation. All evaluative judgements, it would seem, have to take note of the circumstances of particular cases to such a degree that it ceases to be plausible to invoke general principles. However, this is too strong a conclusion to draw. Political principles are not a blueprint, but a standard. They do not tell us what to do in the design of political insti-tutions, since knowing what to do in any particular case always involves a great deal of local and contextual knowledge, but they do provide a criterion for assessing whether what we are doing is aiming in the right direction. The circumstances of politics set constraints on what it is feasible to expect from the construction of any set of political institutions. However, a great variety of political institutions can be constructed in accordance with the characteristics so far identified. Even if we limit ourselves to recognizably democratic political institutions, they are still a diverse set. The circumstances of politics should lead us to be cautious in our evaluations, but not normatively agnostic.

The definition of democracy

So far I have referred to the global growth of democracy and assumed a notion of democratic government without offering a formal definition of what we are discussing. The definition I shall use is intended to capture the thought that democracy is best defined by contrast with non-democratic forms of government and it also attempts to identify elements that are common to the variety of forms that democratic government can take. Accordingly, the definition should be regarded as stating the minimal conditions for a system of government to count as democratic. The definition I offer may be stated as follows: in a democracy important public decisions on questions of law and policy depend, directly or indirectly, upon public opinion formally expressed by citizens of the community, the vast bulk of whom have equal political rights.

In this definition government policy depends in some formal and regular way on the state of public opinion. It is precisely the dependence of government upon opinion that was the object of the critiques of the earliest forms of democracy in classical Athens written by Plato in *The Republic*. For Plato, knowledge (*episteme*) of the wise, not the opinion (*doxa*) of the people, should steer the ship of state. In offering this definition, I therefore seek to defend the role of popular opinion as a source of political authority, but I do not intend to assert that in a democracy public policy always needs to track public opinion unerringly across the full range of decisions that governments make. I merely mean to assert that if we came across a system of government in which there was no dependence at all in important public choices on public opinion, then we would withhold the name 'democracy' from that system.

This definition of democracy uses the concept of public decisions being dependent upon public opinion rather than the stronger idea suggested by Beetham (1999, p. 5) of democracy as popular control of a collective system of decision making. Although there is much to be said in favour of the criterion of popular control, it is, I suggest, too strong a requirement for a number of reasons. In the first place, it might be taken to imply that elections were systems of popular control in the sense that they determined which parties were to form the government of the day. However, as Lijphart (1999, pp. 6–7) has argued, although this test would suit Westminster systems of government, it would preclude some long-standing democracies from being classified as such. Thus, between the 1940s and the year 1996 neither Germany nor Luxembourg, and neither the Netherlands nor Switzerland experienced a complete change of party composition in government as a result of an election. Moreover, the notion of control is too strong for the activities of citizens participating in rule-governed processes such as elections. Elections simply record the aggregated judgements of many millions of citizens; they cannot determine a coherent set of principles of public action, which is what would be required for the notion of popular control.

Dependence of political choice upon public opinion may be either direct or indirect. A direct dependence exists when choices on law and policy are made by citizens themselves participating in processes that determine a political choice, for example by voting in a binding referendum. However, political choices may be only indirectly dependent. Provided that political representatives can effectively be replaced through reasonably regular elections, the political system is a democracy according to the definition I am working with. However, such indirect links must involve a recognized and authoritative rule of the political system. Someone once said of government in late eighteenth-century Britain that it was 'despotism tempered by riot'. But according to the definition I am offering, even when effective in changing government policy, rioting crowds are not democratic citizens exercising their rights. So in saying that the link is formal, there is no implication that it is ineffective. Rather, on the claimed definition, a democracy achieves its effectiveness through the formal features of the relevant institutions, and this is what helps to define the system of government as democratic.

The proposed definition of democracy also requires an equality of political rights among the vast bulk of the citizens in a democratic community. How stringently one should insist on this criterion is a matter for judgement in particular cases, and it is difficult to come up with a general formula (neither is it necessary). However, even in the absence of a definite criterion, we can still make distinctions. Thus, I take it that many states in the US were not democracies until African-Americans obtained the effective right to vote and organize politically on a par with other citizens after the civil rights legislation of the 1960s, but that Britain was still a democracy when university graduates had two votes compared with everyone else's one. Similarly, political systems that deprived women of the vote, even if there was a high level of partici- pation among men in political decision making, were not democratic, a possibility exemplified in the case of Switzerland at the federal level until 1971. For a democracy to exist, it is not necessary that all exclusions are unjustifiable. Whatever may be the rights or wrongs of excluding prisoners from the vote, for example, a system that did impose such an exclusion would still properly be called a democracy according to the definition advanced here.

It will be helpful in seeing the force of the definition to identify cases with which democracy in this sense is contrasted. The defin- ition excludes two possible systems of government from being called democratic (there are many others, of course, that could never aspire to the title). The first is benign or soft authoritarianism, or what Finer (1970) termed 'quasi-democracies', a type of political regime that is supposed to prevail in some east Asian societies influenced by Confucianism. Under soft authoritarianism, it is asserted, govern- ments take decisions in the interests of the citizens, but they substi- tute their own judgement about what those interests are for the views of citizens themselves. By contrast, on the definition I offer, democ- racy is a system of government in which the policies and decisions of government on an important range of issues depend, to a greater or lesser extent, on public opinion as expressed in elections or other forms of aggregating opinion.

The definition also denies the title of democracy to what has been termed 'vanguard democracy' (Macpherson, 1966). Vanguard democ- racy is simply the former Communist Party's version of benign authori- tarianism, on the understanding that the scientific insight of the party leadership into the march of history replaces the wisdom of the rulers. One might extend the courtesy title of democracy to this system of government, if it were clear that it was aiming firmly at the inaugur- ation of a democratic regime. However, as Trotsky notoriously pointed out about Lenin's version of vanguard democracy, it too ends up as a sort of 'substitutionism' (see Knei-Paz, 1978, pp. 192–9), in which the views of an elite replace those of the population at large.

In defining democracy I have been referring to systems of govern- ment. The main reason for approaching the topic in this way is that, whatever else we might want to do with a theory of democracy, we cer- tainly need it to evaluate governments. Does this imply, however, that there are no other social institutions that we might wish to classify as democratic or non-democratic? What about the democratic workplace, the democratic school, the democratic university, the democratic church or the democratic family? If we say that the principle of democracy applies to systems of government, should we not also say that it applies to these other institutions, and, if so, should we not also expand our definition to include these other institutions?

There is a perfectly clear sense in which we can distinguish such institutions as being democratic or non-democratic. For example, we can say of a firm either that its organization is based on principles of worker democracy, in which those in the firm choose who is to run it and what decisions are made, or it may be based on the non-democratic principle of hierarchy. The same can be said for the other institutions I have mentioned. However, it does not follow from this definitional point that we should seek to construct a normative theory of democracy on the assumption that all these institutions are covered by the same arguments. There are a number of reasons why this is so.

Even if we do not define the state along with Weber (1947, pp. 154–7) as that association with the legitimate monopoly of coercive force in a given territorial area, no other association typically rivals a stable state in its ability to raise revenue, impose laws and fight wars. It would seem to be an obvious question to ask how the distinctive power that is generated by the state should be used and directed. Secondly, governmental politics deals with the articulation and aggregation of what are relatively permanent interests. With their retentive memories, human beings may be able to recall for some time their being jostled out of turn for a place in the bus queue or the kindness of strangers who shared their firelighters at the camp-site (compare Leftwich, 1983, pp. 11–12). But these memories are not part of the fabric of basic and long-term interests – such as the conditions of employment, the provisions made for economic security in the event of loss of earnings or the character of an educational system – that are the elements of political contestation within systems of government.

Both these features – the distinctive powers of the state and the relevance to permanent and basic interests – distinguish the activity of government from other spheres of human activity and, taken together, they mark government out as a significantly distinct institutional realm. Provided we continue to remain open about the possibilities of seeing analogies between politics and other forms of activity, it is simply intellectually confusing not to distinguish issues that arise in the practice of government from issues that arise from other practices.

By extension, one should remain open-minded about the degree to which we can carry over arguments about the justification and form of democracy from one sphere of human activity to another. Participatory democracy in, say, the university need carry no implications about the form of democracy in the nation-state in the absence of any special argument to show how the former could be a model of the latter. Conversely, democracy in the nation-state need not imply, again in the absence of special argument, democracy in the workplace or the church. To be sure, there may be a frame of mind we could call, to use Davie's (1963) term, a 'democratic intellect' that is constant across different areas of activity. However, unless we wish to say that members of churches whose government is non-democratic cannot be good political democrats, we have to acknowledge that arguments about the principles of government do not have straightforward application to other spheres of activity and vice versa.

The definition offered is intended to be minimal, in the sense that it designates a class of political systems without distinguishing among the members of that class. Hyland (1995, pp. 49–50), however, reminds us that definitions can involve 'scalar' as well as 'sortal' concepts. Sortal concepts designate a class, for example sortal concepts distinguish lions from tigers, whereas scalar concepts identify a characteristic, for example warmth, that objects can have to a greater or lesser degree. Why should we regard democracy as a sortal rather than a scalar concept? Why not say that political systems can have certain characteristics, for example their degree of inclusiveness or their extent of citizen participation, and such systems are more or less democratic depending upon where they are located on the appropriate scale? In this approach we would not be looking for the minimum conditions that a political system would need to satisfy in order to count as democratic, but the ideal scheme of democratic political organization against which actually existing examples could be assessed.

The answer to this question is complex, but I suggest that it falls along the following lines. From the point of view of making practical decisions of political morality, there is some value in distinguishing democratic from non-democratic political systems in the sense that the democratic systems meet some minimal conditions that are stipulated. For example, such distinctions may be important in answering the question of whether international aid should be made conditional upon the accomplishment of democratic reforms in some countries. In such contexts, it would be impracticable, and perhaps counterproductive, to set the standard so high that imperfect human societies could not reach it. Even if our underlying notion of democracy is scalar rather than sortal, we may still need to impose some cut-off points on the scale.

In addition, to define democracy in scalar terms carries the implication that having more of a certain characteristic, for example citizen participation in the making of decisions, makes the political system more democratic as such. Yet we should at least be open to the possibility that representative government is in some cases as democratic a form of government as direct democracy, even if there are good substantive reasons for wishing to increase participation. There are a variety of conceptions of democracy that have been advanced as justifiable all of which are compatible with the definition I have offered. The definition is intended to be a criterion, distinguishing democratic from non-democratic regimes; it is not intended to be a full characterization of the full range of democratic polities. In the next chapter, I consider how we might understand this range of possibilities and how we might begin to understand the way in which we could evaluate their respective merits with some intellectual plausibility.

2 Forms of Democratic Government

Democracy, I have suggested, is a form of government in which public policy depends in a systematic, if sometimes indirect, way upon public opinion. However, even accepting this definition, there are various ways in which democracy can be thought of. Indeed, looking at the literature on democracy, it is clear that it reflects this diversity with classifications, categories and typologies in abundance. We read of pluralist democracy, radical democracy, liberal democracy, socialist democracy, deliberative democracy, elitist democracy, equilibrium democracy, cosmopolitan democracy, and so on (for a good discussion in this mode, see Held, 1996). It may seem that the task of a democratic theory is to identify which of these differing conceptions of democracy has the greatest claim to justification or is most defensible in intellectual terms. Why do we find the theory of democracy discussed in this way, and how should we deal with the problems that this proliferation of categories raises?

It is not hard to see why there should be a proliferation of conceptions of democracy. First, democracy, whatever it is, is a complex phenomenon, and it is bound to take a variety of forms. To understand and account for this complexity requires some typology to reduce the complexity and clarify thinking. Secondly, given the favourable connotations the term 'democracy' often seems to possess, it is not surprising that many people from different ideological persuasions have wished to identify their preferred arrangement of political life with democracy as an ideal. Whatever the merits of liberalism, socialism, capitalism, republicanism, and so on, each ideology will receive considerable intellectual and moral support from its being associated with a plausible account of democracy. In consequence, ideas such as 'liberal democracy', 'social democracy', and so on are bound to flourish.

There is therefore a considerable element of persuasive definition at work in the production of these typologies. Consider the example of the notion of 'deliberative democracy', which has been much discussed in recent years (see, e.g., Bohman and Rehg, 1997; Elster, 1998; and Fishkin and Laslett, 2003 for collections that offer various points of view). Proponents of deliberative democracy fall into various camps, but their views are often presented in terms of an understanding of what democracy is supposed to be in its essence, namely a political system in which issues of public policy and political choice are resolved by discussion. Yet, it is clear that this definition is supposed to function not as the description of any actually existing democracy (indeed, deliberative democrats are typically critical of the performance of such democracies), but as a normative account of how a well-functioning democracy would institutionalize decision making. Within this account, it is assumed that, at the core of political legitimacy, there is a process by which reasons are offered and exchanged among citizens, and that a legitimate democratic government would institutionalize such reason giving.

As a normative account, the insights of deliberative democracy have considerable merit (see Chapter 4). However, such a conception orientated towards a persuasive definition cannot be the whole story about how to understand democracy, since many other important issues are left out. For example, within the deliberative tradition, some writers stress the importance of popular deliberation (Dryzek, 2000), whereas others see constitutional courts as being the sites of public reason (Rawls, 1996, pp. 231–40). These are two quite distinct accounts, and the question can therefore be raised as to how consistent with one another they are. Similarly, deliberative democrats accept that there are important questions about voting and participation that are not determined solely by the commitment to a deliberative account of politics. If we were simply to discuss the merits of deliberative democracy without considering these other issues, then we should have merely a partial account of what democratic theory involves.

Moreover, to base the discussion upon accounts of democracy that advance a persuasive definition reinforces the view that democratic theory is the comparison of conceptions that, in their basic logical characteristics, are essentially contested. Compare, in this regard, the contrast between deliberative democracy on the one hand and radical democracy on the other. Whereas deliberative democrats stress the extent to which politics is the search for consensual reasons, radical democrats stress the agonistic elements of democracy, drawing attention to the way in which differences of value and perspective are an ineradicable part of politics. As Chantal Mouffe (2000, p. 99) has written, the deliberative model of democracy 'is unable to acknowledge the dimensions of antagonism that the pluralism of values entails and its ineradicable character'. So, if we simply compared these two conceptions in terms of their logical structure and key concepts, we would be forced to conclude that, in some sense, proponents of the two views were talking past one another, drawing upon such different conceptions of politics that their accounts could not be rendered commensurable with one another.

Yet, conceptions of democracy can be compared and evaluated because they are not simply theoretical exercises. They are intended in some way to relate to political practice. Even an account of politics based upon a persuasive definition has to provide an understanding of how political practices and institutions function, if only to contrast practice with favoured norms. So one way of seeking to render different accounts of democracy commensurable with one another, enabling us to compare their relative merits, is to focus upon those institutions and practices. In other words, rather than beginning with a particular conception of democracy and asking what account that conception might offer of political practice, we can begin with the varieties of political practice and ask what reasons drawn from different conceptions might suggest our favouring one of those practices over others. From this point of view, we develop an account of the variety of institutional forms that democracy can take and then consider those institutional forms in the light of normative arguments drawn from political theory. One merit of this approach is that we can relate discussions in normative political theory to discussions in the literature of comparative politics, the latter being a literature that has sought systematically to define different institutional arrangements for government and politics.

Institutions, behaviour, social structure

An institution can be defined, in the words of Oran Young (1989, p. 5), as 'identifiable practices consisting of recognised roles linked by clusters of rules or conventions governing relations among the occupants of these roles'. Institutions in this sense may be highly informal. The practice of leaving your coat on your seat in the train when you want to keep your place is an institution in this broad sense, as is the practice of shaking hands when meeting people. However, institutions may also be formalized into organizational structures such as firms, political parties or systems of government. If we offer an institutional account of democracy, therefore, we essentially make our typology turn on the way that we characterize and categorize the rule-governed and convention-governed system of roles and practices that constitute action in politics. Examples of institutional rules and convention in this sense include the following: the scope that the rules of decision making assign to popular participation; the role that political representatives are supposed to play within the scheme of public decision making; the division of authority between the legislature and the courts; the ways in which membership of the polity is assigned or denied to individuals; and the processes by which statements of popular preference are amalgamated into a collective choice.

The distinction between a normative and an institutional typology in part relates to the interpretation of such rules and conventions. A normative typology picks a favoured rule or set of rules and suggests that the norms associated with that rule have special status. For example, participatory accounts of democracy give special importance to rules that enable citizens to participate directly in the making of law and public policy. By contrast, an institutional typology in itself is agnostic on the normative status of the rule. Within an institutional typology we can certainly see rules and conventions as embodying or corresponding to more general political principles. Thus, a rule that made certain issues the subject of popular referendums, for example, would correspond to participationist principles of politics. But the typology itself is based upon the institutional features, not their underlying normative rationale.

Neither does the typology turn on the behavioural dimension of political practice. Behaviour differs from institutions by specifying the ways in which actors use the institutionally defined powers and opportunities available to them. A behavioural typology of democracy would thus focus upon how people act within institutional constraints and possibilities. It would ask whether citizens at large avail themselves of the institutional possibilities open to them to influence public policy, or whether decision making in practice is largely concentrated in the hands of a few people. It would examine the ways in which powerful political actors use the rules of the game to maintain or enhance their own strategic advantage, say by moving amendments and procedural motions during the passing of legislation. It would assess the extent to which social agents have the ability to ignore, bend or alter the rules to their own advantage given the political resources they are able to mobilize. In short, a behavioural account shifts attention away from the institutional structures of government to the actions of individuals and groups within those structures. The contrast between elitist and pluralist accounts of democracy is a behaviourally based typology in this sense. Pluralists think that various groups are able to use political institutions, and conclude that power is dispersed. Elitists think the opposite. Yet, both are characterizing their accounts of democracy in terms of putative behavioural patterns.

There is a strong intellectual current in the history of political science which argues that in studying politics we should look at behavioural and not institutional questions. In part, this emphasis arises from an aspiration to liberate political science from legal studies, and to study not what the legal and constitutional rules say should happen but what in practice does happen. A good example of the attempt to get behind the appearance of modern politics in order to understand how things work in practice is provided by Bagehot's (1867, p. 61) distinction between the 'dignified' and the 'efficient' elements of the English constitution. According to Bagehot, although the formal rules of the nineteenth-century constitution stipulated that parliament was sovereign, if one looked at how decisions were made in practice it became clear that it was the cabinet which governed. Many British political scientists have embraced a similar 'realism' (compare Gamble, 1990, p. 410).

There is a temptation in discussions of political science for the choice between institutional and behavioural approaches to be polarized, so that one approach comes to dominate the other. This can even apply to authors who show great sensitivity to institutional questions. Thus, in the heyday of the behavioural revolution in political science, Robert Dahl argued that 'in so far as there is any general protection in human society against the deprivation by one group of the freedom desired by another, it is probably not to be found in constitutional forms. It is to be discovered, if at all, in extra-constitutional factors' (Dahl, 1956, p. 134). Among these extra-constitutional factors Dahl included such things as the distribution of preference intensities in society, a factor that is unrelated in any straightforward way to a society's institutional arrangements. Yet, without seeking to underestimate the importance of behavioural accounts for political science generally, there are powerful arguments for taking an institutional focus within normative political theory when constructing a typology of democratic forms.

One important reason for taking such an approach is that political choice can be exercised over institutional arrangements in a way that it can not easily be over behavioural regularities. Countries can adopt systems of proportional representation where previously they had used first-past-the-post electoral systems. They can open up their decision making to the greater use of referendums or other forms of citizen participation. They can entrench a bill of rights. They can extend the franchise to resident aliens. They can adopt a constitution that gives a supreme court restraining powers in the action of a legislature, and so on. By contrast, it is more difficult to change behavioural regularities and the results, when tried, are likely to be unpredictable. Occupational structures, the division of labour by gender, the ethnic and linguistic composition of a community or the popular balance of religious sentiment are clearly important in shaping political behaviour, but they are influential precisely because they are the unintended consequences of multiple interactions among members of society that take place over time in a myriad of different settings. Moreover, the causes of political behaviour are only partially related to political decisions. In designing political institutions we may hope that certain patterns of behaviour will result, but we have to reckon with a number of other influences, some of which may be deeply rooted in social structure.

To accept this argument, however, is not to imply that understanding political behaviour is irrelevant to normative theory. In particular, behavioural considerations can enter as evidence within a normative theory relevant to the choice of institutions. Consider, as an example, Arend Lijphart's account of consociational democracy (Lijphart, 1968, 1977). Lijphart argued that there was a class of segmented societies in which the behaviour of their members was defined and constrained by close social ties based upon language or religion. Patterns of work organization, marriage and recreational life were structured by the existence of segmented groups, so that in the Netherlands, for example, Catholics did not marry, form trade unions with or spend much of their free time with Protestants. Lijphart argued that in such circumstances a political system built upon the principle of simple majority rule would not work, because the members of each group would fear that the other group would take too much advantage of the opportunities for power that were offered in a winner-takes-all system. In this context institutions were needed that were built upon a super-majority principle with opportunity for each group to veto the political proposals of the other.

In this sort of argument behavioural and historical evidence is clearly relevant to evaluating the merits of alternative political institutions, but it is taken as a given and attention is directed at the choice of a pattern of institutions rather than at questions about how one might go about changing the underlying social structure that gives rise to the problem. This is not to deny that the structures will change, as indeed they have in the Netherlands, the paradigm of the consociational state, where religious differences have weakened and the traditional 'pillars' have ceased to play the dominant role in shaping behaviour. But it is to say that, in so far as any political prescriptions do emerge from normative argument, they are more likely to make sense when applied to institutions than when applied to structured patterns of political behaviour.

It might be thought that, if social structures shape behaviour in so strong a way, they leave little room for political choice. To speak about institutional choice related to behavioural evidence is to reject that form of sociological determinism which asserts that political institutions are simply a manifestation of underlying social forces in relation to which institutional design is purely epiphenomenal. However, a rejection of sociological determinism in this strong form is not a rejection of the claim that there may be social conditions that facilitate or enable, on the one hand, or prevent or inhibit, on the other, the adoption of certain institutional arrangements. Lijphart's own argument essentially turns on considerations of how social conditions may prevent the emergence of one stable pattern of institutions. More generally, the statistical association between economic development and democratic stability is strong and well documented, and it is not difficult to think of reasons why this association should hold, as well as reasons why it is sometimes overridden (for discussion, see Rueschemeyer, Stephens and Stephens, 1992). To reject a strong form of sociological determinism is merely to say that there are degrees of freedom within socially and economically defined boundaries and that choice within these degrees of freedom is politically important. It may also be true to say that there can be an obligation upon policy makers to bring about the social conditions – such as generalized prosperity or higher levels of popular education – that make democracy easier to maintain.

An institutional typology

If we are to examine institutional alternatives in the way I have suggested, then we shall need some classification of the possibilities in order to make our task manageable. In this section, I suggest one such classification, and provide some account of the traditions of political thought with which each alternative is associated.

The general concept of democracy is given by the criterion of a systematic and non-trivial relationship between public policy and public opinion formally expressed by the bulk of citizens with equal political rights. What variety of institutional conceptions is compatible with this view? The typology I offer is built upon two stages of classification. The first stage is simply defined by the familiar distinction between direct and indirect democracies. In a direct democracy the people choose the content of public policy by voting on that policy or participating in public deliberation, or by some mixture of both of these activities. In an indirect democracy the people choose representatives who then in turn determine the content of public policy. This is so obvious a distinction in the way that political arrangements can be organized that it is difficult to see how any institutional account of democracy could ignore it. Moreover, the distinction between direct and indirect democracy has implications for other aspects of institutional arrangements. For example, it is impossible to practise direct democracy on a large scale (views differ as to exactly how large the limit may be), and so a choice for direct democracy involves a choice for decentralization. Similarly, direct democracy involves an unmediated relationship between the people and the process of government, so that although there can be representation in a direct democracy, say in respect of particular political tasks such as that of magistrate in classical Athens, the practice of representation will be very different in a direct democracy from that in an indirect democracy.

Thus, if one became convinced, on normative grounds, that the arguments for popular participation were so strong that direct democracy should be implemented as far as possible, this decision would have extensive consequences for the way one thought about other values in political life. Similarly, if one were convinced that indirect democracy could be defended in normative terms, then a different set of values would be invoked, perhaps including those of constitutional constraint and the protection of individual rights. In short, the distinction between direct and indirect democracy marks a significant distinction in the range of values and principles that may be thought applicable to political life.

Building on this fundamental distinction between direct and indirect democracy, the second stage of the typology divides the two categories into sub-categories. Two forms of direct democracy are identified. The first is unmediated popular government, the central idea of which is that citizens themselves make laws and rules to govern the terms of their association when gathered in assemblies. The second is party-mediated popular government, in which there is political representation, but fundamental decision power is given to the people at large by the extensive use of referendums.

The classification of indirect democracies builds on work in comparative politics, including Lijphart's (1984, 1999) distinction between consensual and majoritarian forms of representative government, and Powell's (1982, 1989, 2000) scheme for classifying modern democracies, which itself draws upon the work of Lijphart. Liphart distinguishes two main classes of representative democracy, classifying them by a combination of their electoral rules and the extent to which the elected chamber is dominated by or shares power with the government. Majoritarian democracy, according to Lijphart, is characterized by plurality of electoral systems and control of the legislature by the executive. Consensual systems are characterized by electoral laws based on proportional representation and parliamentary chambers in which executives are counterbalanced by parliament. These two forms of government, according to Lijphart (1999, p. 2), embody two different views of the nature of democracy. According to the majoritarian view, all that is required for political legitimacy is that a majority agree on a particular course of action, and it would be undemocratic for the majority not to get its way. The consensual view, by contrast, says that as many people as possible should agree to political measures if those measures are to satisfy the conditions of democracy.

These two dimensions of government are associated with one another, and this is well brought out in Powell's (1989, 2000) cross-classification. Powell shows that countries cluster into two broad groups, one of which is defined by plurality election rules and executive dominance, the other of which is defined by proportional election rules and the sharing of power in the parliament. In detail, the bases of the classification change between the 1989 paper and the book in 2000 since in the 1989 paper election rules are defined by the extent to which they encourage parliamentary majorities, whereas in the 2000 book they are defined directly by their type. However, the striking feature of the two analyses is that, even with these changes in definition, the clustering remains quite stable. The countries with plurality election rules or election rules that encourage legislative majorities tend also to be the ones that encourage executive control of parliament. They include the Westminster systems of Australia, New Zealand (presumably before 1996) and the UK, as well as the Fifth Republic in France. Countries that use PR and encourage the sharing of power in the elected chamber are the continental European democracies, including Austria, Belgium, Denmark, the Netherlands, Norway, Sweden and Switzerland (Powell, 1989, p. 113; Powell, 2000, p. 39).

The 'off-diagonal' countries, such as Canada and Finland, can be understood in terms of their distinctive institutional features.

The changes in classification of particular countries between the 1989 paper and the 2000 book are generally easily explicable in terms of the political history of the particular countries in the 1990s. Japan changed its election laws; Greece strengthened the role of the executive in the elected chamber; and the break-up of the Christian Democratic control of the Italian political system led to greater opposition power in parliament. The one interesting change in classification that is not so easily accounted for is the USA, which in the 1989 classification was in a position of its own, with a plurality electoral system encouraging party majorities together with opposition participation in legislative processes. By the 2000 book opposition power in the Congress is classified as being weaker, placing the US in the same category as Canada.

Now far be it for a humble underlabouring political theorist to disagree with one of the world's leading comparativists, but I wonder whether the change in the classification of the US is really correct. There has been a rise in majority party control of representatives with the rise of the more disciplined Gingrich Republican Party after the 1996 election, but that would not of itself indicate greater executive control of the legislature, so long as there were divided government. Moreover, Powell (2000, p. 39) has a footnote to the key table, which says of the US, among others, that the upper house 'occasionally provides added possibilities for dispersed power in policy-making'. This seems a somewhat coy description of the US Senate. If George W. Bush cannot secure passage of his social security reforms, even when he shares power with a Congress of the same party, there is some reason for doubting whether the US executive has moved in the direction of greater control of the legislature.

The case is interesting, because if the US is more singular than Powell's 2000 classification would have us think, then we can see a distinctive third institutional form of representative government. One reason for thinking this might be so is the extent to which Lijphart (1999) has added important institutional dimensions to his own 1984 classificatory scheme, including the extent to which there is an independent supreme court and an independent monetary authority. Clearly, the US has historically had both a strong Supreme Court and a strong Federal Bank. Although Lijphart wishes to make the place of the courts and the central bank aspects of his own dichotomous classification, the distinctive role of these institutions historically in the US is at least suggestive of a third variant of representative government.

How then can we name these three categories? One category Powell (1982) once called 'representational government' and it corresponded to Lijphart's category of consensual systems. I shall follow Powell's earlier usage and refer to representational government. (This is an ugly neologism, but there is no alternative. 'Representative government' refers to all forms of indirect government, whereas 'representational' highlights one important distinctive feature of this government, namely that decision making reflects a broad range of opinions and social groups.) I prefer this to 'consensual' because in many continental democracies, although decision making encompasses a wider range of groups and interests than a bare majority, it typically falls short of anything approaching, say, four-fifths of an electorate. Moreover, since plurality systems almost always fail to secure government majorities based upon a majority of the electorate whereas continental systems generally do much better in this regard, it seems inappropriate to deny the latter the title of majoritarian. By the same token I agree with Nagel (1998) that a more accurate term for Westminster systems is 'pluritarian'.

Following from the argument about the distinctive institutional arrangements of the US, I shall also distinguish a third form of representative government, namely liberal constitutionalism. This is a form of government in which various decision-making institutions that are not responsive to popular preferences, most notably supreme courts, play an important role in policy decisions. In other words, there are strong counter-majoritarian institutions at work in liberal constitutional systems. With this third category of indirect democracies, and simplifying somewhat, we can group the various types of democracy into five categories: unmediated popular government; party-mediated popular government; representational government; Westminster systems; and liberal constitutionalism. To the description of each I now turn.

1. *Unmediated popular government*

The first form of democracy that we can envisage is that of unmediated popular rule. The modern image of this type of government is heavily influenced by the form in which it was conceptualized by Rousseau (1762). Strictly speaking, Rousseau does not offer a theory of direct democracy as a form of *government*, since Rousseau is clear that the tasks of government, by which he seems to mean administration, cannot be carried on by citizens but have to be undertaken by specialized institutions. However, Rousseau's account of popular rule has been so influential both theoretically and ideologically that it needs to be considered as a distinct account of what is involved in democracy.

Central to Rousseau's conception is the idea that political legitimacy will only exist if citizens determine for themselves the rules and laws that they will be obliged to follow. Citizens assemble together and decide on the content of laws and public policy without the mediation of political representatives. In making their decision, each citizen seeks the common good or what Rousseau terms the 'general will' of all. Persons are naturally free, and their moral autonomy requires that obligations are self-willed. Under certain conditions (notably a rough equality of economic circumstance and willingness on the part of citizens to think about the general interest), these separate autonomous wills combine into the general will. Under the same conditions the obligation of citizens to obey the law is complete in the sense that they can properly and legitimately be forced into compliance, in a way that would not be possible before the expression of the general will.

One important element in Rousseau's conception is the prohibition upon factionalism. His distinction between the general will and the will of all is precisely that the latter is simply the sum of wills, when people vote thinking of their own interests, whereas the general will arises when people think of the public interest. Rousseau's own example of a decision on whether or not to have the death penalty provides a good instance of this distinction (Rousseau, 1762, pp. 189–91). Likely criminals, consulting their own self-interest, would vote against it, and likely victims, consulting their own self-interest, would vote in favour. Citizens, seeking to identify the general will, say to themselves that they could fall into either category, and will balance the competing interests and perspectives involved. Such balancing seems both psychologically possible (think of the way that causing death through drunken driving has attracted less penalty than other ways of causing death, presumably because those responsible for making a decision, including juries, think that they themselves might be guilty on some occasion) and is part of the reason why Rousseau values economic equality (since the ability to put oneself in the shoes of another is likely to be easier when all share similar circumstances).

Since autonomy is the central underlying value constraining the construction of political institutions in the Rousseauian conception, it follows that participation is an essential element in the justification of legitimate government. When Rousseau wrote that, though the people of England regarded itself as being free, it was in fact free only during the election of its members of parliament (Rousseau, 1762, p. 240), he was expressing this sentiment. Without participation by citizens in the formulation of the general will, there can be no legitimate way of making public decisions. In this sense the connection between public opinion, suitably defined, and the making of rules and laws is direct and constitutive. Public opinion defines the content of the laws and rules by which citizens are to be governed.

Rousseau is clear that there is a moralization of individual human beings in the process of social life. The social contract transmutes natural freedom into moral obligation by the participation of citizens in forming the general will. Moreover, the scope of the general will is in principle unbounded. It has to be. Since persons are morally autonomous, there can be no *a priori* limitations upon what they might will (for example there can be no requirement that their choices be consistent with the demands of a traditional religion). Hence the only source of obligation is the general will as defined by a majority of those voting. Those who are in the minority simply realize that they have mistaken the general will.

Although this last element of Rousseau's thought has often been held to have totalitarian implications, it is in fact no more than a logical inference from the strong assumption of moral autonomy. If strong moral autonomy exists in the way that Rousseau supposes, then moral rules and principles can be nothing other than conventions adopted by societies for the regulation of their conduct. This conventional character of morality means that a majority will be right, since conventional behaviour is simply what most people will do under given circumstances. To see this, consider a case that we recognize to be purely conventional. If I turn up at a party wearing a suit and others are in jeans and a T-shirt, I have simply mistaken the operative convention, and in this sense I have mistaken the general will.

The conception of democracy that emerges in the Rousseauian tradition is both an ideal and an idealization. It is an ideal in the sense that its proponents have thought that it incorporated the value of moral autonomy, and it is an idealization in the sense that it does not describe any particular functioning democracy, but is meant instead to identify some important characterizing features. Rousseau's own models were ancient Sparta and republican Rome, though the dedication to Geneva at the beginning of *The Social Contract* suggests that Rousseau also thought that there were contemporary examples that approximate the ideal. In the twentieth century, it has been argued, certain forms of African democracy had Rousseauian elements, in particular Julius Nyerere's conception of *ujamaa* in Tanzania, with its emphasis upon consensus and the outlawing of factions, supposedly building upon what were taken to be traditional African forms of government (see Nursey-Bray, 1983, pp. 101–3). Neither is it difficult to see Rousseauian elements also in a number of radical social movements in liberal democracies. Maier (1992, p. 145) has drawn attention to the echoes of Rousseau in the 1962 Port Huron statement, which was a rallying cry for American radicals, and there are certain styles of Green politics that stress consensus and absence of factional struggles as central to their way of working – at least as an ideal.

Among the other sources of inspiration for ideas of direct democracy, the model of classical Athens is important. Urbinati (2006, p. 2), for example, writes that Athens was a genuine democracy and 'is the touchstone for our thinking about democracy (and the undemocratic character of representative government) ... Democracy meant that each and every citizen had an equal and meaningful chance to take part in lawmaking and to address the assembly.' In a similar vein, Finley (1985, pp. 18–19) pointed out that the Athenian Assembly made the final decision on many matters, including war and peace, finance, public works and legislation. Open to all citizens it met frequently throughout the year – at least forty times. Everyone had the right to participate in debate and decisions were carried by a simple majority. It is this notion of citizens assembled in debate to discuss and decide on matters of common concern that has come down to us as the authentic model of democracy.

In fact, the historical form of democracy in classical Athens was more complicated than this picture would suggest. Participation rates in the Assembly (*ekklesia*) were lower than the idea of the body of citizens joined together would suggest. Hansen (1991, pp. 130–2) estimates that some 6,000 from a possible 30,000 citizens regularly attended the meetings and that the physical space would not have allowed much more. Moreover, Hansen's general thesis is that there was a shift in power between Periclean Athens in the fifth century BCE, about which there is little reliable historical information, and the fourth century down to the ending of Athenian independence in 322 BCE. In particular, after the defeat in the Peloponnesian War and the restoration of democracy in 403, two legislative bodies were set up, one connected with the preliminary publication of the laws, the other with an evaluation of measures passed by the Assembly (Hansen, 1991, p. 163). Any decrees of the Assembly had to be consistent with the established laws, which were higher than any decrees. Moreover, even in the fifth century, any matter that came before the Assembly had to be discussed by the Council and it could be overturned by the People's Court. Although membership of these bodies was by lot, thus preserving in the eyes of contemporaries the principle of political equality, it was also true that there were certain important offices, most notably military generals and the chief financial officers, who were elected. Nevertheless, and despite these qualifications, the openness of political decision making to participation by citizens in classical Athens is remarkable by contemporary standards.

A similar point can be made about the other obvious model of direct democracy in contemporary theory, namely the New England townships from the seventeenth century. In these communities the principle of public decision making was that communal decisions, about such matters as taxation, schooling, roads or water management, should be decided by a meeting of all qualified adult males in the town. As with Athens, the image of the New England town meeting, as much as its reality (Mansbridge, 1980, ch. 11), has been enormously influential on certain types of political theory. The notion of a town meeting, however, underlines the extent to which influential models of participatory democracy are often tied to political decentralization. What of direct democracy in large-scale societies?

2. *Party-mediated popular government*

Instead of democracy in its Rousseauian version, it is possible to imagine a form of direct democracy that took to their limits participatory devices, such as the referendum or the citizen initiative, that currently exist only in restricted form in representative democracies. Ian Budge (1996) has proposed a conception of democracy along these lines, arguing that information and communications technologies now make possible extensive citizen involvement in the making of public policies, even in large-scale societies.

How would such a form of democracy differ from its Rousseauian variant? One important difference is that, contrary to Rousseau's strictures on sectionalism, a direct democracy of the sort that Budge envisages would still have political parties, who would perform their traditional functions of organizing the agenda, defining alternatives, seeking for compromise packages and offering candidates for executive office. The chief difference from their role in existing representative democracies is that instead of providing the representatives who decide legislation, voting on laws, rules and policies would be done by the people at large registering their preferences electronically. This characterization of a direct democracy looks more like the example of ancient Athens, where there were clear factions organized in the Assembly meetings, than it looks like the idealized version of Rome or Sparta that Rousseau envisages.

One of the principal differences between unmediated popular government and party-mediated popular government is that there is no need in the latter account to imagine that voters go through the mental exercise of seeking to find the general will. Just as party representatives at present vote for measures for a variety of reasons, not all of them by any means related to an attempt to define a public good, so citizens in a party-mediated direct democracy might in some cases vote from high motives and in others from considerations of self-interest or partisan advantage. No doubt, if there is a refining and elevating effect from having to present one's arguments in the forum of public opinion, as a number of deliberative theorists suggest (a view well discussed by Elster, 1997), this process would operate too in a party-based direct democracy. However, we should not have to make it a defining requirement of such a system. In such a system public policy could be regarded as a balancing of interests as much as the expression of a view about the public good.

Budge argues that such a system is feasible given new information and communications technologies. He cites the growth of citizen participation in the United States through such means as referendums, citizen's initiatives and the recall of representatives, to show that some of the obvious practical objections to such a scheme can be overcome. He is also insistent that direct democracy of this sort is quite compatible with the familiar range of constitutional devices – the separation of powers, the provision of checks and balances, the existence of bills of rights, the power of courts to engage in judicial review of measures that are passed, and so on – that are intended to control the abuse of legislative power. It is simply that the controls are exercised on the people at large rather than upon their representatives. Here again there is a significant contrast with Rousseau. There is no assumption that the 'general will is always right' (the logical consequence of Rousseau's commitment to a strong form of moral autonomy). Instead, the assumption is that though public choices should properly be made by only those people who experience the consequences of the choice, it may be necessary to constrain the operation of electoral decision making through constitutional means.

Again by contrast with Rousseau, there is no commitment in such a model to equalizing the economic circumstances of citizens. Such an equalizing of material circumstances was necessary for Rousseau so that each person could have the imaginative identification with others necessary to form a general will. Within the party-based model of direct democracy factions would still presumably reflect associations of citizens with similar interests and perspectives to each other and distinct interests or perspectives from competitor groupings. Such groupings would presumably include factions based upon economic differences, though no doubt these would not be the only source of difference and political competition.

Almost by definition, it is difficult to find examples of this conception of democracy in action, since its operation depends upon the advancement of new information and communication technologies that, though in existence, are not yet widespread. However, the combination of aspects of representative politics with the extensive use of referendums can be found in practice. One obvious example is Switzerland, where referendums at all levels of government are used to ratify acts of elected bodies. Until quite recently, a high proportion of the referendums held in the modern world had been held in Switzerland. Cronin (1989, p. 48) points out how the Swiss experience influenced US reformers in the 1890s, which in turn inspired populist reformers, who were anxious to break the power of monopolies and corrupt political practices. Bowler and Donovan (2000, ch. 1) point to the extensive use of the initiative and the referendum in California and the more general growth of direct devices in the US in the latter part of the twentieth century after a decline in the middle of the century.

In fact, the idea of party-mediated direct democracy has been even more widely discussed in political theory than these examples would suggest, but the tone of evaluation has generally been negative. Party-mediated populist politics has been seen as a form of politics in which notional representatives manipulated mass electorates by using referendums to their own advantage. One statement in such a mould is to be found in Marx's *The Eighteenth Brumaire of Louis Bonaparte*, where Marx (1852) sees the isolated condition of the French peasantry as providing the conditions within which their votes could be manipulated by Louis Napoleon as a way of bringing him to imperial power. Finer's (1970, ch. 7) account of de Gaulle's use of the referendum in the Fifth Republic just over one hundred years after that of Louis Napoleon echoes criticism of the manipulative possibilities.

The democratic credentials of party-mediated popular democracy are not clear from these writings.

3. *Representational government*

The countries that form the principal instances of representational governments as classified by Lijphart and Powell are the north European democracies. They combine electoral systems that encourage a wide range of political parties in the legislature representative of different social groups. They also encourage a sharing of power between executive and legislature, primarily in the form of relatively strong parliamentary committees. A central principle of representational government is that major decisions should be taken by political representatives meeting in a legislative chamber, who reflect in their characteristics and opinions a wide variety of views and experience. The idea in this conception is that, for various reasons largely to do with size, we should not expect the people to rule directly, but nevertheless policy choices should still reflect opinions that are representative of a broad swathe of opinion in society.

If we ask what political theory might justify such a form of democracy, then one place to look is John Stuart Mill's *On Representative Government* (Mill, 1861a), but without the fancy franchise that Mill thought necessary to give the more able and intelligent a greater say in political power than others. Undoubtedly, the central institutional mechanism for Mill in achieving proportionality between electoral opinions and the balance of representatives is a system of proportional representation in the electoral law (Mill, 1861a, ch. 7). For Mill the chief reason for wanting proportionality is that it is the only way of ensuring that a majority, rather than a minority, of the electorate actually decide policy through their representatives. Moreover, Mill supported Thomas Hare's proposed electoral reforms, in which there was an (impractical) attempt to allow the free association of voters in the selection of candidates, because of the diversity of views that could be expressed in society.

Mill's account of the functions of a representative assembly in chapter 5 of *Representative Government* reflects the parliamentary experience of mid-nineteenth-century Britain with which he was familiar. Many of the distinctions he makes now strike us as so obvious that they hardly need repeating. The function of parliament is not to do government business, but to control it. Representatives should vote on matters of taxation, but not draw up estimates. The job of parliament is not to supervise or control administration, but to appoint suitable persons for those tasks. Parliament decides who should be prime minister, but does not select the members of the cabinet. There should be a commission to codify the laws, rather than this being a task of parliament. All these distinctions of function are familiar today, and we can understand them as simply reflecting the exigencies of time and attention span. The main positive account that Mill gives for the functions of parliament is a deliberative one. Parliament is a congress of opinions in which not just the general sense of the nation, but every section of it, can engage in discussion. In addition, the job of parliament is to control the government, to 'throw the light of publicity on its acts' and to compel the executive to give an account of its actions.

There are two respects in which Mill's normative theory goes beyond the practice of some of the European democracies. The first is his stress upon popular participation in politics at local level, not as a rival to representative government but as a complement to it. It is central to this conception that public spiritedness can only be built through the experience of citizens' participating in the processes of government, so that in consequence there is an emphasis upon local democracy and other forms of citizens' participation, for example in the jury system, that would promote increased civic awareness among citizens. Such a conception does not go as far as Rousseau in thinking that citizens can so internalize a sense of the common good that there will, in effect, be unanimity, but it does stress the extent to which citizens must learn to put their own prejudices and partial sentiments to one side when participating in the making of public decisions.

Because Rousseau thought that the people should be the sovereign, he saw no possibility that the people would pass laws against their own interests. Mill saw much greater scope for the tyranny of the majority and for the need to protect individuals from any harmful effects of collective decision making (Mill, 1859). It is therefore consistent with Mill's theory of democracy that there should be some separation of powers and protection of individual interests through a bill of rights. Nonetheless, these individualistic elements of this political theory should not detract from the distinctive democratic conception that he also advances.

4. *Westminster systems*

Taking the polar opposite group in Powell's classification, we find political systems built not on the idea of representativeness but on that of elections as devices for choosing governments. As with the system of representational government, the principles of the Westminster system assume that elected officials, rather than the people themselves, make the most important political decisions. However, the Westminster system differs from the conception of representational government in thinking of the legislative chamber not as a mirror or microcosm of the population, but instead as a device for choosing a team to make decisions for a limited term of office at the end of which they render an account of their tenure to the electorate in a competitive election. Thus, behind the institutional differences, there are differing conceptions of political representation.

A distinctive feature of Westminster systems has been the lack of proportionality between electoral opinion and the choice of representatives. This feature of the electoral system makes sense if the purpose of the system is to choose a government rather than mirror opinion. From this perspective, typical features of the Westminster system have a coherent logic and rationale. For example, it is a feature of first-past-the-post electoral systems that they magnify the share of the vote that locally strong political parties receive in the share of the seats in the legislature they are allocated. If the point of elections is to choose a government, rather than reflect popular opinion, this will be a desirable feature, since it will serve to make those governments that are elected more stable.

Moreover, within this conception of politics, it is clearly desirable that the government be able to get its way in the legislature, through control of business, again so that responsibility cannot be confused. So, by delivering a larger House of Commons majority to the winning party than would be implied by its share of the popular vote, the electoral formula puts the winning party in the best position possible to form the government. There is thus a direct connection between the choice of the electorate, as represented by the plurality rule, and the choice of government. The preference for clarity in government is seen also in the fact that when the electoral system has failed to deliver a legislative majority, the preference has been for one-party minority governments (Pulzer, 1975, p. 40). According to its inner logic, the institutions of the Westminster system are therefore justified by offering a programmatic choice to the electorate by competing parties, where the terms of the competition are simplified by a bipolar party system and where the concentration of power, facing institutionalized opposition, is an essential device for ensuring that accountability is maintained.

The notion that political choice is essentially bipolar is one that has pervaded defences of the model of responsible government.

The historian Macaulay, for example, sets out the notion particularly clearly in a passage that was referred to but not cited by Duverger (1964, p. 215). Writing of the Long Parliament of 1641 Macaulay says:

> The recess of the English Parliament lasted six weeks. The day on which the Houses met again is one of the most remarkable epochs in our history. From that day dates the corporate existence of the two great parties which have ever since alternately governed the country. In one sense, indeed, the distinction which then became obvious had always existed and must always exist. For it has its origins in diversities of temper, of understanding, and of interest, which are found in all societies, and which will be found till the human mind ceases to be drawn in opposite directions by the charm of habit and the charm of novelty... Everywhere there is a class of men who cling with fondness to whatever is ancient, and who, even when convinced by over-powering reasons that innovation would be beneficial, consent to it with many misgivings and forebodings. We find also everywhere another class of men sanguine in hope, bold in speculation, always pressing forward, quick to discern the imperfections of whatever exists, disposed to think lightly of the risks and inconveniences which attend improvements, and disposed to give every change credit for being an improvement. (Macaulay, 1906, p. 82)

Though a striking expression of this view, Macaulay's account is by no means an isolated one (Pulzer, 1975, pp. 42–4).

Bipolarity is built into the question of confidence in government. As is well known, British political parties are top-down entities, becoming mass parties as an extension of their parliamentary activity. In parliament, the overarching question is whether 'the King's government must be carried on' (Pulzer, 1975, p. 43). This is a question to which there is only a yes or no answer. It was the role of executive formation, rather than the representation of public opinion, in the legislative chamber that Sidgwick (1891, p. 568) saw as the basic impulse to duality in the party system. Similarly, Amery (cited in Pulzer, 1975, p. 43) says that the natural concomitant of a political tradition in which government as such is the first consideration is that the views of electors and parliamentarians are limited to the simple alternative of being for or against the government.

In Lijphart's classification of political systems, one distinguishing feature of Westminster systems is the absence of checks and balances on the operation of legislative majorities. It has certainly been a feature of Westminster systems that they have made less use of formal institutional and judicial constraints on legislative majorities than other political systems have. For example, the UK has traditionally not had a written constitution or a bill of rights (though the Human Rights Act of 1998 has now altered the situation), and second chambers are relatively weak or non-existent in Westminster systems. However, it may well be that the formal institutional measures are rather misleading in this respect, in the sense that there is nothing intrinsic to the idea of accountable government to prevent the use of checks and balances. Dicey certainly argued that individual rights were better protected in the Westminster system than in political systems in which there were formal bills of rights on the grounds that where the law was silent there was a presumption of non-interference (Dicey, 1915, p. 195). Whatever may be one's views of the merits of Dicey's argument, it does at least suggest that a notion of minority protection is not inconsistent with the principles of accountable government.

5. *Liberal constitutionalism*

The use of the term liberal constitutionalism in the sense I intend it here is supposed to reflect the use of the notion of Whig constitutionalism in Riker's (1982) *Liberalism against Populism*. It refers to a form of government in which the emphasis is upon the capacity of electorates to turn politicians out of office, rather than upon their capacity to achieve an expression of their views in public policy. It is also sometimes known as 'protective democracy' and is the sort of view that one might associate with Schumpeter's (1954) writing on democracy.

A distinctive feature of this view is that popular participation is, and should be, low and decision-making power is exercised by a political (and in Schumpeter's view at least social) elite. In this form of democracy the people do not rule, they merely choose who is to rule them. Indeed, the stress on the lack of popular participation can be taken a stage further, with the thought that the task of the electorate on the constitutional view of democratic government is negative rather than positive. If we ask where the democratic element is in this theory, the answer is that it lies in the capacity of the people 'to throw the rascals out'. In other words, the purpose of making government depend upon popular elections is not to guide the government in the choice of policies, but instead to provide an incentive for rulers not to become tyrannical.

One reason why it is assumed that it is not the task of government to pursue the will of the people is that it can be held that the popular will is not coherent or stable. On classical versions of liberal constitutionalism, for example the *Federalist Papers* (1787), the popular will is not stable or coherent because the people in general are assumed to be turbulent, with fickle preferences. In modern versions, such as that of Riker, other reasons are invoked for being sceptical of the idea of a popular will. So, unlike those versions of the Westminster system in which it is assumed that it is a mandate that the government should implement, Whig constitutionalism may (and in Riker's version does) assume that there is no underlying popular will, and that the task of government is to govern in the sense of maintaining a certain pattern of inherited rights and duties in being.

If constitutionalism sees a small role for popular organization and politics (even smaller than in the Westminster system of accountable government), it sees a correspondingly greater role for judicial and other counter-majoritarian devices. Typical institutional proposals that emerge from the constitutionalist perspective include: an elaborate system of checks and balances to prevent majorities using political power to their own advantage; independent judicial systems with the powers to strike down legislation that is unconstitutional; constitutional restrictions on the powers of legislatures to raise taxation, via such devices as the requirement to maintain a balanced budget; control of the money supply that is independent of the legislature; reductions in the role of parties in the conduct of government; and insulation of decision makers from the pressures of social groups and interest organizations.

Evaluating forms of government

In setting out the above typology of forms of government, I have been describing ideal-types, in Weber's (1947, p. 92) sense, namely simplified descriptions of the distinctive characteristics of each form. There is no supposition that any of these ideal-types either do exist or can exist in anything resembling this ideal form. We have seen that Powell's typology clearly distinguishes actually existing systems, with a core of Westminster systems on one side and the parliamentary systems of the European democracies on the other. Yet, we should also recognize that there are variations in practice within these two broad classes. Among political systems that have inherited the Westminster pattern,

some are federal (Australia and Canada) and others are unitary.
Similarly, the degree of popular participation through institutionalized devices such as the referendum varies among the representational democracies, for example between Switzerland, where it is
high, and the Netherlands, where it is low.

One obvious way in which actual examples of political systems
depart from the ideal-types is that different institutional rules and
practices may operate at different levels of government. Typically, for
example, sub-national governments offer more opportunities for participatory devices than national governments. Thus, the use of devices
such as the referendum and citizens' initiative is well developed in
many states of the USA, but not used at all at the national level.
Similarly, in international systems of governance different institutional
principles may operate in structuring patterns of decision making that
operate at the national level. Thus, the EU may be compared to a system
of liberal constitutionalism, with elaborate checks and balances and a
leading role given to the judicial institution of the European Court of
Justice, even when the political systems of member states are based
on models of accountable or representational government.

Despite the fact that the typology is built on ideal-types, with real-
world analogues being only imperfect replicas, the models of democracy are intended to be alternatives, resting on distinct assumptions
and principles about such matters as the value of political participation, the role of representation, the definition of the popular will, and
so on. In other words, in so far as we are confronted with a choice
about institutional arrangements, each of the models implicitly
involves distinct principles of organization. It follows that each will
appeal to distinct and incompatible evaluative criteria and standards.

We can pick out from our institutional analysis the main respects in
which the organizational principles vary and therefore the dimensions of assessment that are most important in terms of coming to a
normative judgement about the comparative merits of the different
institutional arrangements. I have already suggested that the centrality of the direct/indirect contrast is linked to fundamental views about
the importance or otherwise of political participation by citizens. So,
questions of participation and representation are important. Each of
the models will have something to say about deliberation and the way
in which the differing opinions of citizens are to be aggregated into a
collective decision. Liberal constitutionalism is marked out by the
special place it gives to the separation of powers and the constitutional control of everyday politics, but all the models contain an

implicit rationale of the role that constitutions play in politics. All the models also presuppose political identity in the sense that the body of citizens is defined, so that those who are included in the polity are distinguished from those who are not included. Finally, all the models think that political choice at the collective level makes a difference to the way that democracies behave in their international context. So, the dimensions of deliberation, participation, representation, aggregation, constitutionalism, as well as inclusion and international relations are all relevant to overall evaluation. However, before looking at these different dimensions of democracy, we need to consider what some might regard as the most basic question for any normative theory of democracy: why might democracy be thought a better form of government than the alternatives? In other words, any conception of democracy requires some form of justification. To that central question we turn in the next chapter.

3 The Justification of Democracy

To justify democracy as a form of government is to show either how its practices conform to a principle of right in political morality or how the consequences of those practices lead to a state of affairs that can be judged good in principled terms or by reference to important political values. In this chapter I consider what kind of justification may be offered for a belief in democracy as a form of government superior to other forms of government. For the purposes of this chapter, then, I shall be treating the competing conceptions of democracy identified in the previous chapter as members of the same class, contrasting the notion of democratic government, whatever specific form it takes, with that of non-democratic government. At this stage, therefore, the stress is upon what elements these varying conceptions have in common rather than the features that distinguish them.

Political theorists have advanced a large number of principles aimed at the justification of democracy. In a useful summary Pennock (1979, pp. 130–60) cites the principles of human worth, autonomy, freedom, distributive justice, equality and the rejection of tyranny as grounds for favouring democracy. Such a list might suggest that the practice of democracy could be justified not by reference to one principle but by the fact that it was at the confluence of a number of distinct principles. Moreover, if we can invoke a range of principles in the justification for democracy, this might in itself suggest an interesting point of interpretation. The collective justification might be more powerful than the justification in terms of one particular principle, by analogy with the methodological principle of triangulation in empirical research: the fact that a finding is established by different methods of inquiry makes its more plausible precisely in virtue of that fact.

Despite the appeal of this approach, one must be careful in simply seeking to amalgamate different arguments purporting to justify democracy. When examined in detail the premises of the arguments within which different principles are cited may not be compatible with one another, so that we may find ourselves invoking contradictory conceptions of society, citizenship or other features of political life if we simply amalgamate different principles. This is not to say that we should adopt a monistic, rather than a pluralistic, justification of democracy. It is merely to say that such pluralistic justifications should contain elements that are compatible with one another.

In this chapter I shall offer such a pluralistic line of argument for justifying democracy. It begins with an instrumentalist approach in the sense that the practices of democracy are seen to be justified because of their role in protecting or advancing certain interests, in particular certain common or public interests. This instrumentalist justification needs to be supplemented, however, by the principle of political equality, understood as respect for the dignity of persons. Even with that supplementary assumption, we cannot justify democracy unless we also adopt an assumption of fallibilism, understood as the belief that no one person occupies a privileged position with respect to political knowledge or judgement and that contestation and criticism of what at any one time is judged to be in the public interest is therefore necessary. In sum, therefore, democratic institutions are justified as those practices that promote and protect the common interests of the members of a political community, when those persons regard themselves as political equals under conditions of human fallibility.

To establish the first part of this argument I shall begin with the shortcomings of a purely protective justification of democracy of a traditional sort. Even if we grant that democracy is not always needed for protection from tyranny, as the traditional argument assumes, we shall still need democracy for other purposes. At this instrumentalist stage of the argument, the primary mode of analysis is what I shall call 'derivation'. Derivation requires us to imagine a possible world in which democracy did not exist or was at a minimum, and then to consider what would be missing in such a world. It is not a state-of-nature theory of the sort that Nozick (1974) used to derive his account of the legitimate functions of the state, since it does not purport to offer a hypothetical explanation of how an outcome arises. It is rather akin to Feinberg's (1970) notion of 'a world without rights' in providing us with an intellectual device for highlighting what would be missing from a political morality if certain concepts were not available.

Feinberg argued that in a world without rights persons would not be able to insist upon their claims but would be mere supplicants, so that such a world would be missing an important moral dimension. I shall argue that in a world without democracy it would be impossible to articulate and act in favour of certain sorts of interests. Of course, this notion of justification via derivation suffers from the weakness that it is always open to someone to say that a world without X, whatever X was, was perfectly all right as it was. But then this is no more damaging to justification as derivation than someone saying of state-of-nature theory 'why should I begin from there?' No pattern of justification is immune from questioning by the determined sceptic. Derivation as a method, however, at least has the merit that it is an extension of familiar modes of inquiry in comparative politics, drawing upon the idea that we have greater understanding of any particular instance when we place it alongside contrasting cases. To examine this mode of analysis further, we first need to look at the traditional argument for democracy in terms of protection from tyranny.

The protective case for democracy

If we ask what the varying conceptions of democracy that I identified in Chapter 2 have in common, it is that they all share the feature that the law, rules and policies that define the public life of a society – including the rules that define what is to count as part of that public life – should be the product of decision making by a body that is, in some systematic way, dependent upon the views of those who are citizens of that society. Even in constitutional democracy, where a central fear is that ordinary citizens will engage in too much back-seat driving, there is still an insistence that the device of elections is the principal means by which citizens can 'throw the rascals out', if that is what they judge their professional politicians to be. So, in all the conceptions of democracy, there is some systematic link between the views of citizens and decisions on matters of public policy. Obviously, in the other conceptions that I discussed, there is a more positive view of citizen opinion, culminating in the Rousseauian conception of a society which moralizes its members through the collective self-determination of its general will. Thus, we may say that what the varying conceptions have in common is the idea that the resolution of political questions is made by a body that is at some point dependent upon the views of citizens.

In treating a variety of conceptions of democracy as a class, it is helpful in clarifying our thoughts to ask what the members of that class are being contrasted with, since finding that contrary of a concept is often a good way of defining its meaning. Here we come across an interesting question of method: should we contrast democracy with its historically most prevalent alternatives or with its theoretically most plausible alternatives? If we choose the former, we shall be looking at what can be plausibly taken as feasible alternatives to democracy; if we choose the latter, we shall be putting up the most stringent test that the justification of democracy will have to face.

To see this point, first consider the option of contrasting democracy with the historically most prevalent alternative forms of government in the modern world. These alternatives have been, in the classification due to Finer (1970), façade-democracies, quasi-democracies and military dictatorships. In terms of political morality, none of these is likely to be a serious alternative to democracy, as Finer's account of façade-democracy serves to illustrate:

> until recently most of the Third World was as though stuck in the first, pre-Reform Bill stage of British parliamentarianism – compounded, however, by a marked scarcity or total absence of indigenous liberal institutions; a disregard for civil liberties; a high degree of formal centralization; assiduous and ruthless police; and the pretensions of large standing armies. (Finer, 1970, p. 444)

This could hardly be described as an appetising prospect by comparison with functioning democratic regimes, whatever the faults of the latter. Thus, if this is the sort of political system that is being contrasted with democracy, then democracy wins hands-down. Totalitarian systems and military dictatorships, the other two specimens in Finer's classification, would hardly do better in the competition.

More recently, Dahl (1998, pp. 44–61) has brought together the evidence relating to the comparative evaluation of democratic and nondemocratic governments. As he argued, that evidence suggests that the performance of democratic governments relatively speaking is good judged by a number of plausible criteria. Democratic governments enhance prosperity, maintain civil and political rights and contribute to the maintenance of international peace, and in particular tend not to fight wars with one another, in a way that other forms of government do not. To be sure, these results are statistical. There is currently, for example, a vigorous debate in the literature on comparative political economy as to whether, at certain levels of economic development, authoritarian governments might not be better than their democratic alternatives at promoting prosperity. Yet, even if this particular debate in political economy turns out to favour the proposition that at certain levels of economic development authoritarian governments may be superior to their democratic alternatives, this would not in itself be a very strong argument. *As a general rule*, it would be unwise for citizens to entrust their prosperity to authoritarian elites, even if on some occasions it might turn out to be true that such elites perform relatively well.

Even allowing for the statistical nature of the argument, the sceptic can of course challenge the consequentialist justification of democracy. Perhaps there is a problem of spurious correlation so that societies are democratic because they are prosperous, rather than prosperous because they are democratic. The sceptic might then urge that a stringent consequentialist justification of democracy is one that would make the instrumental role of democracy robust with respect to a wide range of circumstances. One way of doing this is to ground the instrumentalist argument in a more general theory of political behaviour, and this is just what the tradition of thinking that informs the protective theory of democracy has sought to do (compare Held, 1996, pp. 70–100; and Lakoff, 1996, pp. 99–117). Theorists in this tradition start from the Hobbesian assumption that government is necessary in order to avoid civil war and social breakdown and to these ends governments with enough power to enforce order are needed (Hobbes, 1651). But at this point democratic theorists note a problem which Hobbes paid less attention to: if governments have enough power to stop civil war and social breakdown, they almost certainly have enough power to exploit their own populations. A government needs power to protect you from the theft and violence of a lawless neighbour, but what if government itself becomes a source of theft and violence?

Locke's famous comment on this dilemma is worth quoting. Assuming that the deficiencies of the state of nature are sufficient to induce its occupants to set up a system of political authority, he rejects the claim that people would sensibly contract into a form of government with absolute power:

> This is to think that men are so foolish that they take care to avoid what Mischiefs may be done them by Pole-Cats, or Foxes, but are content, nay think it Safety, to be devoured by Lions. (Locke, 1690, p. 372)

Madison developed this thought further, posing it as a problem of political design in paper No. 51 of the *Federalist Papers*:

> In framing a government which is to be administered by men over men, the great difficulty lies in this: you must first enable the government to control the governed; and in the next place oblige it to control itself. (*Federalist Papers*, 1787, p. 322)

Madison argued that the solution to this problem was to establish divided government founded on the principle of checks and balances. The protective theorist of democracy argues more generally that institutions of political accountability in democracy are necessary to avoid tyranny.

The most systematic presentation of this argument was provided in the *Essay on Government* by James Mill (1820). Mill seeks to derive the necessity of democracy from the effects of what he takes to be universal propositions about human nature. In schematic form, his argument can be stated as follows:

1. In order to build up prosperity in a community, people need to be assured of the fruits of their own labour.
2. Government is necessary to enforce rules of property and protection of the person.
3. The whole of the community cannot be expected to defend itself, because people acting together in an assembly simply cannot conduct business effectively.
4. A self-appointed minority cannot be expected to protect the people from tyrannous government.
5. But the people can elect a set of representatives whose function is to check the abuse of power, and if those representatives are subject to sufficiently frequent re-election, then their interests would be brought into accord with the interests of the community as a whole.

Human motivation being what it is, Mill argued that, in the absence of any restraint, those who governed would simply abuse their powers to appropriate to themselves as much of the cooperative surplus of society as they could. Thus, Finer's characterization of non-democratic systems is just what we should expect without any institutionalized system of political accountability. Democracy, on James Mill's argument, is just such a system of political accountability through the institution of elections.

I noted earlier that one of the ambitions of the protective theory of democracy is to rest the case for democracy on a general account of political behaviour, so that the justificatory argument should ideally be robust with respect to a wide range of conditions. In other words, the idea is to make the case for democracy independent of assumptions concerning the circumstances of particular societies. However, it can be argued that this strategy gives rise to a serious problem, namely the extent to which the argument's general and abstract form disguises the partial and one-sided empirical generalizations upon which it rests. The historian Macaulay, commenting upon Mill's *Essay*, notoriously pointed out the problem in a barbed way:

> We have here an elaborate treatise on Government, from which, but for two or three passing allusions, it would not appear that the author was aware that any governments actually existed among men. Certain propensities of human nature are assumed; and from these premises the whole science of politics is synthetically deduced! (Macaulay, 1829, p. 101)

Macaulay goes on to point out that there were non-democratic societies in which people were well governed, a fact that even Mill himself acknowledged in the case of Denmark. So, Macaulay alleges that Mill's method not only leads him to adopt a theory that is contrary to the facts, but also to adopt a theory *because* it is contrary to the facts – a form of argument that is clearly absurd (Macaulay, 1829, p. 102). Claiming that Mill's theoretically derived account of government simply failed to take into account those non-democratic forms of government that were not tyrannous, Macaulay argued that Mill had not demonstrated a general reason why democracy is the only response to the problem of tyranny.

Yet Macaulay's criticism, while it strikes home in some respects, is not entirely fair. To be sure, Mill does admit exceptions to his generalization, such as the state of nineteenth-century Denmark, but he also cites what might be termed 'crucial cases', one of which was the English practice of slavery in the West Indies. Appealing to the prejudices of his readers, Mill assumes that they will agree that English gentlemen are likely to be as civilized as one can imagine slave-owners to be, and then goes on to point out that in the English West Indies slaves were mercilessly exploited and oppressed (James Mill, 1820, pp. 15–16). In other words, even in favourable circumstances, so Mill's argument runs, we cannot guarantee freedom from oppression when some people are given absolute power over others. At this point, then, he appeals to what he takes to be a decisive empirical example. Lively and Rees (1978, p. 33) point out in their introduction to the debate between Mill and Macaulay that Mill became more defensive and in his reply, in the *Fragment on Mackintosh*, was forced to rely upon Hume's principle of the supposition of knavery in institutional design, according to which we should assume the worst of those who hold power. Perhaps this indicates doubts about the extent to which one can generalize even from a crucial test case. Even if Hume's principle were allowed, however, the argument would still suffer from the defect that it only shows democracy to be superior to historically observed alternatives or to the worst feasible alternative. It does not show that democracy has merits against the theoretically most compelling alternatives. Suppose we could contrive non-democratic checks on government to circumvent the problem of tyranny. How would democracy perform against that sort of alternative? In other words how does democracy fare against the best form of non-democratic government that we can envisage?

From adjudication to democracy

Since all the varying conceptions of democracy have in common the idea that decisions should be made by legislators who depend upon the views of citizens about collective choices (including the case where citizens are the legislators), one obvious way of finding a theoretically plausible alternative to democracy is to consider a form of government that reduces or dispenses with the function of legislation. One such alternative would be a judicialized form of government resting upon a body of rules governing social relations, where the rules evolved incrementally over time on the model of the English common law. Sidgwick described such a possibility with his usual clarity:

> a great part of the rules enforced by Government in our own society have not had their origin in express legislation; they have been gradually brought to the degree of precision and elaborateness which they have now attained, by a series of judicial decisions which ostensibly declared and applied rules and principles handed down from time immemorial. And it might be held that this judicial quasi-legislation is, even in a highly civilised society, the best

machinery for introducing such improvements as may be required in the definition of the fundamental rights and duties that constitute the 'individualistic minimum'. (Sidgwick, 1891, p. 324)

As the reference at the end of this passage to the individualistic minimum suggests, the conception of government that most naturally fits with such an institutional structure is that contained in the idea of the minimal or night-watchman state (not an alternative that Sidgwick was advocating incidentally). In this conception, the function of government is to define a framework of rights and obligations that enables individuals to interact with one another to their mutual advantage, but without prescribing some common course of action upon those individuals that they would not themselves choose when exercising their rights.

Jeremy Waldron (1999b, ch. 2) has pointed out that there is a long tradition of political and legal theory, one still active, that is sceptical of legislative activity and that prefers to ground law in tradition or the common law. Moreover, if the close association that Sidgwick identified between the idea of a judicialized, non-democratic, form of government and the idea of the individualistic minimum is correct, then we should expect to find in libertarian writers a theory of government in which the opportunities for democratic choice and deliberation were attenuated or reduced and in which control of social relations was conceived primarily in terms of adjudication among individuals by reference to a customary or otherwise implicit body of rules, akin to the English common law. And indeed, if we turn to libertarian writers such as Nozick or Hayek, or even Oakeshott in his libertarian moods, this is exactly what we do find.

Consider, for example, Oakeshott's discussion of the 'civil condition' (1975, pp. 108–84). According to Oakeshott, the distinguishing feature of the civil condition is the way in which its members, whom he calls *cives*, are related to one another. In particular, the members of the civil condition are not related to one another as partners in an enterprise, but in terms of their subscription to a common practice. At the centre of this common practice is a system of rules, the chief characteristic of which is not to tell *cives* what to do but to prescribe the obligations of *cives* in respect of one another in the pursuit of their self-chosen purposes. As Oakeshott clearly puts it, 'it belongs to the character of *cives* (as it does not belong to the character of agents joined in an enterprise association) to be related as suitors to a judicial court' (1975, p. 131).

According to Oakeshott, legislation does take place within a civil association, but the most striking thing about his own discussion is how little he has to say about its basis and character. He does speak about what the basis of law in civil association is *not*. Thus, for him, it is not the expression of preference, the exhibition of a will, it cannot be deduced from reason, it is not the pursuit of common purposes or interests, it is not 'managerial', and there is no ready and indisputable criterion for determining the desirability of a legislative proposal (1975, pp. 139–40). The list does not end in anything positive, however, and though he later specifies three conditions on legislative deliberation (1975, p. 178), these are largely formal conditions that many rules could satisfy, since what is required is that the rules be enforceable, be related to harm and be accommodatable to the particular political system for which they are proposed. Most importantly, there is no account of how those legislating are supposed to be chosen and to whom they are accountable. Indeed, the 'glimpses', to borrow his metaphor, of civil association that Oakeshott sees in the work of political theorists make it clear that democratic responsibility is not an essential element of the civil condition (1975, p. 181). Sidgwick's non-democratic judicial form of government then is clearly represented in Oakeshott's account of civil association.

It may be that Oakeshott's view of government is compatible with democracy, if we hold with Mapel (1990, p. 405) that an Oakeshottian perspective enables us to see democracy with a certain detachment and irony. Yet, it is equally true that democratic forms of government are not implied by Oakeshott's conception of politics. As noted in Chapter 1, similar points could be made with respect to Nozick's account of political authority (Nozick, 1974). Although Nozick's basis for the political morality is founded in a notion of pre-existing rights rather than in customary law, the function of government, in his view, is adjudicative. Protective agencies emerge to adjudicate, and the dominant protective agency that ultimately becomes the state is the body best able to provide adjudication for its subscribers.

What distinguishes this judicialized form of government from all the varieties of democracy that I identified in the previous chapter? The first distinguishing characteristic is that the principles of adjudication that the judges are supposed to use are derived either from a pre-existing notion of rights or from a customary, traditional code, the basis of both of which are beyond the scope of discussion and deliberation of a legislative assembly. For someone like Oakeshott this is, of course, an advantage, since it means that the development of political principles does not rest upon a constructivist rationalism which seeks particular ends, but merely states the general conditions in which individuals can pursue their own ends (compare Waldron, 1999b, p. 17). The second distinguishing characteristic is also one that Oakeshott and others, including Hayek (1973, ch. 2), have found attractive, namely that it rests upon a conception of society as being made up of a collection of individuals with their own, typically divergent, purposes, rather than a conception of society in which individuals are conceived to have purposes in common. On this conception of the social order, the principles that judges apply impose limits on the freedom of action of individuals, rather than prescribing a substantive purpose. Thus, the law will forbid theft, force and fraud, but within the limits implied by these proscriptions individuals are allowed the freedom to pursue their own individual purposes. In the pure form of this doctrine, the only substantive performance that the law will prescribe is the fulfilment of contractually incurred obligations, a substantive performance that could notionally be rendered as simply forbidding one individual to defraud another.

The third distinguishing feature of this conception of government is that those with responsibility for formulating principles for the regulation of public affairs are not to be made dependent upon an elected assembly or the opinions of citizens at large and so rendered accountable for their decisions. This absence of democratic dependence makes a great deal of sense within the overall conception of society and government, not least because judges are conceived of as developing a customary or otherwise pre-legislative code of principles, rather than implementing the decisions of a legislative assembly or popular referendums. Since the source of judicial authority is to be found in custom, not the resolutions of a legislature, it would simply be otiose to make judges accountable to an elected body. Indeed, since the chief means that a legislature has for controlling governments is to dismiss them on a vote of confidence, this prospect of dismissal is thought to be the best way to control democratic governments. By contrast, the traditional means for securing judicial independence is to ensure that judges cannot easily be removed from office.

In characterizing a plausible theoretical alternative to a democratic system of government, I have of course only provided a sketch, rather than given the full picture, but it is, I think, suggestive even so. For if the *most plausible* alternative to a democratic form of government we can find has the characteristics identified, then it is already possible to see how it is in fact implausible as a conception of government.

The first problem is one that Sidgwick himself recognized in his own discussion. In any system of government in which there is no legislative body, and consequently in which there are no explicitly formulated legislative rules, there is a large penumbra of uncertainty surrounding individual legal obligations. Courts proceed by making decisions on individual cases that are brought before them, and although their decisions are binding as precedents within a common law system, courts do not seek to anticipate future judgements on related matters by making rules that clearly demarcate the class of cases that are covered. Thus, for example, in matters of product liability, a court may well decide that widget manufacturers are liable for defects in their widgets, but it will not be clear if consumers are able to claim reparations for purchases of goods that are like widgets in some respects but unlike them in others. In other words, in quite ordinary transactions, there will be uncertainty about where the borders of liability are to be drawn, and there will be no general principles governing exchange and transactions. This uncertainty may make it difficult, perhaps impossible, for individuals to coordinate their activities with one another for mutual advantage.

This problem of uncertainty is related to the second problem with our hypothetical form of judicialized government, which is its inability to anticipate, rather than merely react to, problems. Consider the problems associated with environmental protection. Experience in industrializing countries with the growth of pollution in the nineteenth and twentieth centuries shows that the control of pollution through the legal remedies of actions under the tort of nuisance must always wait until the damage has been done before a rule is formulated. If we now think about emerging technologies with environmental implications, most notably biotechnology and genetic manipulation, it is clear that an anticipatory capacity is needed to deal with the problems that might arise.

In the third place, a judicialized conception of government has no way of dealing with the cumulatively undesirable consequences of individual interactions. Social problems such as environmental pollution, traffic congestion and urban sprawl arise as the cumulative effect of a series of individual actions each one of which is entirely legitimate taken on its own. In the absence of any governmental capacity to take stock of the whole series of actions, individuals will find themselves worse off than they otherwise need be. In effect, each individual is locked in an N-person prisoners' dilemma with every other individual, where the only rational action is to free-ride on the efforts of others. In Fred Hirsch's (1977, p. 49) evocative image, when all stand on tiptoe, no one sees any better.

It is helpful at this point to introduce a distinction between inter-active choice on the one hand and social or collective choice on the other (Hargreaves Heap *et al.*, 1992). Interactive choice is typified by the pattern of behaviour in a market. The outcomes of a market are a result of the interactions of buyers and sellers with one another, and no individual has a particular overall outcome in mind. Although the individual transactions in a market may be planned, the sum of trans-actions is not. In a social or collective choice, by contrast, the aggre-gate outcomes are planned, though the individual outcomes may not be. Thus, a local authority imposing planning controls on land use will limit the number of houses to be built in a given area over a given period of time, though it will not typically say which builders shall build the houses or which occupiers shall buy them. In other words, the authority constrains the aggregate results of the individual transactions with some overall goal in mind. It is just this collective perspective that a legislative capacity in political decision making provides.

This, in turn, suggests another function for which a legislative cap-acity is needed. When individuals interact with one another, they do so under the terms and conditions that are already established. For example, when traders bring a product to market, its value is determined by the prevailing demand for their products. Even when individuals suc-cessfully bargain to mutual advantage, there is no way in which the structure and form of the background circumstances to the trade can be adequately addressed within the process of interactive bargaining itself. The only way possible is through legislative action that changes those terms and conditions. This is particularly important in labour markets where, for obvious reasons, employers usually have no incen-tive to have regard, for example, to the family circumstances of their workers, so that wage-rates will not normally compensate workers for the number of dependants that they have.

Thus, there are matters of common concern that need to be resolved if successful cooperation is to take place, but which cannot be resolved by individuals in the conduct of their own business. These common matters include the institutional preconditions for economic and social life, including the system of property rights and civil liability prevailing in the community, as well as the provisions to be made for dealing with the cumulative consequences of individual interactions, of which environmental protection is the most conspicuous. Although we can imagine a form of polity that dispensed with a legislative function in respect of the resolutions of disputes between individuals, it would by its nature be incapable of satisfactorily resolving the collective problems to which any system of interactive choice gave rise.

Democracy and political equality

The argument so far has been that in order to promote or protect certain common interests, it is necessary for the members of society to establish a legislative capacity that can remedy the defects that arise from interactive modes of choice. Whatever the merits of this argument, it may be thought to neglect something of importance, namely why that legislative capacity should be democratic. To be sure, we can always reintroduce the protective argument, but this would throw us back onto empirical generalizations and so weaken the case for democracy against the most plausible alternative. Perhaps, if we are considering the most plausible alternative, we should consider a self-perpetuating meritocratic elite, with a strong internalized sense of the public interest acting on behalf of citizens at large. Some have argued, for example, that this was just the view that inspired the creation of the Commission of the European Community (Hayward, J., 1996, p. 252), and it is arguably the view of government that has underpinned the soft authoritarianism of east Asia.

By contrast with this meritocratic notion, democracy is founded on the idea that each citizen is to be given an equal status within the system of collective political authority. This may be thought of as a deontological claim to supplement the teleological justification of democracy as serving common interests. The political equality of democracy is not simply that everyone is equal before the law, or, to put it differently, that as a subject of political authority everyone should be treated equally. It is also that everyone should have a place in the exercise of political authority, even if this only means electing one's own political representatives. To deny the validity of an idealized meritocracy is thus to assert that political equality is a central component of democracy. Yet what, exactly, is the ground of this claim?

One version of the principle of political equality can be expressed in the maxim that each citizen is as well qualified as any other to contribute to the formation of a political community's decision making and policy making (compare Sidgwick, 1891, p. 587). This maxim denies the claim that there is a special political faculty of governing possessed by some people but not others. It also denies the claim of a 'ruling class', for example an heredity caste, that is entitled to enjoy privileged access to the political machinery of the community. Sidgwick points out that the institutional embodiment of the principle of political equality in Athenian democracy was selection by lot among the whole citizen body for certain offices. We can note an analogous institutional embodiment in modern democracies in the progressive removal of the disqualifications from serving in public office on such grounds as sex, race and property ownership.

This version of the principle of political equality is close to, but not identical with, the principle that Thompson (1970, pp. 13–19) identified as one of the presuppositions of democracy, namely the non-paternalist principle that each citizen is to be treated as the best judge of his or her own interests. (Thompson calls this a principle of 'autonomy' but I shall avoid this term to prevent confusion with the discussion later in Chapter 5.) How does this non-paternalist principle compare with the equal qualification principle that says that each person is as well quali-fied as any other to contribute to the formation of a community's political decision making?

From one point of view the equal qualification principle appears to be weaker than the non-paternalist principle, since the former rests only upon a putative capacity of citizens, namely their ability to make a contribution to collective decision making, whereas the latter claims that persons usually are in practice the best judges of their own welfare. Thus, the equal qualification principle does not say that the democratic capacity of persons is always realized, it only makes the assumption that it could be realized under appropriate circumstances. By contrast, the principle of non-paternalism asserts that persons are typically, not just potentially, the best judges of their own welfare.

This difference most probably reflects the contexts within which the two principles are commonly used. The obvious context for the non-paternalist principle is not that of collective political decision making, but the arrangement by citizens of their private or domestic affairs. To say that persons are the best judges of their own interests is not to say that they are perfect judges. It is to say that no one else is better placed to make decisions on their behalf. Such a principle would appear to be an empirical generalization that is likely to hold under certain circumstances, most importantly when the knowledge required for making a prudent decision is not easily available to anyone other than the person or persons on whom the consequences of the decision might fall. The equal qualification principle, by contrast, does not assume that citizens are always in possession of the knowledge that would best place them in a position to make a decision, merely that there is in principle nothing stopping them appreciating and understanding the relevant knowledge. In this sense, the equal capacity principle ascribes fewer abilities to citizens than the non-paternalist principle.

From another point of view, however, the equal capacity principle rests upon stronger assumptions than the non-paternalist principle. The non-paternalist principle says that in the sphere of their own interests persons are likely to be better than others at making prudent decisions. The equal qualification principle says that one person's contribution to collective decision making is as likely to be as good as that of someone else. Taken in a literal sense, political equality understood as an equal capacity is an implausible assumption. Since in other spheres of life we regard expertise as unequally distributed, why should we regard the capacity for political judgement as equally distributed? It is a point as old as Plato to point out that in steering the ship we trust the captain, who is trained, not the other passengers, who are not. Of course, it is possible to hold that ethical and political disagreement is about ends rather than means, in which there are no specialists (Bambrough, 1956, p. 109). The analogy is not with who should steer the ship, but with the direction in which the ship should head. However, in politics and policy making, ends and means are not always easily distinguished, and if this is so, there surely will be some place for expertise and merit.

The principal argument against privileging expertise appeals to a parallel in political affairs to the principle of non-paternalism more generally. For the non-paternalist persons are the best judges of their own interest (by and large) because only they are in a position to appreciate the consequences of the decisions they make. Even good-natured persons have only a limited incentive to acquire information about the circumstances of others in conditions of bounded rationality. So, in cases of collective decision making, where the consequences are public so that they fall upon all and sundry in a general way, no one person has the incentive fully to investigate what the decision will mean for others. Hence all should be able to contribute to the decision, to ensure that the collective deliberations take account of all relevant points of view. Political equality means here, as Dahl suggests, that no one person is so definitely better qualified as to be presumed capable of acting on behalf of others (Dahl, 1989, p. 98; compare Lakoff, 1996, p. 20).

So far we have considered the ideal of political equality in the form in which it precludes an appeal to the rights of a privileged group to control the machinery of political decision making within a community. This approach is most at home in a context where we might be thinking of the political rights of the general body of citizens against the claims of a 'ruling class'. However, we also have to consider the value of political equality as it applies to the relations of citizens to one another. In this context, there is a purely deontological element to the concept of political equality, based on the idea of respect for persons, even though the notion of respect for persons is notoriously vague (compare Larmore, 1987, p. 61).

Respect for persons cannot simply mean acting in the interests of another. To see why not, consider the example of proponents of various forms of restrictive legislation in the fields of censorship and sexual behaviour. Such people often argue that they are seeking to show respect for persons by compelling people to act for their own good, despite any protestations on the part of the individuals concerned to the contrary. To act in this way may be a case of loving the sinner while hating the sin, but it is not the notion of respect for persons that I am seeking to define here.

Larmore (1987, pp. 64–5) comes closer to the relevant notion when he says that equal respect means that, whatever we do when we affect others, we must deal with them from within their own perspective. This involves explaining our actions and acknowledging an obligation of justification towards others. There are, I suggest, two ideas contained in this formulation. The first is a form of non-paternalism, in which there is an unwillingness to see elites impose solutions on others. The second is a commitment to the principle that we have an obligation to explain, discuss and negotiate about proposals with others before we put them into practice. Yet, even this latter formulation does not capture the minimum sense of political equality founded on a principle of respect. The extra requirement is that the common enterprise of political life is one in which all members of the community have a place. Hence, the requirement of political equality is not simply that there is a mutual obligation on persons to justify their policy positions to one another, but it also involves the acknowledgement that each member of the community has a place in the determination of the common interest.

If political authority is thought of as something that is exercised by citizens collectively to promote and pursue their common interests, then a failure to include all citizens as equals in the possession of that authority is an assault upon the dignity of the excluded. Beitz comes close to this notion when he identifies an argument for political equality

arising from the higher-order interest in recognition. Political procedures, on this view, define the terms on which citizens recognize one
another as participants in the public processes of deliberation and
choice. To be excluded from the public forum is to be 'socially dead'
(Beitz, 1989, p. 109). However, it is unnecessarily restricting to formulate the point about dignity in terms of a 'higher-order interest'.
For Beitz this formulation is important because his general account of
political equality is contractarian, and in such a contractarian framework it is important to be able to identify, notionally, the interests on
which citizens would not compromise in agreeing to a social contract.
But if the notion of recognition and the importance of upholding dignity that underlies it could be a reason for agreement within a process
of contractual negotiation, there is no reason why it cannot be treated
as a first-order moral claim with political argument (Weale, 1998).
If citizens lose their dignity by being treated as less than equal to other
citizens under a set of political arrangements, we add nothing of moral
force to say that they would not have consented to such an arrangement
in a hypothetical social contract.

Fallibilism

In some ways, the account of the principle of political equality that
I have offered rests upon a form of fallibilism. Any one of us can make
mistakes, and so even the meritorious cannot be granted unaccount-
able political power because they may err in its use. Fallibilism is the
view that human beings are prone to make mistakes in their estimates
of cause and effect relations, their judgements as to the best course of
action to achieve their goals and their appraisals of the characteristics
of a situation in which a course of action has to be decided. Proneness
to error in theoretical and practical reasoning are assumed by the fallibilist to be a pervasive feature of social and political life. If this is
so, then one of the tasks of political life is to institutionalize procedures
that help correct errors.

The assumption of fallibilism on its own will not yield a straightforward argument for democratic government, however. J.R. Lucas
(1966, p. 9) once pointed out that civil servants or technocrats might
regard themselves as fallible, but think that the only people qualified
to criticize their reasoning and detect their fallacies were other civil servants or technocrats. So, in order to get from fallibilism to a democratic
conclusion, we need some proposition such as Popper's assumption

that we should, if we are rational, consider the argument rather than the person who is making the argument. It requires the view that we must recognize everybody with whom we communicate as a potential source of argument and reasonable information (Popper, 1945b, p. 225). In this sense a commitment to fallibilism and a commitment to political equality are mutually reinforcing.

In bringing attention to the role of fallibilism in the justification of democracy, I am also bringing attention to an aspect of the deliberative component of democracy. The importance of deliberation has been a central theme in many contemporary accounts of democracy, and in the next chapter I shall take up some of the points of overlap, as well as the differences, with the account I am offering here. Anticipating that discussion somewhat, I shall simply say here that fallibilism rests upon more modest assumptions than those typically adopted by deliberative democrats. In particular, in a number of versions of deliberative democracy, consensus on political questions is seen as the ultimate goal of politics, such that the grounds on which political action is advocated are constrained by the requirement to make them acceptable to others. The requirements of fallibilism are less demanding in this respect, since the guiding idea for the fallibilist is not that the reasons for political action be mutually acceptable but that those reasons be open to potential refutation. The fallibilist can therefore say to the decision maker: you should not do what you are doing, but if you are going to do it, your current assumptions as to likely effects are mistaken.

Political fallibilism can in part be traced back to the 'burdens of judgement' identified by Rawls (1999a, pp. 54–8). For Rawls pluralism of conceptions about the good life among citizens is inevitable as a consequence of the normal operation of human reason. Indeed, there are several features about the operation of human reason that lead to differences of judgement among citizens. These features include: conflicting and complex evidence; the weight to be given to diverse considerations; the vagueness of concepts; the varieties of human experience rooted in such things as the division of labour; the difficulty of making an overall assessment of different kinds of normative consideration that bear upon an issue; and the fact that social institutions exclude, as well as include, certain social values. The conjunction of these features means that different citizens will inevitably hold to differing conceptions of the good life. However, strict fallibilism does not have to endorse this inference, for even if all citizens held to the same conception of the good – say by virtue of the widespread adoption of a national religion – mistakes of fact or of interpretation could arise in choosing a political course of action. Thus, if it were accepted that anyone in the society might identify what those mistakes were, then the basic elements would be in place for the justification of democratic institutions.

Common interests and political ideals

On the account of democracy so far, democratic political institutions are to be seen as the means by which citizens advance their common interests, conceiving themselves as equals in conditions of fallibility. However, I have not so far set out an account of what those interests might be. Instead, I have relied on intuitive notions such as 'prosperity' or the *obiter dicta* of theorists such as Locke and James Mill. In some ways such agnosticism about the theory of interests (and related concepts such as human welfare, the public good and human flourishing) is inevitable in any normative theory that is not exclusively devoted to such topics. However, it may be helpful if I set out, at least schematically, what form an account of interests might take.

How then are we to understand the notion of interests? Here is a stipulative definition. Governments protect interests when they ensure the provision of certain classes of goods to members of society. There are three main classes into which these goods fall: public goods, in the strict sense developed in economic theory; those goods that Rawls termed 'primary goods'; and the political goods associated with having disputes about the previous two categories of goods settled in a peaceful and relatively civilized way. I shall say something about each of these three categories in turn.

The category of public goods has been well defined in economic theory to cover those goods that are non-rival and non-excludable in consumption (Samuelson, 1954). A good is non-rival in consumption if its consumption by one person does not diminish consumption by another. A good is non-excludable, if, when it is supplied to one person in a group, it is supplied to all, whether or not they have paid for it. A standard example of a public good satisfying these two conditions is clean air in a city or a region. No one in the city or region can be excluded from its enjoyment and any one person's enjoyment does not diminish the enjoyment of others. Other examples of public goods in this strict sense include a well-functioning system of property rights, the provision of law and order, protection from external threats to a society and many forms of environmental protection. To say that a good is public in this sense is not to say that all members of society place an equal value on the provision of the public good. Usually, for example, some members of a society are more willing than others to put up with dirt and squalor. Rather, goods are public when, at whatever level they are supplied, all members of a group will experience that level.

To the category of public goods we need to add the category of primary goods. These differ from public goods in that they can be supplied in excludable forms, and typically some principle of individual allocation is presupposed in their distribution. The term 'primary goods' was introduced by Rawls, and was originally defined as those goods it would be rational to want if one wanted anything at all. Subsequently, Rawls has moved away from this rational choice conception and has characterized primary goods as 'all-purpose means that are normally needed' for pursuing whatever conception of the good life one has together with maintaining a sense of one's own good and a sense of fair social co-operation (Rawls, 1996, p. 76). The sorts of goods that Rawls has in mind, under either of these two definitions, include basic rights and liberties of the person, for example freedom of movement and free choice of an occupation, along with income and wealth and what Rawls termed the social bases of self-respect. The key characteristic of these goods, therefore, is that they function as multi-purpose goods for individuals, but unlike public goods they do not have to be supplied in equal quantities to all members of society. Indeed, before the advent of mass democracy, political rights and freedoms were unequally distributed, and, after the advent of mass democracy, income and wealth continue to be unequally distributed.

The third category of good that I shall identify as common interests are the political goods associated with having disputes about the two previous categories of good settled in a peaceful and civilized way. I have already noted that the irreducibly collective character of public goods does not mean that there is agreement among the members of society about the level of such goods to be supplied. Such differences of view will reflect differences of opinion and evaluation that it is the task of the political process to deal with. Similarly, there will be disputes over the ways in which primary goods are to be assured to members of society. In particular, there will be disagreements about the extent to which it is legitimate for governments to intervene in markets with the aim of bringing about greater equality in the distribution of income and wealth. The political goods that flow from the peaceful and civilized reconciliation of such disputes comprise not so much the political rights and liberties that Rawls included among his primary goods, but rather the security and ability to plan for one's life that comes to members of a society when they live under a well-functioning system of government. Members of society have an interest in knowing that political disputes will be settled in ways that do not threaten civil disorder.

To ensure the supply of these three categories of good, governments will need to put policies and institutions in place. It does not follow from this truism, however, that the provision of these goods is the direct responsibility of governments, let alone that the goods should always be supplied as public services financed from taxation. Across a wide range of goods, governments will discharge their responsibilities by ensuring that functioning markets are in place underpinned by a regime of legal liability that fairly protects the interests of buyers and sellers. Even in the case of pure public goods, we cannot assume that public supply is the best option. If lighthouses, as a public good, can be supplied through levies among private actors once government has defined a scheme of property rights (Coase, 1974), then a government function has been discharged. The purpose of government is to ensure the supply of the relevant goods, not necessarily to undertake the supply themselves.

To this account of interests there is a significant objection. Let us return to the protective core of the argument. The argument for democracy is founded on a relatively pessimistic view of human nature. It does not assume that people are naturally good, so that they should participate in government as an expression of their self-development. Rather it assumes that people can be predatory and need a representative body to restrain their tendency to abuse power. For this reason some critics have said that a protective theory of democracy 'is neither inspiring nor inspired' and that according to this conception 'government, even to the extent of responsibility to a democratic electorate, was needed for the protection of individuals and the promotion of the Gross National Product, and for nothing more' (Macpherson, 1977, p. 43). To accept this argument is to say that in setting out to protect the sort of goods that I have identified, a protective and instrumentalist account of democracy underwrites an acquisitive view of human nature, and prevents our seeing the positive value of democracy. In particular, it prevents our seeing how democracy provides the conditions for the pursuit of political ideals rather than the protection of interests.

This argument is, I submit, too quick, and part of the problem is contained in the final clause from the Macpherson quotation 'and nothing more'. Macpherson's critique of the protective argument has to assume that the account of interests that we find in the tradition of Locke and James Mill, as well as Rawls, does not simply state the necessary conditions for human flourishing but rather states a set of conditions that, though they may seem necessary, are in fact sources of alienation and discontent. Unless this assumption is made, the proponent of the protective view has an easy response to the critique. If the protection of public and primary goods is a necessary condition for attaining a wide variety of ends, then it will be the function of government to secure those goods under the best conditions possible, for without the securing of those goods, no other forms of human good will be attainable at all. If we think that government ought to protect public and primary goods, it is largely because this is a way of securing to humans the conditions under which deeper forms of fulfilment are to be attained.

Even this reply will not satisfy the determined critic, however. That critic will restate a view that is found many times in philosophy, but whose political effects were explored most extensively by Rousseau and Marx, namely that a focus on tangible public and primary goods tends to a commodity fetishism. Commodity fetishism may be defined as a distortion of human priorities from activities expressing human excellence or the development of human relationships to a focus upon the possession of material objects. In effect, according to the proponent of the thesis of commodity fetishism, the desire of humans to possess objects turns into the possession of humans by those objects. The good is lost in the pursuit of goods.

This is obviously a large topic and it is not possible to do it justice in the space of a short discussion. However, it is possible to make a number of relevant points that weaken this possible line of argument. First, not all the goods that I have identified as part of human interests take a material form. The most obvious example is that of environmental protection, in particular landscape and species protection, which has value by reference to the wider meaning with which human beings invest the world (Goodin, 1992). Secondly, we do not fully have to accept the 'hierarchy of needs' thesis associated with Maslow to accept that many individuals need a certain modicum of private goods in order to develop their higher faculties, a truth nicely captured in Virginia Woolf's (1929, pp. 93–4) observation that what women need in order to be writers is £500 a year and a room of their own. Thirdly, whilst it may conceivably be true that human fulfilment would be higher under a social regime of the communal sharing of goods than under a regime of private property, no one has shown that the control of private property under governments that lack democratic accountability leads to any other outcome than kleptocracy.

A similar point can be made in respect of the claim that a protective theory, modified by political equality and fallibilism, places too great a focus upon interests rather than ideals. From the viewpoint of individual citizens, much that is a matter of the common interest is an issue of political ideals. Thus, it may simply be a matter of common interest that there be a system of property rights or that there be the means of environmental protection, but each individual will be living up to an ideal of citizenship when he or she acts in order to promote and protect these common interests. Hence, from one point of view, we cannot make too sharp a distinction between ideals and interests.

Democracy and consent

One frequently used argument in favour of democracy is that it is government by consent. If we hold to the Jeffersonian principle as set out in the US Declaration of Independence that just governments derive their powers from the consent of the governed, then democratic government will be justified if it alone can be said to be government by consent.

In speaking of government by consent, we need to distinguish two ways in which the idea can be used, as Bryce pointed out (1888, pp. 14–23) many years ago. In the first sense the idea is used in relation to consent to a system of government; in the second sense it can be used to refer to a system of government in which decisions taken by governments are subject to the consent of citizens. It should be clear that the distinctively democratic claim is that governmental decisions should be subject to popular consent, not that the system of government should be subject to consent. If it were merely the latter, then it would be impossible to distinguish the legitimacy of democratic and non-democratic government. After all, Hobbes's (1651) theory of political obligation grounds the authority of government in the consent of those subject to it, but the form of government may as well be authoritarian as democractic on Hobbesian premises. Hence, there does not seem to be a special connection between the requirement that the system of government be subject to the requirement of consent and the requirement that the system of government be democratic.

The conclusions of authoritarian versions of social contract theory have to rely of course upon the fiction of a hypothetical social contract, and it might be open to someone on this basis to argue that the hypothetical reasoning has been misconstrued. But, as anarchists are fond of pointing out, justifications of democratic government in terms of consent to the system also have to rely upon notions of hypothetical consent, since even within the most democratic governmental system there is never a device for expressing continuing consent over time. Indeed, there is a serious argument to the effect that even in *prima facie* obvious cases constitutional rules and conventions cannot be understood on the model of a contract.

To illustrate the importance of this point consider the establishment of the US constitution in the 1780s. In 1787 there was the constitutional convention in Philadelphia and in 1788 a series of popular votes to elect representatives to ratifying conventions. This process look as though it is a contractual one, in which the members of one generation were agreeing with one another to establish the rules of their common association. Yet, as Hardin (1999) has persuasively argued, the arrangements negotiated at Philadelphia are better seen as the outcome of a process of coordination among powerful actors than as a constitutional contract. To establish this conclusion, Hardin builds on an insight from Hart (1961, p. 113) to the effect that all that is needed for a functioning system of law is that enough people within a community are willing to recognize a set of rules as authoritative. If there is some level of agreement, then everyone else faces a collective action dilemma in overturning the arrangements on which the powerful have converged. The acceptance of the institution of slavery at Philadelphia shows that constitutions can be established without the consent of the governed.

The claim that democracy has special merits by enabling those affected by particular policy measures to consent to those measures has more attraction. After all, through devices such as elections, referendums, and so on, one might say that actual processes of consent go on in democracy. So this looks to be a more promising line of argument than appeals to hypothetical consent to a system of government taken as a whole, since we can have independent evidence about what it is that people are consenting to by simply observing their choices. So on this argument one of the special merits of democratic government is that it enables citizens to consent to laws, policies and measures in the light of which they will have to constrain their otherwise free behaviour.

One issue here is whether the notion of consent is either necessary or sufficient for us to say that someone has acquired authority by virtue of an act of consent, and the answer to these questions obviously turns on the definition of consent. On one definition of consent it is to be understood as the transference of a right. The idea here is that consent forms part of a broader institutional practice of social cooperation which has its own constitutive rules. According to these rules, to consent to an action is to act within the practice in such a way that a right is transferred. This was the view of consent taken by John Plamenatz in the postscript to the second edition of *Consent, Freedom and Political Obligation* (Plamenatz, 1968, pp. 163–82).

If we take this view of consent, then it seems natural to think that an act of consent is criterial for our appraisal of political institutions. By this I mean that once the condition of consent has been satisfied, the right has been transferred and no further questions need to be asked. The only problem then is whether we can find a process within the activities of modern government that functions like an act of consent in this way. One candidate for such a process is participation in elections. According to this view participation in an election is a form of consent to the outcome, and since consent is the transference of a right, participation in an election establishes the right to govern. Since elections are one of the principal devices of modern democracies, it would seem by this argument that only democracies can be classed as falling in the category of governments that rule by consent.

The obvious problem with this approach is that electorates are often divided and many people do not bother to vote. How can we say of those who have not voted or who have voted against the party or candidate who won that they have consented to the outcome, even though it is contrary to their wishes? Some people who are in the losing group may say that they are happy to see the winners get their way, but there is no reason to think that this is a widespread or usual attitude. People may have participated in an election solely with the intention of securing the election of their party or candidate, and have no reason to think that they have consented to the actual result. If we are to maintain the idea that participation in the democratic process is a form of consent, it is therefore going to be necessary to distinguish that part of the meaning of a person's act that derives from his or her intention and that part which derives from the meaning that is attached by the institutional context within which they act. Here we should need to use the institutionalist account of consent to say that participation in elections carries the meaning of transferring a right to govern to the winners irrespective of the intention of those voting.

One analogy would be with ordinary legal processes. Consider the process of making a will. If I transfer ownership of some asset to a beneficiary after my death, then I cannot circumscribe the uses to which the asset shall be put. I may intend that the transfer entail the obligation that the family house is always to be maintained as a single dwelling, but I cannot impose these conditions on beneficiaries. Once they have legally acquired the asset it is theirs, and if they wish to turn it into flats they have the legal freedom to do so. So, whatever my intention in making the will, the institutional meaning of my act will trump the meaning derived from my personal intention. In just the same way, someone might argue that participation in an election carried a series of institutional meanings. It meant not simply the transference of a right to govern in the event of one's preferred candidate being elected, but also such transference in the event of any qualified candidate being elected. If consent is the transference of a right, then there would seem to be no reason why we could not construe electoral participation as such a form of consent. This would give meaning to the idea of tacit consent.

This is clearly a logical possibility, but I doubt that it can explain how the notion of consent functions standardly within liberal democracies. If we take the analogy to legal processes seriously, then it is clear that the ascription of intentions by virtue of undertaking certain legally defined acts is possible only because there has been some legislative or judicial interpretation explicit to that effect. Moreover, those who undertake legal actions such as making a will would be imprudent if they did not take specialist advice on the meaning of what they were doing. The ascription of meanings independently of intentions is not arbitrary but takes place within an institutional setting in which there are well-developed and agreed techniques for working out what the meaning of particular acts is (and of course well-developed techniques for settling disputes about the meaning of acts when they are in question).

Taking the analogy to the political case reveals that there is not this hinterland of institutional provision for settling the meaning of particular acts. By analogy with everyday legal processes, we should require something like a constitutional convention or constituent assembly to define explicitly the meaning of crucial political acts such as voting, as well as continuing provision for resolution of differences of interpretation. But in the political case there is simply not this rich institutional background to provide an authoritative interpretation of the acts of individuals, and a great deal of politics consists precisely in the unresolved dispute of questions about the meaning of such actions as not voting in an election, not paying one's taxes, occupying a building as part of a political protest or taking up a seat in the legislature. In short, to justify democracy, we cannot appeal to the notion of government by consent. We need the more complex notions of common interests, political equality and fallibility.

4 Deliberation, Consensus and Political Equality

In the previous chapter I sought to justify democracy as a form of government in terms of the requirement to attend to common interests that would otherwise be neglected. The argument moved from the need to institute protection from arbitrary government through a thought-experiment about the most plausible alternative to democracy to considerations of political equality under conditions of human fallibility. This last point has particular implications. The principle that any conception of government needs to recognize the fallible character of human judgement is especially related to that class of goods that I have identified as distinctively political, involving the provision of institutions to settle disagreements in situations where a common policy is essential. If there are disputes about the supply of public and primary goods, and if each member of society has an interest in the peaceful and civilized resolution of those disputes, then no one person or group of persons will have sufficient knowledge to secure the right answer to any particular problem. Some form of public reasoning about feasible alternatives, involving citizens in general, will have to be instituted. From this point of view, the problems of politics are problems of deliberation. That is to say, where there are differences of opinion about what collectively is to be done, then some set of institutions will be necessary to deliberate about the different points of view that are advanced. Just as individuals confronted with the need to make a practical choice in the face of conflicting reasons will need to deliberate on the relative strength and force of those reasons, so the members of a political community will need to deliberate about their common course of action in the face of competing opinions.

Understanding political problems as stemming from a situation of practical reasoning and deliberation already suggests a rationale for a number of democratic practices: the representation of a range of legitimate interests in the making of decisions; public consultation on policy proposals; the use of intersubjectively testable evidence in policy making; the requirement that decision makers be accountable for their decisions; and requirements of openness and transparency in processes and arguments leading to a decision on items of public policy. In these ways, democratic government may be conceived of as a system of public discussion, designed to deal with the deficiencies of decision making that arise as a result of human fallibility.

Seen from this point of view, the account of democracy that I am offering may seem to overlap with contemporary accounts of deliberative democracy that are currently influential, and indeed there are many points of contact. It would be wrong to suppose, of course, that there is a unified and coherent school of deliberative democrats holding to an agreed body of propositions. However, one influential strand of thinking about deliberative democracy stresses the importance of basing political decisions on reasoned argument leading to general agreement. If we were looking for a single slogan to summarize this school of thought, it would probably be Cohen's (1989, p. 22) formula that political outcomes are legitimate 'if and only if they could be the object of free and reasoned agreement among equals'. This principle is echoed in Dryzek's claim that deliberative democracy holds 'that outcomes are legitimate to the extent they receive assent through participation by all those subject to the decision in question' (Dryzek, 2001, p. 651).

There are a number of ways in which this claim might be motivated, but one important strand of thinking has been to link the search for political legitimacy with a putatively basic requirement of moral reasoning. Thus, Nagel (1991, pp. 36–7) explicitly ties the notion of political legitimacy to the idea of voluntary participation in a practice and invokes Scanlon's (1982, p. 110) criterion of an action's being wrong if it would be disallowed under a system of rules that no one could reasonably reject. Behind this line of argument, of course, there is a liberal view of the person as an inherently autonomous being. It is not difficult to see how this account of political legitimacy can be linked to the idea of deliberative democracy as reasoned agreement. Richardson (2002, pp. 62–5), for example, associates the view of the free person with the idea of government through public discussion by suggesting that the liberal demand that persons be treated as autonomous gives rise to three requirements. The first is 'that the political process publicly address each citizen as someone capable of joining in discussion'. The second is 'that the political process solicit the participation of each citizen as a potential agent of political decision', which is tied, thirdly, to the idea that each person is to be treated as a self-originating source of claims. For Richardson, the first two claims together imply that government should take the form of rule by the people.

Making deliberation central to an account of the values of democracy is not a new idea, however. Sir Ernest Barker (1951, pp. 67–8), in a flowery, but insightful, passage, advanced just such a view, arguing that, when faced with the need for a common course of action, people pooled their minds and put forward a point of view for others to consider. He argued that such processes of common reasoning were widespread in many societies, citing tribal gatherings, folk-moots and modern parliaments as examples. He connected these ideas to the values of democracy as follows:

> Any society, to be worthy of the name, must consist of *partners*, who enjoy a say in the affairs of the society. When a society ceases to be that, it ceases to be a society. It becomes a mere heap of the leader and his followers – followers strung together, like so many dead birds on a string, by the compulsion of leadership. (Barker, 1951, p. 68)

For Barker, then, as for modern deliberative democrats there was a commitment to the idea that reasonable discussion contributes to making a democracy a free society.

Proponents of deliberative democracy seek to provide a theoretical account of democratic politics in which reasoning and the exchange of viewpoints provide a way of understanding the values of democracy and the sources of its political legitimacy. One theorist who has sought to work out such a theoretical account in recent years is Habermas, especially in *Between Facts and Norms* (Habermas, 1996). Habermas sees the legitimacy of a legal system as depending upon the engagement of citizens communicating with one another. He traces this conception of social order to the democratic theorizing of Rousseau and Kant, to whom he ascribes the idea that 'the claim to legitimacy on the part of a legal order built on rights can be redeemed only through the socially integrative force of the "concurring and united will of all" free and equal citizens' (Habermas, 1996, p. 32). As this quotation shows, for Habermas political systems are democratically legitimate if and only if they involve agreement among equals, where the agreement is reasoned in a situation in which the participants are uncoerced.

An alternative, but in some ways complementary, way of seeing the centrality of legitimacy through discussion and public reasoning arises from the claim that a political association satisfying the requirements of deliberative democracy is one whose members are disposed to seek for fair terms of cooperation with one another (Gutmann and Thompson, 1996, p. 53). If we think, along with Rawls (1996, p. 4), that moral and religious pluralism is the inevitable result of the powers of human reason at work in the context of free institutions, then it seems natural to say that common political decisions need to reflect the inevitable differences of viewpoint to which moral pluralism gives rise. In turn, this would suggest the principle that Gutmann and Thompson advocate in relation to deliberation within a democracy, namely that of reciprocity, according to which political legitimacy rests upon decisions that derive from mutually acceptable reasons among citizens who nonetheless differ in their moral and religious viewpoint. According to this account, the requirement is not one of an actual consensus, but rather a reasonable consensus grounded in the requirements of fairness.

At one time, it was common for proponents of deliberative democracy to advance their theory by contrasting it with a (somewhat ill-defined) model of aggregative democracy, implying that deliberative democracy and aggregative democracy were competing and opposing modes of political organization. However, since those early heady days, many deliberative theorists have recognized that in the absence of complete consensus (perhaps even in the presence of deep disagreements) voting and other aggregative methods will continue to be necessary (Bohman, 1998). One inference some have drawn from this concession is that there is nothing intrinsically undesirable about aggregation, merely that what is aggregated should be reasoned and reflective preferences rather than raw or uninformed preferences. The problem is not with aggregation as such but with what Goodin (2003, p. 12) calls the 'mechanistic and meat-grinder aspect of the aggregation of votes into collective decisions'. If we allow deliberation at the pre-decision stage and aggregation at the decision stage, we do not have a contest between the two models of democracy, but merely different aspects of a not very complex story. When we vote we do not reason, but if we cast reasoned votes our aggregation scheme will be improved.

A further development of this thought can be associated with a third way of thinking about deliberative democracy, distinct from that of either Habermas or Gutmann and Thompson, namely that of proponents of greater deliberative opportunities for citizens within a representative democracy. One leading advocate of this position has been James Fishkin (1991, 1995), whose work is particularly associated with deliberative polling, in which a representative sample of citizens is brought together to discuss and deliberate on some matter of public concern.

However, there are other forms of deliberative citizen participation associated with other theorists advocating various forms of deliberative citizen engagement in policy making. On these accounts, deliberation does not replace the familiar institutions of politics, in particular political decision making by representatives selected through a process of competitive elections. Rather it supplements those processes, with the aim of informing the choice of citizens about electoral candidates and informing policy makers about the considered or reflective preferences of citizens.

Although it is convenient to use the expression 'deliberative democracy', strictly speaking this is a misnomer. No democracy could be solely deliberative (compare Saward, 1998, p. 64). Rather what we should speak of is the deliberative component of democracy, with the understanding that institutions and practices of deliberation are an essential part of democracy. One of the reasons why deliberative institutions are necessary in a democracy follows from the fact that citizens are persons who reason in pursuit of their practical ends. This notion of deliberation as central to reasonable human action, including political action, is found in different sources. Aristotle's account of choice as something within our power that we desire after deliberation and his elaboration of that idea in the *Nicomachean Ethics* (Book III, iii, 19) is one obvious source. Another is J.S. Mill's insistence in *Utilitarianism* (Mill, 1861b, p. 135) that it ought to be possible to conduct political arguments by reference to considerations 'capable of determining the intellect'. The idea here, then, is to see distinctively human action as the product of reasons and reasoning, contrasting it with an account of action that sees it as the outcome of conditioned reflexes or habits induced by socialization. From this perspective, the notion of deliberation is tied to a very general account of human action at the level of the individual, an account that is nonetheless distinct from competing characterizations.

However, we can bring this rather general idea closer to the specific claims of deliberative democrats if we see this account of action as forming a critique of what Sen (1977) once termed the 'rational fools' conception of human agency. Sen's critique was aimed at those rational choice conceptions of the person, in which persons were seen merely in terms of preference orderings, without their having the ability to shape or redirect those preferences. Once we allow for deliberation, however, we have put in place the conceptual element that will allow for preference alteration. Then, if we imagine deliberation taking place through political discussion, we have in place one of the building blocks for a deliberative conception of democracy. Democracy is not simply about the aggregation of given preferences. It also involves processes of discussion and the exchange of information through which preferences are formed.

Even in this brief summary of the claims of deliberative democrats it is possible to see an attempt to bring together a number of distinct ideas. Government through unforced discussion is a way to secure reasonable agreement among citizens. Such reasonable agreement is necessary for government by consent, and it embodies the idea that persons are autonomous at least in the weak sense of being capable of willing favourable conditions for their own lives. However, in addition to these claims about the person, there is also the idea of fair social cooperation, an idea that is intended to bridge the gap between what is in practice accepted and what might be reasonably acceptable.

Although these claims have been typically advanced by political theorists, it is not only theorists who have been concerned to promote political deliberation among citizens. At the practical level many experiments have taken place in the last few years across different democracies involving such innovations in public decision making as citizen juries, deliberative polling and other forms of participatory decision making. Even as august a body as the UK's Royal Commission on Environmental Pollution (1998) argued in its report on standard-setting that, though the regulation of environmental hazards inevitably involves specialist scientific judgement, the setting of standards has to go beyond science through a publicly open process of discussion and consultation since the setting of limits for acceptable risks is inevitably value-laden (compare Weale, 2001). In many other realms of public policy, in many democracies, there are well-established deliberative devices intended to secure public participation in the making of collective decisions.

The claims of deliberative democracy are important, then, both theoretically and practically. However, it is one thing to state the general ambition behind the idea of deliberative democracy; it is another to develop a theoretical account of the practice of democratic deliberation that can withstand criticism. Can we really use the ideas of deliberation, public discussion, autonomy and fairness to make sense of the idea of democratic government? How do these ideas comport with a theory of democracy in which common interests, political equality and fallibility are the central ideas? Even if we accept that the rational fools conception of agency is a gross simplification, can the emphasis upon the deliberative basis of political decisions be provided with a normative justification and rationale?

Consensus and deliberation

One central strand of thinking among deliberative democrats is to assert the principle that public deliberation should be aimed at securing the agreement of all. There are many aspects to this aspiration, but an important theme has been the desire to ground political action in a process of non-coercive reasoning. However, there is no one account of what this might mean and there are in principle various ways in which a model of public reasoning could be constructed.

As a preliminary way of fixing ideas, it is useful to compare deliberative democracy with the decision-procedure that Brian Barry (1965, pp. 87–8) once called 'discussion on merits'. Barry defined the notion as follows:

> As an 'ideal type' this involves the complete absence of threats and inducements; the parties to the dispute set out ... to reach an agreement on what is the morally right division, what policy is in the interests of all of them or will produce the most want-satisfaction, and so on. (Barry, 1965, p. 87)

There is, of course, nothing intrinsically democratic about the procedure of making decisions by discussion on merits. Such a procedure could be used by Lucas's meritocrats (discussed in Chapter 3) who took one another's opinions seriously but did not care about the views of the general public. However, although not essentially tied to the idea of democratic decision making, it is an idea that can be applied to it.

One way of understanding the view that decisions should be made on their merits is as follows. There are reasons and evidence that bear upon a particular problem, and the best policy in relation to that problem, and discussion is the best way of ascertaining not only what these reasons are but also what weight should be attached to them. This account would be consistent with an objectivist view of practical rationality of the sort discussed by Raz (1990, p. 17), according to which it is not the beliefs of actors that make action reasonable but the state of affairs to which those reasons point. Thus, it is not my belief that it is raining that makes it reasonable for me to carry an umbrella, but the fact that it is raining. On this view, methods of inquiry and decision making are justified by their tendency to track objectively valid reasons more accurately than alternative methods. It is of course an open question as to how far existing political procedures are successful in tracking the reasons that would justify any particular decision, but at least one proponent of a deliberative interpretation of democracy has argued that in practice representative democratic institutions are capable of identifying and responding to valid reasoning in the making of decisions. Bessette (1994, p. 46), for example, writes: 'The deliberation that lies at the heart of the kind of democracy established by the American constitutional system can be defined most simply as reasoning on the merits of public policy.'

_ The fundamental idea in this approach, then, is that the open political procedures associated with well-functioning democratic practices are the best way of arriving at the reasons for action that would enable decision on the merits of the case. On this account, there an analogy between scientific procedures and democratic procedures. Scientific procedures are a way of ascertaining true states of affairs, whilst democratic procedures are a way of discovering the valid reasons for a course of action. It is important in this conception that there is an external relationship between the procedure and the truths or reasons that were being sought. That is to say, truth or validity is not viewed as constituted by deliberative procedures, but deliberative procedures are understood as ways of attaining truth or validity. Richard Braithwaite (1953, pp. 272–3) once pointed out what this meant in the case of scientific truth when he said that if some method other than science – say heavy breathing followed by free association – had such good results, then we should be obliged to investigate that method. Similarly, on the decision-on-merits view of politics, if some method other than free and open discussion enabled good decisions to be made – say priests consulting the entrails of slaughtered beasts or the elite of a political party discerning the meaning of history – then we should be obliged to consider that as a method of making political decisions. In short, on this view, the connection between deliberation and truth in science or validity in decision making is empirical. Institutionalized discussion, in suitable form, simply has the consequence of leading to better results.

However, although this view of public deliberation as tracking objective reasons is a possible account of the basis of deliberative democracy, it has not been a prevalent one among theorists recently, in part because there is a general scepticism about the representational theory of truth and reasons on which it depends. To say that a theory of truth or reasons is representational means, among other things, that the putative truths or objective reasons can be represented in a way that is independent of the procedure or process by which human beings come to hold to propositions as true or reasonable. Habermas (1996, pp. 12–13) appears to argue this point in a somewhat obscure passage, where he writes:

> The semantic critique of representational thinking holds that the sentence 'This ball is red' does not express a particular representation of a thing, that is, a red ball. Rather, it is the linguistic representation *of the fact* the ball is red ... Otherwise one is misled, along with Frege, Husserl, and later even Popper, to a Platonic conception of meaning, according to which thoughts, propositions, or states of affairs enjoy an ideal being-in-themselves. (Habermas, 1996, pp. 12–13)

Although it is difficult to reconstruct his exact meaning in this paragraph, he seems to be claiming that any correspondence theory of truth has to posit the existence of what Popper (1972) called a 'third world' in which thoughts and propositions enjoyed an existence in themselves. For Habermas this is no more plausible than Plato's realm of forms. In place of such an account, we need a post-metaphysical account of reason. It is not that open discussion discovers the truth of the matter or the objectively valid reasons for a course of action, but rather truth and validity emerge from the process of deliberation itself.

How does Habermas develop this claim theoretically? The general contours of Habermas's own approach to this problem are pretty well known by now, but it will still be useful to set them out, so that the difficulties with a supposedly post-metaphysical account of public reasoning can be understood. Habermas bases his account upon a series of arguments about the presuppositional basis of human communication. For Habermas, claims to truth are not claims to considerations that are independent of language users, but instead are claims that are only valid for the way in which a community of language users engage with one another. Such engagement inevitably involves presuppositions as to the orientation of the agents, including tying their assertions to intersubjectively criticizable validity claims and taking on obligations arising from agreements (Habermas, 1996, p. 4). Even a technical interest in control of the natural world presupposes an interest in communication, the implicit goal of which is consensus.

Locating communicative interaction in the supposed requirements of successful communication, by means of this quasi-transcendental argument, Habermas holds that he has secured an account of rationality and reasonableness via a reinterpretation of Peirce's pragmatic notion of truth. As Habermas puts it, 'Peirce explains truth as ideal assertability, that is, as the vindication of a criticizable validity claim under the communication conditions of an audience of competent interpreters that extends ideally across social space and time' (Habermas, 1996, p. 15). Habermas links this to the claim that for Peirce the reference to an unlimited communication community replaces a metaphysical conception of truth and meaning 'with the idea of an open but ultimately cumulative process of interpretation that transcends the boundaries of social space and time from within', linking this notion interestingly to 'the argumentative practices of a republic of letters' (Habermas, 1996, pp. 15–16). Truth on this account becomes a form of warranted assertability, but warranted assertability in the limit, that is to say what a community of language users would agree to were they able to conduct their exchanges indefinitely conforming to the presuppositions of communicative rationality.

Once the concept of truth is understood as that position to which a community of enquirers would tend in the limit, it is possible (so Habermas claims) to unite the rationality of scientific inquiry with the rationality of normative agreement by means of the constraint of universalizability. This claim has been a theme in his writing over a number of years, and it reflects his acceptance that the Weberian disenchantment of the world means that persons can no longer rely upon preformed notions of the good either of individuals or of the communities in which they live. Since neither individuals nor communities can live by standards inherited unreflectively from the past, they have to engage in a process of reasoning about the principles by which they are to live and this once led Habermas to pose the question:

> In which direction would the structures of the life-world have to vary if the undistorted reproduction of a concrete form of life were to be less and less guaranteed by traditional, customary, time-tested, and consensual stocks of knowledge and had to be secured instead by a risky search for consensus, that is, by the cooperative achievements of those engaged in communicative action themselves? (Habermas, 1985, p. 344)

For Habermas himself, the answer to this question involves imposing a universalizability test upon normative reasoning, leading him to the claim that a 'norm is just only if all can will that it be obeyed by each in comparable situations' (Habermas, 1996, p. 161). Just as truth is to be thought of as that which can be asserted with warrant by a community of enquirers, so the validity of norms is to be thought of as that which is consistent with what can be universally willed. In forming our view of collective choices, therefore, we have to appeal to the results of a social dialogue, constrained only by the requirements that the participants to the dialogue can enter it freely and that the process of collective will formation is uncoerced and undistorted. Whatever emerges from this dialogue will then count as constitutive of human interests.

This approach to democracy via discourse ethics has the merit of showing clearly what is involved in a deliberative conception of democracy that makes the notion of consensus and general agreement central in the absence of an objectivist theory of rationality. The claim goes beyond the familiar observation made by many that democracies function better with high levels of consensus or that decision making suffers fewer pathologies if actors seek to find a consensus among different points of view. Rather it says that the search for truth and validity takes a democratic form, at least as far as that form can be modelled on a republic of letters. Indeed, Habermas's ideal speech situation looks rather like a certain sort of participatory democracy, or at least a representative democracy with high levels of public engagement, so that the gap between the moral concept of autonomy and the political principle of democracy is correspondingly narrowed. We have here therefore the articulation of a theory of democracy in which democracy and deliberation are conceptually linked, so that we cannot have an account of democratic practice without also being able to specify what would be the conditions in which free agents would be able to negotiate with one another and come to a collective decision about their common affairs.

How far can this account of democracy be maintained? Two obvious questions arise: how far is Habermas entitled to rely upon his interpretation of the Peircean account of truth and how far, even if there are no questions about the use of Peirce, can the normative theory stand up?

On the first question, one trouble is that Habermas's theory only seems plausible by overplaying the extent to which the Peirceian pragmatist theory of truth depends upon a pure notion of method. In order to assess the extent to which the Peircean pragmatist theory of truth depends purely on a concept of method, it is necessary only to recall the words of Peirce himself:

> To satisfy our doubts, therefore, it is necessary that a method should be found by which our beliefs may be determined by nothing human, but by some external permanency – by something on which our thinking has no effect ... Such is the method of science. Its fundamental

hypothesis, restated in more familiar language, is this: There are Real things, whose characters are entirely independent of our opinions about them: those Reals affect our senses according to regular laws, and, though our sensations are as different as are our relations to the objects, yet, by taking advantage of the laws of perception, we can ascertain by reasoning how things really and truly are; and any man, if he have sufficient experience will be led to the one True conclusion. (Peirce, 1934, pp. 242–3)

As a number of people, including A.J. Ayer (1968, pp. 17–40) and Mary Hesse (1982, p. 98), have pointed out, Peirce's own conception of truth, as can be seen from this passage, was not a pure consensus theory but had elements imported into it from a correspondence theory, at least in his later philosophy. This is well illustrated in Peirce's inductivist justification for the principle of induction, which rests upon the claim that the principles of induction are justified by virtue of the fact that they have been shown to yield successful predictions in the past. In short, and whatever the gloss that Habermas puts on the theory, although in Peirce's approach the consensus of a scientific community warrants the assertion of certain propositions, this is only because the appropriate methods of science, understood to mean any valid principles of inference, enabled opinion to be chastened by experience.

We are not therefore entitled to infer from the claim that a certain method is necessary for truth that truth may be explicated in terms of that method. Truth may be a form of warranted assertability, in the sense that we are only justified in asserting as true those propositions with some warrant from the practices of a community of enquirers. But our commitment to those practices makes sense only if we in turn think that the methods used in those practices are successful at getting at the truth. Truth cannot be detached from method, in the sense that we have no reason for asserting a proposition as true unless there is some methodological commitment behind our assertion, but this is a long way from saying that truth rests purely on method. Rather, from a pragmatist point of view, our commitment to any method derives from a commitment to the belief that the method is more likely than not to yield something that is true. Recalling Braithwaite, as cited earlier, if heavy breathing were as good, we should feel compelled to integrate that into our theory of truth.

It might be said at this point, so much the worse for Peirceian pragmatism. It does not matter whether Habermas has got his Peirce right. If Habermas wishes to claim that truth is method, then he is entitled to do so. But things are not so simple. In so far as Habermas does advance an argument for taking warranted assertability seriously as a test of the acceptability of propositions (whether factual or normative), he does so via an appropriation of what he takes to be the achievements of Peirceian pragmatism. Moreover, Habermas needs a notion of truth as purely warranted assertability if he is to succeed in his fundamental ambition of undermining the distinction between technical rationality and discursive rationality. If we need the notion of correspondence to get final lift-off with a pragmatist conception of truth, then the task of assimilating technical and discursive rationality is made much more difficult, for it requires us to be able to use a corresponding notion of truth in relation to normative propositions – an implication which even the bravest moral realist might fight shy of.

In this context, what are we to make of the second part of Habermas's argument to the effect that open and unforced communication, when norms are at issue, will show that a norm is just only if it enables us to regulate our common life in the equal interests of all? One obvious problem here is that the Habermasian account seems to replicate a difficulty inherent in the Kantian tradition of moral reasoning, namely that it merely provides a formal account of conditions for legitimate decisions that need to be satisfied, but without indicating what the substantive content of those decisions is. A familiar charge, going back to Hegel and J.S. Mill, against Kant's test of of universalizability is that it offers merely an 'empty formalism', in the sense that an indefinitely large number of principles could satisfy the test. Similarly, one might argue of the test of the ideal speech situation that it too merely provided an empty formalism, since an indefinitely large number of contradictory principles might be regarded as emerging from the ideal speech situation. Indeed, Steven Lukes (1982) pointed out this problem in the Habermasian approach many years ago, and yet the critique does not seem to have had the effect on Habermas's theory that it should have done.

To assume that the universalization test will work in such a way as to lead to consensus has important implications for our understanding of the central practices of democratic decision making. Consider, in particular, the role of majority rule. Habermas accepts the majority principle but only as a second-best. It 'only represents a caesura in an ongoing discussion; the decision records so to speak, the interim result of a discursive opinion-forming process' (Habermas, 1996, p. 179). In short, whilst majority rule may have certain practical benefits, it cannot substitute as a source of legitimacy for consensus brought about through the power of reason. Yet, quite apart from the fact that this interpretation of the majority principle appears to confuse losing the vote with losing the argument, it entirely assumes what it needs to show, namely that universalization will lead to consensus. Assume, on the contrary, that there are good faith disagreements about what is in the interests of all. Then majority decision making may be a fair way to resolve the dispute (on which more in Chapter 7).

I conclude, then, that a model of democracy derived from an account of normative consensus generated by method cannot be successful. One implication of this conclusion is that the ambition to reconcile democracy with a strong conception of autonomy looks implausible, in so far as that reconciliation rested upon a claim about the centrality of method in uniting truth and validity. A second implication is that consensus is not constitutive of democratic decision making as Habermas supposes. This does not mean that consensus and the social dialogue that might give rise to it are unimportant in value terms. It means rather that we need some other account of what the status of that consensus might be. Moreover, we need an account of consensus that accepts that there may be persistent moral disagreements about important matters of public policy. In other words, we need to understand the political culture of disagreement and the principles that ought to govern disagreements within a democracy otherwise committed to deliberative consensus. To a consideration of a theory with these aims in view, I now turn.

Deliberation and fairness

Suppose that the members of a society face some common policy problem about which there is deep, conscientious and persistent disagreement. Such issues can be diverse, including the morality of nuclear weapons, the permissibility of abortion or the justification of redistribution. Suppose also that the citizens of this society wish to act on democratic values. What principles should govern the way in which advocates of different and incompatible positions interact with one another?

One answer to this question offered by Gutmann and Thompson (2004, p. 3) is that citizens should offer reasons to one another that are consistent with a fundamental requirement of political fairness. In particular, they suggest, citizens should appeal to principles that individuals who are seeking for fair terms of cooperation could not reasonably reject. Their argument is that this requirement for reason-giving consistent with fairness is common to many conceptions of democracy, and in particular it expresses the view that in a democracy persons should not be treated 'as passive subjects to be ruled' (compare Sir Ernest Barker's 'dead birds on a string'), but as autonomous agents who take part in the governance of their own society.

On this approach, what does it mean to offer reasons consistent with the requirements of political fairness? In answer to this question, Gutmann and Thompson propose a general requirement of reciprocity, according to which reasons given in discussion must be public and accessible. Rousseau (1762, p. 247) once famously said that in a true democracy the first person to speak merely says what all have felt when arriving at the general will. In other words, decisions in a democracy should not be a product of public discussion but should reflect the private and independent wills of citizens, who would nonetheless converge in their judgements. Gutmann and Thompson, by contrast, see the public stating of reasons as being central to democracy and they suggest that any private reasons used by public officials in a democracy evince lack of respect for citizens (Gutmann and Thompson, 2004, p. 4). They also suggest that reasons that are offered should be accessible to other citizens, in the sense that the reason-giving must be intelligible to those with differing viewpoints. It would not satisfy the requirement of reason-giving, for example, for a public official to say that the reason for a decision of public policy was that this was what God wanted. It is, I think, not difficult to see the rationale of such a requirement within a theory that stresses the test of reasonable rejectability. An appeal to God's will might conceivably be acceptable to those citizens who shared the faith of the official, though not necessarily even to them, but it would hardly be acceptable to those who did not share the faith. (Hobbes, 1651, p. 243, wrote that when a man says that God spoke to him in a dream it 'is no more than to say he dreamed that God spoke to him'.) Reason-giving in a democratic society must meet the test that the reasons are mutually acceptable, at least in the sense that they are public and intelligible to those with different points of view.

This requirement of mutually acceptable reasons can be understood as an attempt to deal with one problem in the view that public choices should be based on a deliberated consensus. That problem is the obvious one that even after discussion citizens may disagree, and disagree profoundly, with one another. In other words, we cannot appeal to the upshot of a hypothetically endless discussion as does Habermas. Indeed, on matters of deep moral importance, for example the legitimacy of abortion or the ethics of nuclear weapons, one would expect disagreement to be not only profound but permanent. In the face of the problem of persistent moral disagreement, Gutmann and Thompson offer an approach based upon what they call the 'moral economy of disagreement'. When citizens disagree with one another on matters of moral choice, they should not merely state their competing points of view, but they should also seek to find points of agreement with one another as far as possible. For example, 'pro-choice' and 'pro-life' advocates on the question of abortion will obviously disagree with one another on the main substantive question, but they can still strive for agreement on certain subsidiary matters. Gutmann and Thompson suggest, for instance, that both sides can agree that if abortion is to be restricted, then there should be adequate programmes of financial support in place to promote the well-being of children (Gutmann and Thompson, 2004, p. 82).

The elements of the moral economy of disagreement can be broken down into a number of component parts, as follows:

- *The minimize disagreements principle.* 'In giving reasons for their decisions, citizens and their representatives should try to find justifications that minimize their disagreements with their opponents' (Gutmann and Thompson, 2004, p. 7). What this means is that when people disagree, that is not a licence to exaggerate those disagreements, or characterize opponents as morally bankrupt or corrupt.
- *The broader implications principle.* '[C]itizens should accept the broader implications of the principles presupposed by their moral position' (Gutmann and Thompson, 2004, p. 82). It is by virtue of this principle that those taking different positions on a question can nonetheless agree on subsidiary matters.

Alongside these claims of principle, Gutmann and Thompson also advance a claim about the way in which public understanding will be promoted in a polity in which the economy of moral disagreement is practised:

- *The partial understandings thesis.* 'By their nature, reasonable differences contain partial understandings. Each alone is likely to be mistaken if taken comprehensively, all together are likely to be incoherent if taken completely, but all together are likely to be instructive if taken partially' (Gutmann and Thompson, 2004, p. 29). This thesis claims that the pooling of different points of view is likely to yield better understanding and decision than views based upon a narrow section of the public.

Gutmann and Thompson do not deny that disagreement may still remain after the practice of the moral economy of disagreement, and so matters will have to be resolved through voting. However, they urge that the deliberative quality of a democracy would be improved if these principles were followed.

The Gutmann and Thompson approach seems to me to be the most sophisticated attempt to date to deal with the problem of deep and persistent moral disagreement within the framework of the deliberative democratic approach that is in general orientated towards consensus, and it is partly for that reason that it has attracted so much critical attention (e.g. Macedo, 1999). There are also obvious points at which it parallels the approach of Rawls to questions of moral disagreement and value pluralism within a liberal democratic polity, particularly with its stress upon understanding the implications for moral issues of the idea of fair terms of political cooperation. Potentially, therefore, any attempt to evaluate their position could range far and wide. To avoid too great a sense of intellectual disorganization, I shall confine my evaluation to a consideration of the extent to which the approach I set out in the previous chapter is or is not consistent with this approach.

Within the framework of the account I have been trying to develop, it is difficult to deny that the fundamentals of the Gutmann and Thompson approach make sense. If one stresses, for example, that the principle of political equality depends upon a notion of respect for persons in which citizens should deal with one another in terms of the perspective of the other and in which there is an acknowledgement that all citizens should have a place in the determination of collective outcomes, then the basic principle of reason-giving is difficult to deny. How else could one deal with people from their perspective without seeking to give reasons for collective action that they can understand?

Moreover, political equality is the basis upon which the principle of fair political cooperation is built, so that some attempt to deal with persons on the basis of explanation and justification is important. It is possible, of course, to understand political equality simply on the model of 'one person, one vote' or more generally according to the principle that all interests should be equally weighed, but this would miss the extent to which a theory of democracy needs a richer conception of the person than that contained in the 'rational fools' account. Moreover, if the justification of democracy in part rests upon the need for a legislative function in government to achieve common interests, then the notion that the pooling of partial understandings contributes to a better collective understanding is attractive. Indeed, Jeremy Waldron (1999a) has argued that this pooling of wisdom principle has played a central role in various strands of political thought about legislation.

However, although the principle of giving reasons for a political decision is difficult to deny, it does not follow that citizens should be seeking either to find and offer mutually acceptable reasons in any stronger sense or be seeking to minimize disagreements or be willing to accept the broader implications of their belief-systems. After all, one can argue that citizens owe one another explanation, without that implying that they owe one another political accommodation. They may act on the principle that each person is entitled to his or her own point of view, and that the best public policy is to decide by means of voting. An unwillingness to be accommodating where it is not necessary may make for a political society in which relations among partisans of different sides are cool and distant, but that is not the same as saying that relations are disrespectful. Indeed, a healthy recognition of difference may be the right way in which partisans of competing and incompatible perspectives relate to one another.

One reason for holding to this view stems from a concern with personal integrity and the integrity of one's own political position and commitments. It is not an accident that the term 'compromise' has an ambivalent position in moral language. Being asked to abandon a principled position in order to minimize differences with opponents can lead, in some circumstances, to a sense of political betrayal. Consider for example the use of deliberative devices in disputes about environmental protection and land use planning. For some twenty-five years, in cases where environmentalists and land use developers have come into conflict, there have been interesting experiments with dispute resolution built upon deliberative procedures. One important norm often found in these procedures is that of finding a mutually acceptable outcome that accommodates the different positions of the parties in dispute. However, even relatively early in the experience of these procedures, observers were noticing that on occasions some of the environmentalists felt that they were under pressure from the process to concede on issues where they felt that no concession should be made (Amy, 1987).

In theoretical terms, it may be that this concern with personal and political integrity is what lay behind Rousseau's concern that there should be no public discussion among citizens in their search for the general will. Given Rousseau's well-known beliefs about the corrupting effects of civilization, it would not be surprising to find a connection between a concern for political independence and a commitment to restrict the ability of groups of citizens to discuss with one another their deliberations and inclinations. I am not saying that this is an explicit element in Rousseau's thought, merely that there is an affinity of ideas that is suggestive.

Another danger with a politics of accommodation is that of lowest common denominator policies. Consider in this context the politics of health care. Within a framework that stresses the mutual acceptability of reasons, it is difficult to avoid the conclusion that, where the poor are denied access to basic health care as a result of their poverty, then there should be some public subsidy. To be sure, there will be some libertarians for whom even this is a bridge too far but the work of Daniels (1985), Menzel (1983) and others makes this conclusion difficult to fault. However, from a social democratic point of view, a public policy in health care in which the poor have an entitlement only to a basic minimum of health care is inadequate. The social democratic aspiration has always been that all citizens should have access to high-quality health care without their facing financial barriers to access. The point here is not which side happens to be right in this particular controversy. Rather the point is that a commitment to a politics of accommodation undermines the aspirational quality of the social democratic position (compare Weale, 2004, p. 94). Of course, it is always possible to say that the requirement of mutual acceptability is concerned with the minimum conditions that need to be satisfied if a society is to be regarded as just and democratic, so that social democrats remain free to argue and campaign for their preferred arrangements, within an agreed framework of justice. Yet, to make the test of justified policy one to which those from different positions could subscribe looks close to constraining the legitimacy of securing changes in health policy through the ballot box on grounds of a competing conception of just health care.

Analogous, if distinct, concerns arise over Gutmann and Thompson's 'broader implications' principle. According to this principle, proponents of different positions should argue with one another in a way that respects the broader implications of their respective principles. This requirement is illustrated in the case of abortion by the claim that those who oppose abortion should be in favour of public support for infant care. The exact chain of reasoning is not spelt out by Gutmann and Thompson, but presumably it runs something along the following lines: being pro-life requires one not only to be opposed to abortion but also to support the conditions under which children can grow up free of disease and squalor, and that in turn requires positive public policies, including financial support for the poor. There clearly are a number of steps in the argument that would need to be spelt out before this was unambiguously an implication of a pro-life position, but that is not at issue here. Rather the point is to notice how this example shows the principle of 'broader implications' to be dependent upon a deductive account of political argument. On this account of political argument, a principle is the major premise and a particular instance the minor premise, and the argument proceeds by bringing instances of particular cases as minor premises under the more general principle as major premise.

Some political argument takes this form, but equally not all of it does. Instead, it can be argued that a great deal of effective political argument consists of persuasive applications of descriptive-evaluative terms (Skinner, 1974) to particular circumstances. Terms such as 'humane', 'prudent' or 'depressing' clearly have a descriptive component, in the sense that their meaning can be given through paradigm cases, but equally a great deal of political argument is taken up with applying these terms to particular cases. For example, in the UK debates over abortion in the 1960s, one of the principal areas of contention between conservatives and liberals, was not over the principle of the right to life (since English law accepted that there were conditions in which abortion was lawful, if the health of the mother was threatened), but whether social reasons such as distress or depression should count as lawful grounds.

Someone seeking to defend the 'broader implications' principle might reply at this point that all the example of descriptive-evaluative terms does is to show that a deductive account of argument is not a complete account of normative reasoning in politics, but that nonetheless where deduction is relevant, then the principle should be applied. Yet, this reply also yields another problem. One complaint that has been made by a number of critics of deliberative democracy is that the whole account of political interchange in deliberative accounts of democracy is too rationalistic. By taking *argument* as the relevant focus of analysis, so this criticism runs, there is a danger of ignoring certain sorts of voices, usually those of the less articulate or those less in tune with the predominant culture. Sometimes political positions and demands are best expressed through action, poetry, song or dance, rather than in the form of syllogistic arguments.

One particular variant of this line of criticism is to be found among agonistic democrats. As with deliberative accounts of democracy, agonistic accounts of democracy are varied, forming a group with a family resemblance rather than a coherent and agreed doctrine. However, one theme that is prominent in agonistic democracy is the idea that the search for consensus and wide agreement can be a mask for the domination of a hegemonic discourse in politics (Mouffe, 2000). In pretending to find points of agreement across difference, the agonist will argue, there will be the imposition of an impartial point of view, presented as though it were universal. In these circumstances, the voices of some groups are not simply marginal, they are repressed through the imposition of a dominant discourse. Both Sanders (1997) and Young (2000, pp. 56f) have pressed this objection further, suggesting that deliberative democrats advocate a position that has a rationalistic bias, so the speech that is emotive or non-rationalistic is discounted. Medearis (2005) has urged a similar point in arguing that, in shifting the frames of dominant public discourse, social movements may have to use unreasonable tactics and forms of speech. Deliberative democracy, in particular, excludes narrative, which is the distinctive way in which certain experiences can be understood (Young, 2000, pp. 73–4).

Too rationalistic and deductive an account of deliberation and political disagreement would obviously be a distortion of the character of controversy in a democratic society. Yet, as O'Flynn (2006, pp. 133–40) shows, it is important not to set narrative and principle in too great an opposition to one another. Narratives may be one of the distinctive ways in which the experience of marginalized groups can be understood, but they can also be devices of exclusion, as endless colonial myths go to show. In so far as the stories that people tell are a way of trying to express their experience, they may not easily be reducible to rational propositions. However, this is not to say that narratives are incompatible with the underlying value of respect for others that is at the basis of political equality. Indeed, political equality can be understood as the willingness to listen respectfully to the narratives of others (O'Flynn, 2006, p. 138). Whilst the form in which people contribute to deliberation may require attention from others for whom it is challenging, this is not to question the underlying value of respect that makes common deliberation a worthy ideal.

Putting all of these points together, we can see where the points of tension in deliberative democracy occur. It can be conceded that a basic obligation to explain one's position comes from the very fact of living in a common territorially based polity, with its attendant common problems. However, of itself, that would not imply the principles of political culture that Gutmann and Thompson advance as being required by the principles of fairness in political cooperation. Indeed, there may well be reasons of political integrity, aspiration or rhetorical style that make a politics of accommodation unattractive. But even a politics of difference has to draw upon the principle of political equality and the underlying value of respect that gives it substance.

Institutional dimensions

There is an interesting, if not exact, parallel between this dispute over the merits of deliberative democracy and the institutional character-ization of political systems as being either a representational or a Westminster system. Lijphart's characterization of what he calls the consensus model (his variant of representational government) reads like an account of a system in which differences are minimized and there is an attempt to find common ground across as wide a range as possible. According to Lijphart, the consensus model 'instead of being satisfied with narrow decision-making majorities ... seeks to maxi-mize the size of these majorities' and its institutions aim at 'broad agree-ment on the policies that the government should pursue' (Lijphart, 1999, p. 2). Conversely, the Westminster system is characterized in terms borrowed from Finer as one of 'adversary politics' (Lijphart, 1999, p. 6), a term that would seem suited to a more agonistic view of politics and political discourse and deliberation.

The parallel can be strengthened by invoking Scharpf's (1988) dis-tinction between politics in a problem-solving mode and politics in a bargaining mode. The key point of this distinction is to recognize that political problems typically involve conflicts of interest but they also involve commonalities of interest. A bargaining mode of politics stresses the zero-sum aspect of the situation, and encourages groups to take a view in which they seek maximum gain for themselves. One result of this approach is that those same groups miss out on the opportunities to make the joint gains from the commonalities of interest that they share. One way in which a problem-solving frame of mind manifests itself is the institutionalization of decision making through corporatist modes of consultation, in which the representatives of different social groups, but in particular labour and capital, seek to find points of agreement amid their differences. This is a feature also discussed by Lijphart (1999) for whom corporatist institutions are one of the hallmarks of a consensus political system. Conversely, interest group pluralism, in which groups differ and seek to resolve their differences through bargaining, is one of the hallmarks of Westminster systems.

Another aspect of the distinction between problem solving and bargaining manifests itself culturally and institutionally in differing systems of parliamentary debate. Steiner and his colleagues (Steiner *et al.*, 2004) have sought to develop a discourse quality index of debate and discussion in parliament, and one of their explicit hypotheses is that the quality of debate is higher in consensus systems than it is in competitive systems. Part of their explanation is that in competitive systems there is little incentive for majorities to share information with minorities, whereas in consensus systems the opposite is the case. Even from grand coalitions there may be no obvious exit strategy. Exactly how much weight can be put on this empirical finding, it is difficult to say, since the content-analysis of parliamentary discourse is in its infancy. At the very least, however, the finding is suggestive.

It may seem from this contrast between representational or consensus systems on the one hand and Westminster systems on the other that all the evaluative advantage lay with the consensus systems. However, they have not been without their critics and the criticisms echo the criticisms that have been made of deliberative democracy. One point of criticism for corporatist systems, for example, is that in institutionalizing deliberation and discussion among the social partners of capital and labour, other legitimate interests have been ignored, just as critics have alleged that certain opinions and points of view are marginalized in the attempt to maximize agreement in deliberative democracy. For example, among European consensus democracies in the period since 1945, there is a good case for saying that environmental issues found it difficult to find a place in a discourse of politics dominated by the productivist concerns of labour and capital. Others might argue that the failure to deal with high rates of unemployment in corporatist systems reflected the institutional advantages of insider status that corporatism gives to unionized workers as distinct from non-unionized workers.

My purpose in mentioning these institutional comparisons is not to suggest, however, that considerations of deliberative democracy give us criteria for determining the relative merits of representational and Westminster systems either way. It is to suggest that any choice between representational systems and Westminster ones, to the extent to which changes of democratic arrangements are possible, is also a choice about the type and degree of deliberation that is thought right for the political system. There is no reason why these issues should remain constant over time, certainly as the character of political issues changes. A system that may seem to institutionalize deliberation adequate for a politics of economic management, of the sort that has dominated democratic politics since the first part of the twentieth century, may not be the right sort of system of a politics of identity or bioethical controversy, of the sort that may come to dominate in the twenty-first century.

In this context, I have already noted that at a practical level there have been many experiments with deliberative institutions in relation to public consultation on matters of public policy. There have been citizens' juries on various aspects of health care. Consensus conferences on new technologies are an established feature of Danish policy making. Deliberative polls have been held on crime and healthcare rationing in the UK, as well as the future of the monarchy in Australia. It is possible to give these various experiments in deliberative and participatory policy making a variety of rationales. However, one influential theme has been the idea that it should be possible to improve the quality of representative government by strengthening the capacity of citizens to deliberate about matters of public policy. What is important here is not just that there be deliberation, but that it also involve participation on the part of citizens. In this way, issues of deliberation quickly lead into issues of participation.

5 Participation as Democracy, Participation in Democracy

If we consider the various conceptions of democracy set out in Chapter 2, we see that one central respect in which they vary is the extent to which they presuppose popular participation in the making of policy decisions. At one extreme are those accounts – whether based on classical Athens, the experience of the New England townships or Rousseau's theorizing – in which popular participation is central to the very conception of democracy. From this point of view, participation is thought of *as* democracy. That is why Rousseau was able to say that the British people may think they are free, but they are in fact so only at the point at which they elect their parliament, for in the absence of participation there can be no democracy. At the other extreme is liberal constitutionalism, in which the primary function of democracy is to protect citizens from the power of government, and popular participation through elections is simply seen as a device for control over political leaders to be exercised from time to time. On this latter point of view, there may be participation within democracy, but participation does not define democracy. Contrasting these two accounts, David Miller (1983, p. 133) plausibly characterizes the distinction between protective and participationist accounts of democracy as of 'paramount importance'. Moreover, since there are intermediate positions between a pure participationist account and a pure protective account, controversies over the nature, extent and feasibility of popular participation are going to be a central feature of any normative theory of democracy.

Among the different conceptions of democracy that I have identified, an obvious distinction in the extent of popular control occurs at the

101

break between the direct and indirect forms of democracy. In a direct democracy the extent of popular control is sufficiently great to allow the public to have powers of final decision over important items on the political agenda, using institutional devices such as popular assemblies or referendums on important political decisions. By contrast, in all forms of indirect or representative democracy, the public's power of decision is limited to choosing those persons or bodies charged with the responsibility for making the final decisions. Yet, even within representative democracies, participation is assigned varying roles by different theorists. Schumpeter famously wished to discourage political action by the public at large between elections, holding that a necessary precondition of any stable democracy was a willingness on the part of citizens to refrain from 'back-seat driving' (Schumpeter, 1954, p. 295). Others, by contrast, have seen the willingness of citizens to form pressure groups and to engage in political activity about which they feel intensely as a central element in the flourishing of what Dahl (1989) terms 'polyarchy', a form of representative political system in which there is widespread popular influence in matters of public policy. More recently, theorists of civil society have argued that democracies flourish in conditions in which there is widespread citizen involvement in a wide range of associations, not all of which need be political but which span the full range of social life, including sports clubs, churches and recreational associations (Putnam, 2000), and this has been linked to Tocqueville's account of the merits of democracy.

The issue of participation relates also to the justification of democracy and the extent to which the broadly instrumentalist account of justification, resting as it does on the idea that elections are a protective device, is adequate as an expression of democratic values. It can be argued that an instrumentalist justification makes the institutions and culture of democracy too remote from the identity and self-understanding of democratic citizens. In particular, someone might say that, despite the centrality of political equality in the account I offered, any instrumentalist justification makes the defence of democracy external to the character and dispositions of citizens. After all, for an instrumentalist, democracy is primarily a means by which citizens attend to certain common interests rather than a practice through which individuals develop themselves and their potentialities. Does this not miss certain intrinsic merits of democratic government? Instead of this instrumental argument, should we not seek to ground the practice of democracy in something more internal to the conception of an individual's good? As Hannah Arendt (1958, p. 198) once put it, there is an interpretation of the political, in which the distinctive human capacities of speaking and writing not only have 'the most intimate relationship to the public world common to us all, but is the one activity which constitutes it'.

This Arendtian view of political participation can be related to claims about the extent to which democracy is compatible with autonomy. If it is right to hold, as Habermas (1996, p. 32) said that Rouseau and Kant held, that the legitimacy of a political system can only be secured through the concurring and united will of all, then participation is central to political legitimacy, for it will be only through political participation that legitimacy can be secured. On this account, the engagement of citizens with one another is not only the expression of self-government in a community, but it is also a way in which individual members of a community secure their own autonomy. On this strong view of political participation, authentic self-government is achieved only through political participation. Such a view suggests that there are deep and important questions at stake in the controversy over political participation.

A related question is that of the size of the political community within which it is possible to practise democracy. The classical view of democracy implicit in Arendt's account of the public world identified democracy with the politics of the city-state. The issue of political participation has often been seen as an issue of size. Until the eighteenth century it was an assumption by those who wrote about democracy, whether or not they favoured democracy as a practice, that democracies could only exist in small-scale societies.

One way of understanding the issue of size is to see it in terms of different positions associated with the assertion or denial of one or more of the following three propositions:

1. Democracies can exist in large-scale societies.
2. Democracies require there to be citizen control of government.
3. Democracies can be politically responsible.

Those in the tradition of Rousseau deny (1) and assert the truth of (2) and (3). That is to say, they assert that democracy in the authentic sense requires more than the responsiveness of representative governments to citizens' preferences. Rather they require citizens actually to control and determine the content of public policies and in this way to be responsible for those policies. They deny that this is possible in a large-scale society, however, and favour schemes of decentralization.

Defenders of representative government, in either its Westminster or representational variants, assert the truth of (1) and (3) but deny (2). That is to say, they see citizen control as being channelled through the existence of representation. So, whilst democratic governments can be responsive to popular preferences, this is not to say that there is popular control of government. Liberal constitutionalists in a Schumpeterian mode are even more sceptical about popular control, asserting that only if there is considerable self-restraint on the part of the general population will democracies act in responsible ways. Democracy does not, and should not, mean that the people rule. It means only that the people choose who is to rule.

The only position to assert the truth of all three propositions is that associated with populism of the party-mediated sort. Its acceptance of party political representation enables government to take place in large-scale societies, but its emphasis upon the extended use of referendums asserts the primacy of popular control. It denies that this combination would lead to irresponsible politics. So, of the major forms of democracy, party-mediated direct democracy is the only view that rests upon asserting the truth of all three propositions.

Parry, Moyser and Day (1992, p. 16) define participation as 'taking part in the process of formulation, passage and implementation of public policies', and this is a convenient way of thinking what participation involves. Obviously, in a direct democracy such participation includes involvement in determining the content of laws and policies, and in an indirect democracy such acts as voting for representatives, writing to elected officials, signing petitions, involvement in social movements intending to bring about a change in policy, taking part in demonstrations and canvassing for political parties. It does not consist simply in taking an interest in politics, for example by watching television or following events through newspapers and websites, although these latter activities are clearly related empirically to participation and may be important predisposing interests in respect of participation. One reason for taking the Parry *et al.* definition of participation as a starting-point is that it is clearly relevant to questions of institutional design and reform. Thus, political reform can increase or decrease the opportunities for voting or for taking part in demonstrations, and these changes may well have important implications for the quality of democracy.

If the distinction between participationist and protective versions of democracy is theoretically fundamental, the crucial institutional question is the extent to which there should be a capacity for the public at large to have a final say on issues of public policy. A key question here concerns the use of institutional devices such as referendums in the making of policy. In the US many states now allow a variety of devices (especially initiatives, referendums or the recall of public officials from office) that provide for some element of direct control by the public over policy decisions (Bowler, Donovan and Tolbert, 1998; Bowler and Donovan, 2000; Cronin, 1989). Similarly, member states in the European Union have used referendums to determine whether changes to the Treaty of Rome should be ratified, and some of these referendums have had significant effects, not least those in 2005 in the Netherlands and France which led to the stalling of the proposed European constitution. Indeed, the use of the referendum as a device of political choice, which at one time was largely a Swiss affair, has grown considerably in recent year across many democracies, both new and established. Yet, whatever its popularity, its value in terms of democratic principles still needs to be established.

However, referendums are not the only participationist devices to have grown in recent years. In particular, in relation to issues of land use and pollution control, there has been a widespread interest in forms of public involvement and public consultation in the making of decisions. These 'political opportunity structures' (Kitschelt, 1986) can be important. Thus, one of the explanations for the growth in Germany of direct opposition to the development of nuclear power stations was that there was insufficient opportunity at the policy planning stage for citizens to influence decision making and for opponents to put their case (Paterson, 1989, pp. 278–81). Moreover, if the logic of opportunity structures is taken further, it would be natural to pursue policies of extensive decentralization of decision-making power and authority. Policies that are currently decided at national level, for example many aspects of health and education services, could be conducted at a lower level of political organization.

Both in theory and in practice, therefore, the issue of the range of activities in which the public can engage in the formulation, passage and implementation of public policies is an important one. Not only can we distinguish the various conceptions of democracy in terms of the place they give to popular participation in the making of decisions, but we can also see that, within the broad class of representative systems, there are important differences in the opportunities open to the public to make or influence decisions. There are, then, two sets of questions that we can distinguish. The first concerns the extent to which a conception of democracy is deficient if it does not rest upon the ideal of popular participation. The fundamental issue here is whether the

Rousseauian assumption that any form of democracy that falls short of participation is not genuinely worthy of the name is correct or not. This may be thought of as the question of *participation as democracy*. The second question is whether, even if we think that democracy does not require the degree of popular participation that Rousseau and participationist theorists generally suppose, it is valuable to increase the degree and extent of popular participation in the making of public policies within representative democracies. This may be thought of as the question of *participation within democracies*. I now turn to the first of these characterizations.

Participation as democracy: autonomy

Among the various versions of direct democracy that I identified in Chapter 2, the example of classical Athens is important because it provides an historical instance of a political system, functioning over some two centuries, that succeeded in institutionalizing direct, popular rule. Its defects as a model democracy are, of course, well known. It excluded large portions of the population, including women, slaves and resident aliens. It partly financed its leading institutions, including the payment of compensation for citizens performing public service, by imperial levies derived from dependent territories that it had effectively annexed. It was accused by contemporary leading intellectuals of making serious mistakes in policy, particularly foreign policy such as the expedition of Syracuse, and of administering injustice rather than justice in the case of Socrates. It lost wars to Sparta and Philip of Macedon, thus calling into question the extent to which its institutions fostered citizen loyalty. Despite these charges, classical Athens has regularly been a source of inspiration in political theory, at least since the Romantic idealization of the *polis* by Hegel (1956 edn, pp. 258–62) and others including Hannah Arendt (1958, pp. 192–9). This idealization ignores many of the defects of the historical Athens in order to bring out the distinctive virtues of the democratic Athenian way of life. Moreover, Athenian achievements in politics were accompanied by other outstanding achievements in the arts, science and philosophy, so that classical Greek culture becomes a focal point of more general intellectual inquiry.

One can debate the validity and seriousness of the charges against the historical Athens. Paradoxically, however, the idealization found among theorists in the Hegelian tradition is an advantage in terms of

normative methods. Just as we could use the best alternative to democratic government in the form of a constitutional non-democratic minimal state to highlight the merits of democracy, so we can use the
most favourable interpretation of the Athenian experience to see what
problems there might be in the pursuit of pure participationist principles in a political system. By looking at the most favourable case,
we provide the best opportunity for an account of those principles to
show their worth.

As Shklar (1976, pp. 13 and 75) once pointed out, utopia for Hegel
was the 'spontaneous harmony' of Periclean Athens, by contrast with
which the freedom of his contemporaries was to be thought of as the
freedom of the bourgeois rather than the citizen. The *locus classicus*
for this account of citizenship in Athens is to be found in the funeral
oration that Thucydides, in his account *The Peloponnesian War*, puts
into the mouth of Pericles himself:

> Here each individual is interested not only in his own affairs but in
> the affairs of state as well: even those who are mostly occupied
> with their own business are extremely well-informed on general
> politics – this is a peculiarity of ours: we do not say that a man who
> takes no interest in politics is a man who minds his own business;
> we say that he has no business here at all. (Thucydides, 1954 edn,
> *The Peloponnesian War*, p. 147)

The notion here is that there is no division between the interests of the
private person and the interests of the citizen. Just as the Athenians
made statues of their gods, thus showing no cleavage between the sacred
and the profane (compare Plant, 1973, pp. 17–32), so participation in
the communal life of politics exhibited an excellence of character that
made for personal as well as public flourishing.

One way of interpreting this thought is to associate it with the idea
that liberty consists in 'ruling and being ruled in turn', which Aristotle
(*The Politics*, book vi.1.6–9) picked out as the key principle of the democratic form of government. Aristotle explained this process of self-rule
by reference to the central organizing principles of Athenian democracy,
including among other things the eligibility of all citizens for public
office, the use of the lottery as the way by which many offices were
filled, the short term of public offices, payment for the performance of
public office and the overarching authority of the assembly in making
policy. The idea was thus that political liberty consists in participation
in a practice of government in which all members participate as equals.

The premiss implicit in this account of participation in self-government as a form of political liberty is that individual citizens are sufficiently identified with their community for there to be no distinction between the individual's good and the common good. If the community collectively achieves self-government, this will mean that individuals are sharing in the autonomy of the community. It is worth exploring further the development of the ideal of autonomy that is contained in the idealized Athenian model. 'Autonomy' literally means prescribing a law to oneself (from the Greek *autos* oneself and *nomos* law), so that a democratic community would be one whose members prescribed the laws of their collective life for one another. Yet, as Lakoff (1996) has pointed out, it is possible to distinguish at least three forms of autonomy that have historically been associated with the idea of democracy. The first is that of communal autonomy, or the notion that a political unit should be independent of outside control. This is self-government in the sense that Athens could accurately be described during its life as a democracy as being self-governing. The second form of autonomy is that of plural autonomy, or the idea that different social groups should share in political power. This is an idea not of Athens, but of republican Rome. The third form of autonomy is individual autonomy, resting on the idea that individuals should control their own lives. The Hegelian argument in effect makes the first of these senses a condition for the third possibility, but this rests on a strong principle of identification of the individual with the collective.

Indeed, the difficulty with this position has been known at least since Benjamin Constant made his distinction between the liberty of the ancients and the liberty of the moderns, noting that when the ancients sacrificed their personal independence to their political rights, they sacrificed less to gain more, whereas moderns making the same exchange would give more to obtain less (Constant, 1819, pp. 316–17). In other words, without the spontaneous harmony of individual and collective presumed in the Hegelian idealization of the *polis*, there is simply always a potential conflict between individual personal freedom on the one hand and collective self-government on the other. Of course, it was a central feature of Hegel's broader political theory that the harmony achieved in classical Athens was only a stage in the development of human consciousness, so that in the story of Antigone, who defies the law in order to bury her brother, we see the first, and paradigmatic, split between individual and communal good. Whatever its merits, Hegel himself recognized that classical Athenian democracy was no longer a possibility.

The failure of spontaneous identification marks an important problem for all forms of direct democracy. Consider one of the other models of direct democracy that has often been invoked by those arguing for democracy as participation, namely the New England town meeting. In such communities important questions of common interest were on the political agenda, including such matters as taxation and land distribution. In these communities there were strong ideological and social pressures for attendance at meetings. For example, meetings had the powers to expel those who were held not to have the right values, and there were fines for non-attendance. Yet, in a situation in which the conditions for attendance were most favourable, in a town such as Dedham, Massachusetts, where the records exist, there was a significant lack of attendance, as Jane Mansbridge records:

> Even though no more than fifty-eight men were eligible to come to the Dedham town meeting and to make the decisions for the town, even though the decisions to which they addressed themselves were vital to their existence, even though every inhabitant was required to live within one mile of the meeting place, even though each absence from the town meeting brought a fine, and even though a town crier personally visited the house of every latecomer half an hour after the meeting had begun, only 74 percent of those eligible actually showed up at the typical town meeting between 1636 and 1644. This must come close to the highest attendance one can expect, on average, in a geographically based direct democracy. (Mansbridge, 1980, p. 131)

In other words, in the absence of an assumption of spontaneous identification with the community, there is no reason to assume that individuals will actively participate in shared processes of government, even in a situation in which there is great pressure upon them to do so. The identification of collective autonomy with individual autonomy simply fails.

Apart from Hegel's idealization of the Athenian *polis*, the other major theoretical statement of a conceptual link between participation and autonomy is that of Rousseau. Rousseau explicitly connected the idea of the individual will to the idea of political participation in his argument that political representation was not legitimate, since the will could not be represented. Yet, for Rousseau, participation in the formation of a general will was compatible with freedom, even in cases where one's individual will was at odds with the majority. Rousseau reaches this conclusion by means of a number of distinctive assumptions. He takes political morality to be conventional, in the sense that the right decision for a political community to take in any one instance is given by what its members can agree upon, assuming that they are all thinking about the general interest. He assumes that economic and social conditions are sufficiently equal among citizens, such that they will be able to agree on a common conception of the public interest. And he argues that individuals in the minority, who recognize the conditions under which citizens are seeking to will the common interest, will be prepared to recognize that they have mistaken the general will. Under these conditions, individuals willing their common good together will be acting both autonomously and in conditions of political freedom.

Even if some of these contentious assumptions could be granted, the argument would yield a case for political participation only if Rousseau's claim were true that the will could not be represented. Rousseau's argument at the relevant point of *The Social Contract* is so succinctly stated that it is not clear why he thinks that the will cannot be represented. However, one possibility is that he holds to a Cartesian account of the will, in which willing is an event in the mind of individuals. Any individual act of willing is therefore private to each individual, and features as an element in his or her biography. If this were a valid account of the will, then it would follow that will cannot be represented, since what takes place in one person's mind cannot take place in another. The difficulty here is not with Rousseau's account of representation, but with his account of the will, since there are many reasons for thinking that the will cannot be understood as a form of mental event. If, instead, we regard willing not as a motion of the mind, but a state of the mind in which reasoned deliberation determines the choices that people make (see Kenny, 1975, p. 26), then it can be seen that the will can be represented, since the same reasons can exist in the minds of different people (compare Weale, 2005, pp. 43–6).

Rousseau is in many respects a bridge between the ancients and the moderns. His admiration for Rome and Sparta makes it seem as though he is harking back to the ancients; but his stress upon individual autonomy and the absence of a God-given natural law makes him a modern. How far can his account be used to link the idea of democracy with autonomy? Is it really the case that democratic legitimacy can only be secured, as Habermas insists, through the united and concurring will of all in the participative engagement of citizens? Can the liberty of the moderns be reconciled with the liberty of the ancients in this way?

One interpretation of the principle of autonomy in the Kantian tradition is well expressed by Wolff (1970, p. 14): 'moral autonomy is a combination of freedom and responsibility; it is submission to laws which one has made for oneself'. Autonomy in this sense is thus the idea that persons are by their nature self-governing creatures, that is beings whose moral personality finds its fulfilment in their prescribing principles of action to themselves. Any attempt to link this idea to democracy has to explain how one moves from the ascription to *individuals* of the capacity for autonomy to the conclusion that democracy is an appropriate form of *collective* decision making. In particular, it is not clear why the collective authority implied in democratic decision making should be thought to flow from a principle that stresses individual autonomy. The natural correlate of individual autonomy would appear to be not democracy but anarchy, meaning not chaos but simply a political system in which no one is forced to act against his or her will. Robert Paul Wolff (1970) himself has pressed this argument. As soon as we move from a system in which all collective decisions are determined by unanimity and in which all persons vote directly, we are saying that individuals have to accept the authority of an agency which is other than themselves, and this violates the principle of autonomy.

In reply to these claims, it has been argued that the justification of democracy in terms of the principle of autonomy does not carry such individualistic and anarchistic consequences, since there are inevitably collective choices to be made in the way in which individuals arrange their common affairs. Beetham (1993, p. 62), for example, explicitly refers to Wolff's argument but insists that Wolff's criterion of autonomy 'simply refuses to recognize the necessary compromises and give-and-take that are an inescapable feature of social living, and that make collective necessarily different from individual decision-making'. The same argument is developed by Graham who suggests that collective decision making need not violate the principle of individual autonomy, since there is a distinction between the conditions under which we can truly say that a collective has decided – namely that certain agreed procedures have been followed – and the conditions under which an individual ought to sacrifice his or her view about what is right (Graham, 1986, pp. 112–13). Thus, on both of these views, the value of autonomy remains central to the justification of democratic procedures, since autonomy does not mean that individuals can claim the right to act in accordance with their consciences against a collective decision. Considerations of practicality, if nothing else, mean that the effective scope of individual judgement is limited, but this is not the same as limiting the scope of individual autonomy.

This is obviously an attractive line of argument, but the trouble is that it either demonstrates too little or too much. On the one hand it demonstrates too little in that it is inevitably tied to the prevailing technological possibilities of what is a matter for individual choice and what is a matter for collective choice. There are such goods as those Raz (1986, pp. 198–203) calls intrinsically collective goods (such as the benefits of living in a tolerant society), but a number of other collective goods are such only by virtue of technological limitation. Consider the case of pure water supplies to households. At present this is secured through purification plants that serve whole communities, but technically individual households could install their own purification equipment, thus rendering their decisions about the quality of water they consume independent of a more general social decision. The 'inescapable compromises' of social living need not always be so inescapable after all.

Someone could always argue that the individualistic technology was more expensive than the collective alternative, but as an argument of principle this is too weak to sustain much burden. To say that autonomy is a value in any sense is to say that it should be upheld when it conflicts with other values, such as economy in the provision of material benefits. This is a necessary condition for our saying that a principle had some value at all. So if we are to take individual autonomy as a value, we should be prepared to sacrifice other goods for it. Hence, a community that respected autonomy would impart a bias to its own collective decision making, insisting that as much as reasonably could be should be exempted from the scope of collective responsibility and placed in the hands of individuals. It could do this partly by fostering investment in individualistic technologies or by promoting alternative non-political decision-making procedures, for example the law courts or alternative dispute resolution procedures. There is no reason, however, why a democratic decision-making procedure should want to impart this bias to its deliberations. Full democratic decision making requires that citizens weigh up the arguments for and against certain alternatives, not that they give special weight to one particular value in their estimation of those alternatives.

There is a link between democracy and autonomy but it is a contingent one in the following sense. For those who live in democratic societies that have also undergone modernization, unreflective habit and the unreflective repetition of traditions is no longer a basis for practical decision making. Critical morality is needed in addition to positive morality, and citizens of modern societies need to consider the point, purpose and rationale of the moral and political traditions they have inherited. This is to say no more, however, than that modern societies are open rather than closed. Since modern communities cannot live solely according to their inherited traditions, there has to be scope for democratic deliberation. These democratic choices will concern not simply the regulation of economic activity and contractual relations, but also choices about the political culture by which decisions have previously been taken, including such matters as the place of religion, the expression of sexuality, our place in the natural world and markers of social identity such as language, ethnic group and place. But no political culture can be made afresh in one decision or even one sweep of decisions. Autonomous deliberation does not constitute our interests, but instead operates over conceptions of interests that are previously defined, though constantly being remade.

One possible analogy here is to career choice. In a free society people will choose the careers that suit them best, and will not be obliged to enter occupations that are traditionally prescribed for them. Relations of contract will have replaced relations of status in such matters. Nevertheless, choice is not completely free, since there is only a limited, if large, range of options. The choice is not fixed in any straightforward way. Technical change is encouraging the development of new careers and discouraging the development of others. This is not to say that there is a deterministic process at work, providing slots into which people fit, since those who are especially imaginative, lucky or unscrupulous will be able to invent or conjure up new options for themselves, for example becoming purveyors of bad, if popular, taste in art or fashion. Yet, some careers will be virtually impossible to pursue, such as that of the village blacksmith. There is a sense of autonomy suitable for such a world but it is defined in terms of the principle that generally persons are presumed to be the best judges of their own interests.

Someone might say at this point, however, that I have begged the central question in connection with autonomy, since the notion of common interests that I have so far invoked is not one that can be made sense of unless we also invoke the notion of autonomy. Again the relevant argument has been made by Beetham as follows:

if the idea of interest-maximization is to deliver a defence of democracy, rather than of paternalist forms of rule, then it must contain the implicit assumption that people are the best judges of their own interests; that is it must embody a concept like that of autonomy, on which it is in effect parasitic. (Beetham, 1993, p. 61)

Clearly, the crucial point of this argument is whether there is the close connection posited between the principle that people are the best judges of their own interests and the claim that therefore the concept of interests is parasitic upon the concept of autonomy.

To assess this argument, let us first of all consider the sense in which the idea of autonomy necessarily enters our account of interests. The basic insight here is that interests are never fixed in a rigid way. Consider, as an example, the case of health interests. Most people would agree that health interests are basic in the sense of saying that a policy or practice that had adverse effects on peoples' health would normally provide a reason for not adopting that policy or practice, and conversely saying that a policy or practice that promoted health would normally be a good reason for adopting it. However, even if we accept that the protection and promotion of health is generally in the interests of persons, we cannot infer from this that policy makers or practitioners can move straight from this assumption to a view about what should be done in particular cases. We still need to invoke something like the anti-paternalist principle that people are the best judges of their own interests for one simple reason. There often arise cases in medical practice where the response to a diagnosis involves balancing risks in the treatment of a disease, say between surgery, carrying its own risks, and watchful waiting. How the risks of these alternative consequences are balanced seems to be properly a matter for the individual patient more than it does for anyone else, including medical practitioners.

Similar trade-offs can occur at the collective level. Thus, a community may be faced with the choice of either environmental protection or economic well-being. A particular manufacturing plant in a locality may be an important source of jobs, but also be a source of health risks for the population of the community, as was clearly the case with traditional coalmining communities exposed to not only the occupational risks associated with working in the mines but also environmental risks such as land subsidence or avalanches of waste material. Provided that the risks are bounded within that community, it seems arguable at the very least (many people would take it to be axiomatic) that the members of the community should determine the balance of risks for themselves.

In the sense conveyed by these examples, a non-paternalist principle of autonomy is a necessary condition for acting in the interests of the people involved. Does this mean, however, that the concept of interests is parasitic upon that of autonomy? In the logical sense of the question the answer is clearly 'no'. These are cases of competing interests, the appeal of which we understand before we introduce the notion of autonomy. True, we cannot define the correct policy without consulting individuals and finding out how they balance these competing goods, and in this sense our judgement of interests is dependent upon their choices. This is not to say that the concept of interest is parasitic upon that of autonomy, however. Rather our interpretation of what should be the definition of a person's interest depends upon how that person balances conflicting goods.

Participation as democracy: moral development

The argument that participation as democracy rests upon an implausible account of personal autonomy is not the end of the matter, however, as far as the idea of participation as democracy is concerned. It can be argued that all democracies need a sense of fair play and impartiality among citizens, to both embody the values of political equality and foster an acceptance of collective decisions. In other words, precisely because there is *not* a spontaneous identification of the individual with collective decisions, attitudes consistent with a public orientation need to be fostered in a democracy. If individuals are to lead meaningful lives together, despite their differences, then this can only be built upon a sense of social cooperation in which there is a shared sense of responsibility. Political participation, it can be argued, is an important means by which these civic virtues are developed.

Strong claims have been made for the moral benefits of participation in a decentralized polity. Such participation is supposed to foster citizen involvement with the political process, ending the alienation that exists in representative democracies. Participation will thereby contribute to a heightened sense of citizen responsibility, since citizens will be taking decisions themselves and will therefore recognize the seriousness of what they are doing. Reinforcing this sense of responsibility are the opportunities available for citizens to deliberate together about common problems without the mediation of television and national newspapers, which distort the political agenda. In these ways, participation is said to promote the self-development of citizens, since the processes of democratic discussion and debate foster certain moral capacities (compare Barber, 1984, p. 155).

These arguments have a long history. The thought that the form of government should be justified in terms of the type of moral personality it produced was, for example, crisply expressed by John Stuart Mill:

> The first element of good government, therefore, being the virtue and intelligence of the human beings composing the community, the most important point of excellence which any form of government can possess is to promote the virtue and intelligence of the people themselves. (Mill, 1861a, p. 226)

Tocqueville (1835, pp. 246–63) too discusses this argument, suggesting that by exercising their political freedoms, citizens acquire a loyalty to their country that they would otherwise lack. 'At the present time', he wrote, 'civic zeal seems to me to be inseparable from the exercise of political rights' (Tocqueville, 1835, p. 252).

It is important to remember the limited scope of these arguments. Tocqueville was contrasting representative government with what he termed aristocratic government, by which he meant any system of government in which political power was vested in an hereditary political elite. His praise of democracy for promoting civic zeal rested upon his understanding of the effects of representative government. Similarly, although Mill had a wider commitment to participation, including the development of cooperatives in the economic sphere, his account of political participation makes it clear that he thinks the activities it involves primarily take place at the local level, and that in national politics citizens are expected to cast their votes intelligently and impartially as their primary responsibility.

Even within these limits, this form of argument has been criticized. Elster (1983, pp. 91–100), for example, has objected to the idea that the educative effects of participation could be the main or sole point of a political system. Taking Tocqueville's claim in particular that democracy is inferior to aristocracy as a decision-making system but excels over it in terms of the popular energy it releases, he argues that unless democracy had a point over and above producing these psychological benefits it could not in fact produce those benefits. His argument here is dependent upon his notion of essential by-products of activity (Elster, 1983), in which certain consequences of action follow only provided that agents focus on something else. (We all know of people who try to be the centre-piece of the party by telling jokes but simply end up being bores, whereas those who are unself-consciously funny will grab attention whatever they do.)

However, as Chan and Miller (1991) have pointed out, Elster rather overstates the force of his argument against the strategy of basing a justification for democracy on its educative effects. They show that all the notion of by-products needs is the assumption that persons pursue concrete goals in politics, and that this assumption is relatively uncontroversial. Self-realization through education cannot be the sole aim of political activity, but when thinking about questions of institutional and constitutional design citizens can appeal quite properly to the educative benefits that democratic governments are supposed to bring. The Mill–Tocqueville strategy cannot, therefore, be ruled out of court *a priori*. Provided we see politics as an arena within which people pursue certain concrete goals, it will be possible in principle to construct an argument for democratic government on the basis that it produces certain types of character and thereby promotes moral development. The question therefore turns on the issue of whether such supposed moral development is something that is so valuable that choices of political institution should be based upon it.

In his discussion of the issue, Dahl identifies a type of moral development that he believes is promoted within democratic political systems. This moral development is impartiality, 'gaining a more mature sense of responsibility for one's actions, a broader awareness of the others affected by one's actions, a greater willingness to reflect on and take into account the consequences of one's actions for others, and so on' (Dahl, 1989, pp. 104–5). Asserting that the qualities of the human beings in a government are the most essential element of good performance, Mill also cites the virtues of impartiality: truthfulness among witnesses, judges immune to bribes, concern for the public good among administrators, calm deliberation among legislators and a spirit of cooperation among elites (Mill, 1861a, pp. 225–6). Similarly, in citing the educational benefits of public service within a democracy, Mill notes that citizens are called to weigh interests other than their own, to be guided in cases of conflict by rules other than those of private partialities, and to apply principles and maxims that have as their concern the public interest (Mill, 1861a, p. 255). These are clearly the virtues of impartiality, and Mill's argument for democracy is that the participation it encourages and requires promotes these sorts of virtues.

However, in addition to the virtue of impartiality, Mill also cites the value of independence of character. He contrasts what he terms the active and passive types of character, and asserts that one of the virtues of democracy is that it encourages the active rather than the passive type. The arguments for the superiority of the active type consists of a series of propositions: all intellectual superiority is the fruit of active effort; enterprise is the parent of both speculative and practical talent; and the character that improves human life is that which struggles with natural powers and tendencies, not that which gives way to them (Mill, 1861a, p. 249). How then does Mill link this notion of active character to the practice of democracy? Essentially he does it through an empirical generalization to the effect that persons who bestir themselves with hopeful prospects of their own circumstances are those who feel goodwill towards those engaged in similar pursuits. In other words, the virtues of impartiality are more likely to be attached to those types of persons displaying independence of character and both sorts of virtues are more likely to be developed in a democracy.

Despite Mill's attempt to link these two sets of virtues together, and to use the cultivation of both as a reinforcing consideration for each, there is much to be said for keeping them separate and considering the merits of the argument in each case, as Dahl does in his discussion. Mill's case for linking impartiality to independence of character via his putative empirical generalization is not helped by the Victorian racism in which he casts the supposed evidence, which consigns orientals and southern Europeans (with whom he is quite happy to lump the French for these purposes) to the domain of sloth and envy. Only the spunky Anglo-Saxons, it would seem, have what it takes to create democracy. But even if the rational kernel of the argument could be extracted from this mystical shell, there would still be good reasons for trying to keep distinct the virtues of impartiality and independence of character.

What then are we to make of the claim that democracy is associated with independence of character? There are good reasons for thinking that the scope for pursuing the result of independent judgement in a democracy is limited, not least because democracies involve the provision of collective goods. Of course, it can be important that individuals express their own views about the nature and character of the collective goods a society needs clearly and forcefully, and in this sense independence of character is important. If individuals think, for example, that their government is committed to an unjust war, then it is important that they have the courage and independence to say so. In a democracy, people cannot literally live under rules of their own choosing, since the rules the winning political forces prefer may not be ones with which they are in accord. They can not, however, live under rules which they resent but from which they have not taken the trouble to express dissent. Participation, even when it is futile in changing rules and policies, can be an expression of political independence.

However, independence of character may not be the unadulterated good that Mill's argument supposes. It seems like a specific virtue which is highly regarded in some moral codes and not in others. (This perhaps is the rational kernel of Mill's argument.) In recent years its value has been challenged by religious conservatives, multiculturalists and feminists. Thus, just as there are some feminists who see the notion of independent character as being necessarily tied to a masculine ethos of individuality rather than a feminine ethos of relationships, so there are feminists who base their critique of patriarchy on its failure to achieve autonomy for women (Phillips, 1993, pp. 50–2). It is certainly not necessary to take sides in the intramural disputes that these challenges have fostered. Whoever is right, it would seem better if one could build a theory of democracy, which after all has to be constructed for a society containing a pluralism of moral viewpoints, on arguments that were not dependent upon particular moral judgements of this sort.

By contrast, a sense of impartiality, of weighing the interests of others as well as the interests of oneself, on the other hand would seem to be absolutely essential if collective action is to be undertaken. Certainly achieving impartiality does require a certain distance on one's own plans and projects, and this attitude of mind looks at least like a close cousin of independence of judgement and character, but the two virtues are quite distinct. There must be strong, biased characters, just as there are mild-mannered impartial ones. Thus, we do have to appeal to the supposed effects of democratic institutions in fostering a certain sort of virtue if we are to have a coherent account of the moral foundations of democracy. However, the most important virtue is that of impartiality, and this in turn we can relate to the requirements of political equality.

Participation in democracy

So far I have tried to show that participation as democracy – in which there is an equation between participatory practices and the good of citizens – rests upon implausible premises. But the arguments about participation do not end there. For it is possible to argue that, even if democracy is seen as a political system in which political representatives negotiate with one another about the fair terms of cooperation, it is still better if there is widespread popular participation in politics.

Although the institutional opportunities for political participation vary within existing representative democracies, it is clear that even those systems in which public participation is at its highest could increase such opportunities even further in at least three ways. First, a larger number of people could take advantage of such opportunities for participation as there are. Empirical studies show that, if we regard participation as a ladder that people have to climb, very few people get above the bottom rung – which is voting – and an extremely small number indeed get above party memberships and some campaigning (Parry, Moyser and Day, 1992, pp. 48–53). Participation could thus be increased by a higher proportion of citizens using existing devices.

Secondly, participation could be increased by using certain devices across a wider range of issues. In most political systems, referendums could be used on a wider range of issues, and called more frequently. In so-called routine administrative matters, such as the setting of standards for environmental protection, there could be a wider use of participatory devices such as regulatory negotiation, public hearings or consensus conferences. In the supply of public services there could be greater use of consumer groups to determine the limits within which professional suppliers worked. All these are institutional devices that are currently in use somewhere within representative systems, but which are not in full use anywhere. It follows that everywhere the level of political participation could be increased above the level that currently obtains.

Thirdly, existing participatory devices could be supplemented by new institutional mechanisms. The use of referendums could be accompanied by the use of the citizens' initiative, by which a concerned groups of citizens, above some specified minimum number, could place propositions before other citizens for decision. Greater use of electronic and information technology would enable an increase in popular participation, helping modern large-scale democracies to replicate the participatory discussions that supposedly went on in the Athenian assembly. Interactive video and televised debates would, on this analysis, overcome the barriers of space and size that modern large-scale societies impose on their functioning democratic institutions. Whatever doubts one might have about the merits of such widespread use of electronic technology, particularly in terms of the quality of public debate it produces, the feasibility of some form of increased participation arising from electronic technology cannot be doubted.

If it is possible to increase participation, and such participation would have beneficial effects upon citizens, would it still be the right thing to do? One way of examining this question is to turn to the most pungent statement against popular participation, that of Schumpeter. In fact, Schumpeter asserts three claims against popular participation: the incompetence of typical citizens; the tendency to irrationality on the part of ordinary citizens; and the opportunities that public participation allows for special interests to pursue their own aims. Thus, in relation to the first claim, Schumpeter writes: 'the typical citizen drops down to a lower level of mental performance as soon as he enters the political field. He argues and analyzes in a way that he would readily recognize as infantile within the sphere of his real interests' (Schumpeter, 1954, p. 262). Secondly, Schumpeter asserts that 'even if there were no political groups trying to influence him, the typical citizen would in political matters tend to yield to extra-rational or irrational prejudice and impulse' (Schumpeter, 1954, p. 262). Thirdly, he infers that 'the weaker the logical element in the process of the public mind and the more complete the absence of rational criticism and the rationalizing influence of personal experience and responsibility, the greater are the opportunities for groups with an ax to grind' (Schumpeter, 1954, p. 263). So, in the context of irrational public opinion, special interests are able to take advantage and press their own claims disproportionately.

It can be clearly seen from these quotations that Schumpeter asserts his claims as psychological generalizations. The tendency to reason in an infantile way, for example, is something that is characteristic of public affairs in general, simply because such matters are outside the everyday experience of most people. For Schumpeter this is not a matter of social position or occupation: those in the liberal profes-sions, who in their working lives are used to arguing rationally, are just as prone to the temptation as anyone else. It is this claim to irrationality and impulsiveness's being a general phenomenon that underlies the supposed force of the argument about the need to limit political participation.

The most interesting response to these claims has come from James Fishkin (1991, 1995). Fishkin does not deny that in the cir-cumstances of modern competitive politics there is a tendency for voters to reason in superficial and inconsequential ways. However, he claims that this phenomenon does not reflect a general lack of cap-acity to reason and deliberate about public affairs. Rather it reflects the institutions and conditions of competitive party democracies operat-ing on a large scale. Since individual voters in a large-scale democ-racy have only a minute probability of being decisive in matters of politics, it is rational for them to remain ignorant of the details of policy, since investing time and effort in acquiring relevant information and understanding is not worthwhile. Their ignorance is 'rational ignorance' in the sense of Downs (1957), a phenomenon also noted by Olson (2000, pp. 93–4) when he points out that the 'man bites dog' criterion of what is newsworthy drives out serious political commentary from the media and that sex scandals among public officials reflect the fact that for many citizens politics is just another form of entertainment. Similarly, to develop this argument, we can understand name-recognition effects in politics in accordance with the same logic. When a large number of candidates stand as governors of California, it is not surprising that a film star turns out to be the winner.

However, according to Fishkin, we can overcome the pressures towards the trivialization of politics in normal life and the media by recreating the conditions of small-town democracy in which individuals are confronted with evidence and argument about public matters and in which those same individuals are required to deliberate collectively with others about important issues. Such a situation not only counteracts the pressures of rational ignorance, but it also restores a strong sense of political equality, in which the views and opinions of ordinary citizens count in the same ways as the views of political professionals. Fishkin's own preferred method for achieving this result is the deliberative poll, which he defines as follows:

> Take a … random sample of the electorate and transport those people … to a single place. Immerse the sample in the issues, with carefully balanced briefing materials, with intensive discussions in small groups, and with the chance to question competing experts and politicians. At the end of several days of working through the issues face to face, poll the participants in detail. (Fishkin, 1995, p.162)

In the original version of the idea (Fishkin, 1991, p. 2), the role of the deliberative poll was intended to supplement the processes of US presidential elections. The deliberative poll was seen as a national caucus, which would interrogate potential candidates and debate the importance of the issues. However, there is no reason why the technique should not be used more generally, and indeed the first deliberative poll in the world was broadcast by UK television network's Channel 4 in May 1994, where participants were asked their views on the most appropriate policies for dealing with crime. Since then, deliberative polls have been used widely in different countries, including the US, Canada, Australia and China. Moreover, although in the original version of the idea the sample was intended to be nationally representative, there is no reason in principle, apart from cost, why it could not be used in a particular locality.

Deliberative polls have the advantage that they combine statistical representativeness with the opportunity for citizens to engage in political deliberation. However, where there is no need for a representative sample or the considered opinion of a small group is what is required, there is no need to stick with the technique of the deliberative poll. Indeed, there is a whole gamut of techniques – including citizens' juries, consensus conferences and citizen assemblies – all of which aim to tap the 'ordinary wisdom' (Davies *et al.*, 1998) of citizens. There is evidence that, if the techniques are used with integrity and understanding, ordinary citizens can exhibit much higher deliberative rationality than is supposed in the Schumpeterian critique of public participation (Luskin *et al.*, 2002).

Scepticism about public participation cannot rest upon the sort of generalizing claims about the absence of political rationality that Schumpeter supposed, therefore. Indeed, the experience seems to confirm Adam Smith's observation in *The Wealth of Nations* that the 'difference between the most dissimilar characters, between a philosopher and a street porter, for example, seems to arise not so much from nature, as from habit, custom, and education' (Smith, 1776, pp. 28–9). The question for democratic theory is not so much whether innovative deliberative techniques can be made to work in fostering meaningful participation. Rather the issue is the value they contribute to the functioning of democracies and what their role might be in decision processes.

One point on which Schumpeter's general characterization of the workings of democracy was wrong was its assertion that between elections the public should not try to engage in back-seat driving. In fact, all well-functioning democracies have extensive procedures of public consultation in the making of policy across a wide range of issues. The reasons for institutionalizing such practices are not far to seek. When governments provide public services such as hospitals, they have to make decisions about the location and configuration of services. Without a price mechanism, there is no opportunity for users of those services to indicate their preferences. To give a typical example, there is a well-known trade-off in the supply of specialist health services between a geographical concentration of care, which tends to improve quality, and dispersion of care, which tends to improve access. Striking the right balance between these competing considerations is not a technical matter, but involves complex judgements about relative priorities. Where there is no possibility of exit for citizens, then mechanisms of voice have to come into play. Similarly, in decisions on environmental policy, for example the setting of standards or a major land use development, consultation is needed to extract relevant information. Public consultation is not simply a recognition of the equal standing that citizens should have in the expression of their interests and their values; it is also suggested by the simplest considerations of fallibility. Where the pooling of knowledge is advantageous, particularly where that knowledge would otherwise remain local and tacit, consultation is necessary.

The use of innovative participatory devices is therefore clearly useful as a supplement to decision making in representative institutions. Can its value be extended beyond that range of functions? In particular, can the results of popular deliberation be given any authority in the way in which citizens in general deliberate about matters of political choice? Fishkin has argued 'yes' to this question at least in respect of deliberative polls:

> A deliberative poll is not meant to describe or predict public opinion. Rather it prescribes. It has a recommending force: these are the conclusions that people would come to, were they better informed on the issues and had the opportunity and motivation to examine those issues seriously. It allows a microcosm of the country to make recommendations to us all after it has had the chance to think through the issues. If such a poll were broadcast before an election or a referendum, it could dramatically affect the outcome. (Fishkin, 1995, p. 162, compare Fishkin, 1991, p. 4)

This claim needs some examination. In particular, it is not clear why a deliberative poll should have recommending force for ordinary citizens, and indeed this claim would seem to take the device beyond its consultative role.

Consider what a well-conducted deliberative poll can tell an elected or appointed official about a decision, say the siting of a medical facility. From the process of deliberation, the official would know what values citizens thought important in relation to siting decisions, and in particular how they weighed accessibility against the quality of care. They would understand the likely concerns that citizens would have, how those concerns might be allayed and what the spread of opinion among the affected population would be. More importantly, they would have the *thoughtful* opinions of citizens. This does not mean that when the decision was taken there would not be opposition, but at least the officials could argue that they themselves had sought conscientiously to understand not only the issue itself but the setting of that issue in the life-world of citizens affected by the decision.

Consider by contrast the position of citizens who learn what other citizens in a deliberative poll thought of a candidate in an election or what their opinion was of a particular item of policy. Such citizens might find the information useful. For example, they might have thought that their opinion of the candidate or the issue was shared by a majority of others, but discover instead that they are in a minority. Or they might be struck by the way opinions had changed over the course of the poll. However, there is no reason why any particular determination of a deliberative poll should have recommending force. In the first Channel 4 deliberative poll, although the respondents generally moved in a more liberal direction on crime policy, there was a two-thirds majority in favour of capital punishment after the event just as there had been before (Luskin *et al.*, 2002, p. 469, reports the average values; the percentage response was in the television broadcast). Although there was some switching of individuals, the aggregate figures remained constant. Why should this result have any effect on someone's judgement about the rights and wrongs of capital punishment? That opinion should be better decided by conscientious consideration of the evidence for deterrent effect, the probability of being wrong in any particular or the intrinsic cruelty of the practice. Here is a case where Mill's independence of character is called for.

Why not populism?

I pointed out in the introduction to this chapter that the populist position was the only one to combine a belief in the possibility of democracy on a large scale, an expectation that populist decision making would be responsible and an assertion of the value of popular control over the determination of important items of public policy. The populist can therefore agree that the images of Athens, New England or Geneva have haunted democratic theory for too long, but disagree with the view that the role of popular decision making, particularly through the use of referendums, should be solely consultative. Why not make popular decision making mandatory? Moreover, if we take the principle of political equality seriously, it might be argued, does this not imply a commitment to widespread political participation? Since no citizen is better than another citizen, according to the principle of political equality, no citizen should rule over another.

One traditional objection to increased participation is the amount of time it would consume. No technology can expand the amount of time available to earthly communities to discuss their common affairs, and, as Dahl (1970) once showed, even a moderate amount of discussion with, say, six or seven points of view represented would quickly consume large amounts of time. Moreover, many of the most satisfying and fulfilling of non-political human activities (playing a musical instrument, writing poetry, climbing mountains, sports and dinner-table conversation, to name but a few) are also time-consuming, so that democratic political participation is likely to be in fierce competition with them for the ultimate scarce resource. The argument for representation therefore is that citizens have a generalized interest in preserving time for the full range of activities in which they might engage, and direct democracies would erode that time.

Budge (1996) argues that modern communications technology renders this problem less serious than one might think. He points out that for many today politics is a form of entertainment to be followed on the radio or television, and that the understanding of issues is likely to arise as a by-product of following the news and current affairs that people will do anyway. Let us suppose, then, that communications and electronic technology have enabled modern political communities to overcome the barriers of space and size that have hitherto prevented modern large-scale democracies from replicating the participation practised in Athens or New England townships. One might then say that there was a *prima facie* argument for expanding the range of issues on which citizens could vote directly.

One important objection to this line of argument concerns the quality of the public debate that typically emerges from the modern forms of communication. I have said that one of the classical arguments for participation is to promote a sense of impartiality that will carry over into social life in general, but it has been urged that this can only arise if political decision making involves deliberation, and intelligent deliberation is something that electronic forms of communication do not foster. So the implication of this view is that participation is desirable where there is an opportunity for deliberation, but it should not be pursued where deliberation is excluded (compare Fishkin, 1995, pp. 40–3). It is better in those circumstances to allow the deliberation to take place in a representative assembly.

However, at this point, the participationist can always reply that this is to make a false comparison, setting the probable functioning of electronic democracy against the ideal functioning of a representative system. In practice the quality of deliberation in a representative system is likely to depend upon such circumstances as the degree of partisanship, the historic traditions of parliamentary practice, the character of the issues being debated and the sense of responsibility of the representatives. Certainly, an Italian elector contemplating in recent years the inability of the parliamentary system to root out corruption might well be excused the thought that even a moderately well-functioning system of electronic democracy would be better than a poorly functioning parliamentary system.

The consequences of bounded rationality play a role of particular importance in a democracy above a certain small size. Such systems will require full-time bureaucratic officials to run and implement the policies and programmes decided politically. Given the conditions of bounded rationality, such officials will come to have detailed knowledge of what they are doing. Unless they are confronted by political actors who are equally knowledgeable, then their monopoly of information will undermine the scope for democratic control. But the most plausible way to confront this specialist monopoly of knowledge is to have political actors who themselves have sufficient opportunity to take advantage of the division of labour to acquire the specialist knowledge, and this in turn requires a system of political representation. Hence, representation has the advantage over direct democracy that democratic authority can best be maintained in complex matters by representatives who themselves are able to challenge the specialism of unelected officials. This does not mean that they have to have the same degree of specialism as the officials (compare the way that well-trained barristers can often demolish so-called 'expert' testimony, even though they are not experts themselves). But it does require that they have the opportunity to acquire the relevant skills, and this can only come with time. Equality is quite compatible with the acknowledgement that time and training is necessary to be able effectively to challenge those who would otherwise have a monopoly of information.

In commenting on this point, Ian Budge has pointed out to me that the argument from the division of labour, whilst it may be good against a Rousseauian conception of democracy, would still be consistent with the model of party-mediated direct democracy. Once political representatives had carried out their tasks of holding officials

to account and reporting their opinion, the final decision on any matter could be put to the people, just as professional lawyers undertake
the questioning in a trial, but the jury decides whether or not the
defendant is guilty. This is of course true, if we think that the time
cost of decision making is primarily related to the tasks of assembling
and presenting the relevant information. But there are also advantages arising from the division of labour to the people at large, since
business can simply be remitted, as a whole, to political representatives. There are savings in time to be made from the need not to have
to take a decision as well as from the need not to have to assemble and
make sense of the relevant information. The jury analogy is not
entirely convincing, since the jury in a criminal trial is asked a very
specific question about the guilt or innocence of the accused, whereas
in matters of public policy the questions to be answered are rarely so
well defined. In the public policy case, there is a more complex
weighing of factual and evaluative elements in the overall judgement
about the advantages and disadvantages of alternative options.

Moreover, there are occasions when the opportunity costs of political participation can be pure loss. The sort of occasions I have in
mind here are what might be called cases of 'defensive participation'.
These are cases where one participates only to prevent other people
from damaging one's own interests. It is quite possible to find oneself
locked into a series of meetings because you know that others whose
interests are in conflict with yours will turn up and in your absence vote
for something that is damaging to you. Unless we can be sure that the
promotion of impartiality and a sense of common purpose will operate on every occasion in politics, such defensive participation is pure
loss for all participants. All would be better off if none participated.

The issue of time should really be seen as related to a more general
point. The development of varying forms of human excellence is
incompatible with the development of other forms of excellence.
Time is standing duty as a proxy for the thought that, for individuals,
the varieties of goodness present mutually exclusive forms of life.
Constant's (1819) thought that the independence that now would be
given up for the ancient form of liberty can be explained in this way.
The loss of the spontaneous harmony of Periclean Athens is not
something to be regretted, but something to be celebrated. It opens up
the possibility of persons developing in different and distinct ways. It
requires, however, that those same persons keep in mind the requirements of fairness in the social cooperation that is the necessary condition for individuals to lead meaningful lives together.

6 From Conceptions of Representation to Systems of Representation

If we accept that there has to be some division of labour in politics and public participation in politics needs to be set in the context of representative government, then we need a theory of what political representation involves. That is to say, we need an account of what representatives should do, what sort of people they should be and how they should discharge their duties. Representatives undertake those tasks that citizens lack time or opportunity to undertake, but upon what understanding of representation should the design of a system of representative government be based? On the answer to this question hangs the issue of how we evaluate the competing models of indirect democracy that we have identified.

These various models of representative government were distinguished from one another by the extent to which they offered competing accounts of representation. Within the Westminster conception of democracy the emphasis was placed on the importance of governing political parties being accountable to the electorate, and this involves the idea that the electorate chooses the government. This in turn involved relatively few political parties competing for office, with parties in office enjoying the conditions that would enable them to govern effectively, in particular a secure parliamentary majority and control over the legislature. We can call this the 'responsible government' model of representation. In the representational model of democracy, by contrast, the emphasis is upon seeing the legislature as broadly representative of varieties of political opinion. In consequence,

129

representational systems typically have a relatively large number of political parties competing for office, shared executive authority, broad representation on legislative committees and an emphasis upon compromise among competing opinions in the construction of governing coalitions. The distinguishing characteristics of these two conceptions, therefore, turn on the competing conceptions of representation that each contains. Moreover, it is clear that these conceptions are also related to the role that the electoral system is expected to perform.

As Lijphart (1994, p. 10) has noted, there is broad agreement among electoral system experts that the two most important dimensions of electoral systems are the electoral formula and district magnitude (that is the number of representatives elected per district). The two main varieties of electoral formula are the winner-takes-all, first-past-the-post system and various systems of proportional representation. In the former, candidates win office by securing the single largest share of the vote, whereas in the latter candidates are elected in proportion to the votes they receive. However, it is also clear that the exact effects of the different formulae interact with the size of the typical district, with a larger district, for example, reinforcing the trend in first-past-the-post systems towards disproportionality. Thus, in the limit, in an at-large election covering the whole country the simple plurality formula would give all the seats to the party with the largest share of the votes.

If we focus simply on the electoral formula, thinking of single-member district systems, then the 'mechanical effect' of the first-past-the-post system alone will create conditions in which there is a tendency towards the underrepresentation of smaller parties in the legislature. Moreover, there is also a 'psychological' effect arising from the desire of citizens not to waste their votes, which will reinforce the original mechanical effect (Duverger, 1964, pp. 216–28). Thus, a central feature of the responsible government model of democracy is the first-past-the-post electoral system in which winning parties acquire the right to govern, but are held accountable for their performance at election time. Conversely, the emphasis in the representational model of democracy on the importance of having a broad sweep of public opinion influencing the making of law and public policy is naturally associated with proportional representation schemes of elections, giving rise to the large number of political parties many of which will represent only small segments of public opinion.

The constitutional model of democracy shares with the Westminster model the notion that governing parties should be made accountable to the electorate, and in this respect the two models possess similar conceptions of political representation. Where they are likely to differ from one another is in relation to the interpretation of the act of voting. Proponents of constitutional democracy, such as Riker (1982), criticize the Westminster model for resting on the false notion that it is possible to identify a popular will to which public policy should conform. Instead, according to Riker, the key function of elections is to provide the opportunity to 'throw the rascals out'. On this view, therefore, the electorate does not mandate a prospective political programme, but rather makes a retrospective judgement about the tolerability of past performance. The relevant notion of political representation is then one of retrospective accountability rather than of prospective accountability operating through the influence of the dominant strand of public opinion on the election of a governing party.

Party-mediated populism is at the other end of the spectrum from liberal constitutionalism, at least as far as the role of party representatives is concerned. On the populist view, the function of parties is to formulate alternatives, develop programmes and offer policy choice to the electorate. Important issues, however, are to be decided through popular referendums and those in government are expected to implement what has been decided popularly. Their role as representatives in this regard is one that stresses responsiveness rather than merely accountability. Accountability allows elected political officials to depart from popular opinion between elections, but requires them to explain at elections how and why they behaved as they did. Responsiveness, by contrast, implies that even when in office, elected officials should implement the popular will.

By a similar token, the populist party-mediated conception of democracy shares with the representational model the idea that parties should be broadly representative. It differs from the representational model by seeing political representatives more as delegates than as trustees. One of the principal features of representational systems is that, because there is a need typically to form coalitions, political parties require some freedom in their post-election coalition bargaining, at least in those cases where they have not already formed pre-election coalition pacts. In this sense, although parties in a representational system need to respond to their supporters' demands, they cannot respond to only their supporters' demands. In contrast, in a party-mediated direct democracy, parties are little more than ciphers for the wishes of the electorate.

Although electoral laws are crucial in distinguishing different models of democracy, the evaluation of their relative merits in full raises more issues than can be considered here (see Grofman and Lijphart, 1986). Accordingly, rather than consider the case for and against proportional representation as such, I shall simply consider the merits of alternative views of political representation that fit, to some extent at least, different types of electoral law. It is clear that a general theory of political representation will have implications for the way in which we evaluate electoral rules, for on some accounts of representation the effects of the first-past-the-post electoral system are seen as desirable, whereas on other theories of representation the more broadly based view of representation is seen as preferable. But how far are we able to make a principled choice among the competing conceptions of representation?

The concept of representation

The general concept of representation is that one thing 'stands for' another. Contour lines thus represent hills, in the sense that they stand symbolically for the hills on the map. Similarly, plastic pieces in a board game can represent armies, navies and the like. In cases where one physical system represents another, the only thing that needs to be established, by convention, is a one-to-one correspondence between selected elements of the represented system and the elements in the representing system that are designated to correspond. Provided we know that the lines are supposed to be contours standing for points of equal height above sea level on the land, we shall not mistake them for footpaths.

Representation as such typically involves selection and a corresponding loss of information. No matter how good you are at reading contour lines on a map and figuring out in your mind how steeply the path climbs, you will not be able to envisage everything about the terrain. Even highly complex computer models of the economy will not contain a representation in their system of equations of all elements in the economy. In this most general sense, representation as such is always partial. Moreover, when we turn to political representation, we see that the 'standing for' can take a variety of forms. How are we to distinguish these forms?

In order to answer this question, we need to turn to the defining contemporary discussion of political representation, which is to be found in Pitkin's (1967) *The Concept of Representation*. Pitkin's method of analysis was to examine the way in which the concept of representation was used, and to identify the different senses that the term carries in different contexts. She was concerned in particular to distinguish different claims that are made about the role of representatives. Thus, she pointed out that one influential strand of thinking, inaugurated by Hobbes (1651), sees representatives in terms of authorization. A representative is someone authorized to act for others. However, this sense of representation carries no implications about the extent to which the representative is accountable, and indeed on Hobbes's own account, sovereigns as representatives in the authorization sense are not acccountable to the members of the community that they govern. Hence we need a distinct notion of representation to cover the case of accountability. The accountable representative is logically distinguishable from the authorized representative. By a parallel argument, we can distinguish a substantive notion of representation, according to which someone acts in the interests of another, as a legal representative might, for example, act in the interests of his or her client. This notion, however, is distinct from that of either accountability or authorization, since clearly someone can act in another's interest without being authorized or accountable to that person.

Using this method of identifying distinctive senses of representation through paradigm cases, Pitkin identified five different senses in which we can talk meaningfully about representation. In addition to authorization, accountability and substantive representation, we can also distinguish descriptive and symbolic representation. Each of these different senses of representation are defined in distinct ways. Thus, to be authorized as a representative is to be able to make commitments on behalf of others. To be accountable is to be liable to explain your actions. Substantive representation is to act in the interests of others. Descriptive representation is to be like those for whom you are standing. And symbolic representation is to instantiate some property that enables you to symbolize a group, a nation or set of ideals. In addition, at various points in her analysis, Pitkin also mentions a principle of responsiveness, which she associated with accountability, but which is clearly logically distinct. After all, political representatives can be responsive to their constituents without necessarily rendering them an account or giving an explanation of their actions. Indeed, the increasing use of opinion polling by political candidates in many democracies to provide information in terms of which they adjust their own policy positions is an example of responsiveness in this non-accountable sense.

It is a central claim in Pitkin's overall argument that no one sense of representation can stand duty for all the other senses, and no one sense is to be privileged above the others. Indeed, the constant theme of the work is that mistakes arise when people generalize too readily and widely from particular examples. (It is not difficult to see the shade of J.L. Austin at work in this part of the argument, an influence that she explicitly acknowledged in her introduction.) However, to say that each of the views of representation is distinct is not to say that they cannot be found together empirically in particular circumstances, as Pitkin (1967, 225–6) herself pointed out. Heads of states or elected representatives may be treated as authorized agents for certain purposes, yet in terms of some democratic norms at least they are truly representative only when they account for their actions. Some heads of state, such as the French president, have a role both in terms of authorization, as when they sign international treaties, and symbolically, as standing for the nation on ceremonial occasions. And there is an obvious sense in which political representatives in a democracy are supposed to act in the substantive interests of their constituents.

How then are we to think of these different elements being combined? Here we turn to the familiar distinction between concept and conception (going back to Hart, 1961, p. 156; Perelman, 1963; and Rawls, 1999a, p. 5). A concept offers the general structure of a term, for example the view that a representative 'stands for' the thing that is represented. Concepts in this general sense can be given different specific interpretations, to which we give the name 'conceptions'. In the theory of representation, these different conceptions will explicate an understanding of how the standing for is to be achieved and how the representation takes place. Different conceptions of representation can therefore be defined by the way in which they combine the distinct elements of representation that Pitkin distinguished.

Consider, as an example of this approach, the so-called delegate conception of representation, which we can associate with party-mediated populism. According to the delegate account, political representatives are required to do all and only what their constituents instruct them to do. The delegate account therefore gives high prominence to responsiveness, holding that representatives can act with proper authority only when they are regularly and frequently mandated by their constituents. Such a view of representation is typically associated with institutional recommendations intended to embody these principles, for example short periods of tenure and the possibility of recall during office if sufficient electors so determine, as well as the extensive use of referendums. By contrast, a conception of political representation that stresses responsible government holds that political representatives can sometimes only act substantively in the interests of their constituents when they are free from the obligations of responsiveness. On such accounts, representatives may be accountable, but not overly responsive. Similarly, a 'politics of presence', of the sort discussed by Anne Phillips (1995), stresses the extent to which valid representation depends upon representatives, at least in the aggregate, being a cross-section of their constituents, thus highlighting the element of descriptive representation.

There is no reason to think that there is one right conception of political representation. The appropriate form for representation to take will in part depend upon the political task at hand, the cultural traditions of particular societies and the extent to which putative representatives are willing to think of themselves in some ways rather than others. However, this does not mean that we cannot identify criteria for evaluating alternative conceptions of representation. Although differing conceptions of representation combine varying elements in different ways, they all share one element of logical form. The varying elements of representation are advanced as competing accounts of how best to advance substantive interests. For example, the delegate account of representation does not emphasize responsiveness out of whim. Rather, it proposes a responsive system of representation as a way of achieving better substantive representation. Without institutions that require responsiveness, the populist argues, elected officials will no longer be agents of their principals, but will instead pursue their own interests or act according to their own view. Similarly, the advocate of a politics of presence argues that the interests of socially disadvantaged groups will not be served unless a representative legislature has members who share the characteristics of the disadvantaged.

Given the general idea of democracy as a system of government in which common interests are protected and advanced subject to the constraints of political equality and human fallibility, we have a potential test for the evaluation of different conceptions of representation. Advocates of competing conceptions of political representation are implicitly asserting that their favoured conception is the best way of serving interests. Of course, there may in practice be different assessments about the extent to which common interests are served by different institutional arrangements. For example, there are competing assessments of how far high levels of government turnover in coalition systems do jeopardize achieving the goals of public policy, but such

disagreement is consistent with conceding that if instability had dele-
terious effects then practices that increased instability would not contribute to common interests.

More generally, we can explore, via the method of derivation, what
values would be missing from possible political worlds in which some
elements of representation were absent as a result of institutional
arrangements. For example, we can imagine a world in which representatives were selected by a means other than conventional elections, and
see what would be missing in such a world. This brings us to the lottery
alternative to elections and to the possibility of maximizing descriptive
representation at the expense of other elements of representation.

The lottery alternative

Manin (1997) has shown the extent to which selection of political office
by election is an aristocratic device, and that for a long period of time
the democratic notion was that ordinary citizens, chosen by lot, should
undertake major political tasks. To be sure, as Manin (1997, ch. 1) has
also shown (following Hansen, 1991), the use of the lot in classical
Athens was applied in the case of public offices, rather than appointment of representative to legislative assemblies, because it was assumed
that membership of the assembly was open to all citizens. Just as importantly, Manin was also able to show that selection by lot was used to
fill some offices or perform some functions in republican constitutions
down to the late seventeenth century and modern methods of election
and principles of government by consent evolved from practices and
theories that were originally opposed to democracy.

Suppose, however, that we revert to the lottery principle, but we
imagine that lottery selection takes place for legislative representatives.
Dahl (1989, p. 340) imagines something like this idea in his account
of 'minipopulus'. This would consist of a thousand statistically representative citizens deliberating on an issue for a year, and then announ-
cing its choices. One feature of this body, according to Dahl, would
be that the judgement of minipopulus would represent the judgement
of the demos itself, since its views would be the verdict of the demos,
if it had been able to undertake the deliberation itself. More recently,
Kevin O'Leary (2007) has proposed a national citizens' assembly for
the US in which some 40,000 participants would be given the time
and resources, over a two-year period, to study an issue and make
an informed judgement. In an even more radical vein, Burnheim

(1985, pp. 110–13) has argued that representation should be undertaken by randomly selected volunteers put in control of functionally specific organizations. The idea here is not so much that citizens should rotate in office as they do when they are acting in a legislative capacity but that they should be as much like those for whom they legislate as possible, taking their characteristics as a group.

If we wanted a parliament or legislative chamber to be a mirror or microcosm of the political community, and so be representative in the descriptive sense, then random selection from everyone would be the way to accomplish this. A randomly selected sample of citizens represents the community at large in a statistical sense. Such a random sample would encompass the range of major social characteristics (age, sex, occupation, race, religion, family circumstance, and so on) that one finds in a community. Moreover, the members of such a sample would also be similar to the community at large in the sense that they could be expected to have a wide range of views about the importance of politics, whereas political representatives who compete for office in elections are presumably unrepresentative of the population at large in the interest they display for public affairs.

If political representation could simply be reduced to the descriptive sense, then random selection would not only be sufficient – provided the sample size were large enough – but it would also in fact be the best way of securing descriptive representation. Yet, there would be an obvious loss of political representation in such an arrangement. There would be no mechanisms of accountability and authorization linking the representatives with those whom they are supposed to be representing. Note, for example, that Dahl does not think that minipopulus would make decisions; rather it would announce the results of its deliberations and its verdict would represent the verdict of the demos. However, it would only do this in the sense that it would form the basis for predicting what the demos would have decided. There is no sense in which it will have taken a decision on behalf of the demos.

One reason for this absence of accountability and authorization is that there would be little institutional capacity or incentive among randomly selected citizens to explain or account for their decisions. The price of social representativeness would be a loss of accountability. In being a substitute for the community, the sample would not have to be accountable to the community. Accountability in this regard can be thought of as having two aspects. The first is that related to the provision of incentives to avoid imprudent or counter-productive action. The second is accountability in a deliberative sense. If reasoning about public policy is important, then the discussion and forwarding of opinions about public policy and public choices is important. Accountability is a process of engaging in argument, criticism and exchange of opinions with those who hold a different view. This too requires the organization of opinion into broader programmes or at least principled understanding of what is involved in politics.

The organization of political opinion in the form of political parties certainly narrows down the range of views that are expressed in politics, and in this sense politics is always the mobilization of bias. However, it is this narrowing down of all the possible opinions that could be expressed that is the condition under which any coherent opinion can be expressed at all. One way of seeing this is to note the importance of political parties in reducing the weight of information with which the individual has to cope. The form of proportional representation favoured by J. S. Mill was the Hare scheme under which voters would be allowed to vote for any candidate who might be standing in the country. Clearly, under such a scheme there could be hundreds of candidates, and it would be almost impossible for even a committed voter to make an intelligent choice among them. Since politics is about choice, this is a severe limitation, and so the narrowing of the range of possible opinions by party systems should not of itself be considered a disadvantage.

Someone may urge at this point that accountability through incentives and the mobilization of opinion is unnecessary, since the microcosm of society that is the representative sample can simply stand for society as a whole. We could make minipopulus a decision-making organ, since there would simply be no need for the members of the sample to explain their decisions to citizens at large, as current political representatives attempt to do, given the statistical basis of their selection. Any decision taken would, by definition, emerge from a body that was representative of society taken as a whole. The problem here is that once such a body is seen as a decision maker, it would be taking decisions not simply for itself but for society as a whole. Its choices would therefore be binding on those who were not party to the process, and in that sense would have authority. Yet, it is difficult to see how those who would not be party to its decisions would feel obliged to accept them if there were no explanation or account forthcoming at all. Accountability and authorization are in that sense linked. Interestingly, in this context, those chosen for public office in ancient Athens did have to render an account for their time in office, and could be penalized if that account was not satisfactory (Manin, 1997, pp. 12–13).

In the hypothetical random legislature that is being imagined here, by contrast, there is no corresponding mechanism, and all that is being relied upon is the statistical representativeness of the sample of citizens chosen rather than any specific mechanism by which an account is to be made.

If this line of reasoning is right, it establishes that, although political representation arises from the need for a division of political labour, its existence means that it is not purely a matter of the division of labour. Instead, its existence calls into being the need for distinct dimensions of evaluation and assessment. One of these dimensions concerns the extent to which the political system is representative in the sense of being authorized by the people. Why should this sense of authorization be important? One answer to this question is that social groups and political systems need ways of committing themselves to a common course of action in order to advance their interests. Without the capacity for authorization, it is impossible for a group of people to advance their common interests. This facet of political representation is most clearly seen in the case of international relations and international agreements. Consider, as an example, agreements made between countries to limit pollution affecting one another. International environmental agreements typically take a form in which countries agree to limit their pollution output provided that other countries will do the same. In order for one country to think it worthwhile incurring the costs of reducing its pollution, it will need some assurance that other parties to the agreement will also play their part in reducing the pollution. Unless this happens, the benefits of the agreement will not be realized and one or more of the parties will have incurred costs in vain. Hence each country needs some assurance that its actions will be reciprocated. However, in order to have such assurance, each country will need to know that those with whom it is making the agreement have the authority to commit their constituents, otherwise it will not be able to rely upon reciprocal commitment.

The value of representation in this authorization sense is that collective commitment usually is necessary, and, indeed, is often critical, to political actors securing goods that are in their common interests. This brings out the way in which representation as authorization is related to substantive representation. If representatives are there to play the role of securing common interests as well as the legitimate interests of their constituents, then having the necessary authorization is one means by which this is achieved. Manin (1997) implicitly draws upon this logic in accounting for the way in which the method of election came to replace the method of selection by lot in democratic thinking, relating the process in particular to the need of monarchs to secure taxation. The origins of parliamentary representation can be found in the need for monarchs in medieval Europe to have reliable ways of raising taxation. One way of doing this was to assemble representatives of taxpayers and secure their agreement to the taxes being levied, thus providing some assurance that the taxes would be paid. Thus, although within democratic cultures we are accustomed to think about representation as a movement from bottom up, it can originate from top-down processes, although this is not to say that it does not also serve the interests of citizens when it is top-down.

What we have seen so far are some of the reasons why, when the system of party competition in representative democracies is working well, there can be representation in more than one of Pitkin's senses. Parties can be accountable and authorized, in ways in which a randomly selected legislative chamber could not be, and by these means they can pursue the substantive representation of interests. Of course, there may be a price to be paid for this in terms of the descriptive representation, and this is a matter to which we will have to return. However, there is another aspect of representation that has not been discussed so far, and that is representation as responsiveness. To that question I now turn.

Responsiveness and representation

I have defined democracy as a political system in which there is a formal connection between public opinion and the content of laws and policies. Although this formula does not of itself imply that all changes of public mood ought to be immediately reflected in changes in public policy (if indeed that were possible), it does imply that the formulation of legislation and policy ought to be responsive, in some sense, to public opinion. Within a representative system, such a view implies that responsiveness plays a role in the account of representation.

Responsiveness of some sort is therefore ineliminable from an account of democratic government, but this does not mean that all accounts of political representation share the same understanding of responsiveness. In particular, different accounts of representation rest upon different views about exactly how responsive governments should be to changes in public mood and precisely how much responsiveness is enough. Some views, such as populism, emphasize the

importance of public policy being highly responsive to popular preferences. Other stress the opposite, as the following famous quotation
from Edmund Burke's speech to the electors of Bristol goes to show:

> Certainly, Gentlemen, it ought to be the happiness and glory of a
> Representative, to live in the strictest union, the closest correspond-
> ence, and the most unreserved communication with his constituents.
> Their wishes ought to have great weight with him; their opinion
> high respect; their business unremitted attention. It is his duty to
> sacrifice his repose, his pleasures, his satisfactions, to theirs; and,
> above all, ever, and in all cases, to prefer their interest to his own.
> But his unbiassed opinion, his mature judgement, his enlightened
> conscience, he ought not to sacrifice to you; to any man, or to any
> sett [*sic*] of men living ... Your representative owes you, not his
> industry only, but his judgement; and he betrays, instead of serv-
> ing you, if he sacrifices it to your opinion. (Burke, 1774, pp. 54–5)

From this account of the relationship between representative and constituents, Burke goes on to assert the importance of representatives
making their judgements in the light of parliamentary deliberations
about what is to the common good. In other words, on this Burkean
account of representation, responsiveness to the interests and opinions
of constituents has a relatively insignificant place.

It is possible to read Burke here in at least two ways. On the most
elitist account, the political representative is regarded as independent
of constituents and appointed to deliberate, with there being little or no
element of accountability in his or her behaviour. It is presumably on
the basis of a reading like this that Gutmann and Thompson (2004, p. 8)
describe Burke's account as being more aristocratic than democratic.
On an alternative reading, however, the representative is accountable
but is not responsive. The principle that the representative *owes* a
judgement to constituents would at least be consistent with that representative's offering an account of that judgement come the election;
it would just be that between elections such an account did not have
to be rendered and MPs would be expected to make up their own minds
on what they saw as the balance of the argument.

Birch (1972, pp. 37–40) has pointed out that the notion that legislation is about deliberation to a common purpose was a Whig theory.
However, it was also a view that came to be widely accepted during the
nineteenth century as the one stating the correct account of the functions
of parliamentary representatives. Thus, Sidgwick (1891, pp. 529–33),

who was the epitome of progressive, but moderate, common sense, defended it in his account of democracy. Schumpeter can also be read as endorsing something like this theory. He identifies five conditions for democratic stability: a high quality of personnel drawn from a social stratum for whom politics is a vocation; a small effective range of political decisions; state control of a well-trained bureaucracy; democratic self-control by the people; and tolerance of differences of opinion (Schumpeter, 1954, pp. 290–6). Read charitably, these conditions would be consistent with a Whig theory of representation. (However, my suspicion is that Schumpeter does not even manage to state a Whig view, and that he has no account at all of representation as distinct from a theory of electoral competition.)

In the passage from Burke there are two distinctions being drawn. The first of these distinctions is between deliberation to a common good on the one hand and the pursuit of interests on the other. The second is between representatives as delegates and representatives as trustees. These two sets of categories are logically different, but they are related in Burke's view. To see why this is so, consider the following possibility. Suppose that representation were to be conceived as a system of bargaining among representatives of groups where the groups were pursuing their own interests. Then deliberation would still be required, since the representatives would have to frame proposals to be considered, evaluate proposals that were put to them and consider the implications for their constituents of any likely solution to the bargaining problems that might emerge. If they did not, they would simply be the 'rational fools' that Sen (1977) identified. In other words, deliberation would be required on the part of representatives to assess how far the interests of their constituents were served by any particular proposal. From this point of view, deliberation is just a component of any intelligent action.

However, such deliberation would not be deliberation to a common purpose. Instead, it merely serves the end of negotiation to a mutually acceptable set of separate purposes. Deliberation may also be used to find mutually agreeable solutions to a common problem in which arguments on all sides have to be weighed by different parties. It is this stronger notion of deliberation that Burke seems to have had in mind when he claimed that in parliament it is the interest of the nation, rather than any particular constituency, that ought to be weighed by a representative. But if this is the goal of representatives, then they cannot be delegates, for if you go to a debate with your mind made up and only intending to vote for what your constituents want, you cannot be taking the process of deliberation seriously. A delegate goes to a meeting to state a position and register a vote, not to be influenced by the debate (compare Pitkin, 1972, p. 151). Once the notion of deliberation to a common purpose is introduced, it follows that representatives ought to be able to listen to what is being said, and make a final commitment in the light, partially at least, of the arguments that are advanced.

There is therefore this kernel of insight in the Burkean account of representation. Were parliamentary deliberation and political discussion simply about the representatives of social groups coming to an agreement, then those representatives could act purely as delegates. However, if collective discussion among representatives is to have an independent role in the formation of opinion and decision, then there has to be some gap between the views and wants that constituents express and the way in which representatives form their judgements about what is to be done. If deliberation really is to be given a role in forming judgements, then representatives have to be responsive to the arguments advanced as well as responsive to their constituents' opinions.

We can in part support this conclusion by considering an empirical argument. A delegate view is likely to go along with short terms of office for politicians and the possibility of recall during tenure in office. These are devices for enhancing the responsiveness of politicians. The difficulty, however, is that in putting politicians on a short leash, it becomes more difficult for those politicians to deal with the collective problems for which legislation is needed in the first place. King (1997) has shown, for example, that as US politicians have had to become more responsive to every modulation of their constituents' concerns, so their ability to deal with long-standing collective problems (economic policies, budget deficits and crime) has been undermined. They are running scared in part because so many of them have to run so frequently, and in part because they have an expectation placed upon them that they will be responsive.

There might be a way to rescue a conception of representation based on responsive delegation as follows. Suppose we focus not on the individual representative playing the role of delegate, but upon the set of representatives as a whole, each of whom is taking the role of delegate. Then it might be that the upshot of every representative acting as vigorously as possible as a delegate for sectional interests was better than the result of all representatives seeking to internalize a sense of the public good in a problem-solving way. The analogy would be with the price-system in a market. A market works well when each trader seeks his or her own advantage to the maximum extent possible, within specified limits. Perhaps the political market will work when representatives try to advance the interests of their constituents to the maximum extent possible. Such a view comes close to the way that a pluralist account of democracy has been portrayed, in which representatives do not pursue the public good directly, but a good society is nonetheless one in which such regulated competition of interests occurs.

Such a view is possible, but it runs up a great deal of counter-evidence from empirical political science taken from a variety of situations. Olson's (1982) argument, for example, is that it is precisely the accumulation of concessions to special interests that causes sclerosis in an economy. Similarly, agricultural protectionism in Europe and the US, which has had serious adverse consequences for developing country producers, is a result of responsiveness on the part of political parties to agricultural interests. At another level, Miriam Golden (2003) has argued that Italian legislators have strengthened their own electoral position through a parliamentary system that has created the incentive for members of parliament to pass a large number of small, detailed laws. Clearly, these are only suggestive empirical examples, and a proper balance of account would, of course, need to take into consideration a wider range of evidence. Yet, there is enough evidence in the examples cited to suggest that there is no invisible hand in a system of parliamentary representation to mimic the beneficial effects of the price system in an economy.

By an extension of this argument, the populist account of representation, at least in its party-mediated form, finds it difficult to deal with the role of inter-party deliberation. Party-mediated direct democracy allows for deliberation, but it is the deliberation of advocates drawing up proposals to put to the electorate. Political competition then shifts alternative schemes through popular direct choice. There is no place for representatives to engage one another in evidence, argument and persuasion, or rather, to the extent to which they do, they shift power away from electorates towards institutions of accommodation and dialogue among themselves, in violation of the fundamental principles of populism.

This does not mean that responsiveness is unimportant in the practice of representation. Unless legislators are responsive to their constituents' concerns, they are not fulfilling one central element of their role. However, the responsiveness of representation has to be balanced against its substantive and accountability dimensions, and incentive structures in the design of political institutions need to recognize that some independence of representatives may be necessary for them to do their job. Delegation cannot replace deliberation.

Back to social characteristics?

In making notions of accountability and authorization central to the idea of representation, I have contrasted what these notions share with the view of statistical representation. However, at this point we meet the argument that the best people to express an opinion are those who actually share the social characteristics of those who are being represented. Does this lead us back to social characteristics and, if so, how?

I have argued that there are problems with the idea that it is only social characteristics that we care about in political representation, and that we need to insist that the articulation of a political position and a commitment to authorization are essential elements of democratic representation. Moreover, once we say that one of the functions of representatives is to argue and deliberate with one another, then we reinforce the need for representatives to hold and articulate a political position. However, to say that it is not only social characteristics that we care about is not to say that we do not care about social characteristics at all. There is a way of understanding political opinion such that the best expressions of opinion and a political position will only come from certain sorts of people.

Mansbridge (2003) usefully draws attention to two implications of this view. The first is what she calls 'surrogate' representation. Surrogate representation is representation by an elected official with whom one has no direct electoral connection oneself. For example, in the US, Representative Barney Frank from Massachusetts sees himself as articulating the point of view of the gay and lesbian community throughout the US. There is, then, in this concept of surrogate representation an interesting, if distant, echo of Burke's concept of virtual representation. Burke argued that some growing constituencies in England did not need separate territorial representation. For example, the interests of all industrial areas were adequately represented in parliament by some industrial areas. Clearly, there is a lacuna in this particular argument, but the thought that the representation of one's own distinctive opinion does not have to be the special province of one's own territorial representative is an important aspect of the deliberative dimension of representation.

The second aspect of opinion representation to which Mansbridge draws attention is one in which voters select representatives who are chosen because they can be expected to act on opinions and principles that voters share, independently of any electoral incentive. Mansbridge calls this 'gyroscopic' representation, because it is as though the representatives rotate on their own axes maintaining their own built-in momentum of movement. The point about such gyroscopic representation is that, provided the voters can identify a characteristic of candidates that enables voters to have a reasonable prediction of how that representative will behave, then less weight needs to be placed on the effectiveness of electoral control. The simplest way of identifying someone whom you think will act in ways of which you approve is to select someone who shares your attitudes and values. And to do this, the simplest rule is to choose people like yourself.

Clearly, the representation of attitudes and values need not entail that those doing the representing share the same characteristics as those whom they represent. You do not have to be sick to speak up for those who favour more spending on hospitals, nor old to think that retirement pensions are too low. However, it may be that without there being some political representatives who share certain characteristics with the electors whom they represent, certain points of view will simply be ignored. John Stuart Mill put the point well, back in the 1860s:

> In this country, for example, what are called the working classes may be considered as excluded from all direct participation in government. I do not believe that the classes who do participate in it, have in general any intention of sacrificing the working classes to themselves ... Yet does Parliament, or almost any of the members comprising it, ever for an instant look at any question with the eyes of a working man? (Mill, 1861a, p. 246)

Some years previously, Tocqueville had had a similar thought, arguing that though the ruling English aristocracy was perhaps the most liberal that had ever existed, under its government it 'cannot escape observation ... that in the legislation of England the interests of the poor have often been sacrificed to the advantages of the rich' (Tocqueville, 1835, p. 250). So while it may be true that to represent someone's opinions you do not have to share their social characteristics, it is not unreasonable to say that it helps to have patterns of political representation that broadly reflect that statistical distribution of politically salient characteristics in the population.

In effect, this is a sort of negative conclusion. It amounts simply to the thought that political representatives who are drawn exclusively from a limited social stratum are unlikely to be able to represent all points of view fully. In a way, this turns a Schumpeterian protective argument on its head and is akin to our earlier assumption about political equality, that no one group of people can be guaranteed to be politically competent on behalf of others. Is it possible to go beyond this rather negative statement of the case to a more positive view, which says that there is a definite virtue in having a representative chamber that contains the representatives of a wide variety of social groups, and in that sense represents the distribution of social characteristics within the community? As Anne Phillips (1995) has put it, how far do we need to complement a politics of ideas with a politics of presence?

The question is pertinent because representative chambers are often highly unrepresentative, in a statistical sense, of the populations from which they are drawn: they are more male, better educated, from more prestigious and better-paid occupations and older than the average. John Stuart Mill argued for the extension of the franchise to women and working-class men as a way of ensuring that certain points of view were articulated within parliament. Subsequent experience would appear to show that the mere formal inclusion of groups in the process of electoral competition is insufficient to secure the representation of those groups in the process of legislation. Thus, even in systems of proportional representation, which are better than first-past-the-post systems at securing the presence of women in parliament, it has proved necessary to supplement the voting rules with rules about the party selection of candidates to increase the number of women MPs. Similarly, in the US redistricting has been necessary in order to ensure that African-Americans could be represented by members of their own ethnic group (Tribe, 1988, ch. 13). But, of course, these extra rules would only have a justification if there really were a case for the politics of presence.

One argument that can be advanced at this point is that political presence may be necessary in order to establish a symbolic move away from exclusion. Seeing members of one's own social group participating as representatives in the process of government is a way of enhancing one's own sense of dignity and political status (Phillips, 1995, p. 40). Where previously social groups have been denied the vote or effective political representation, then it seems right that great importance is attached to members of those groups seeing people like themselves exercising political power. Pitkin's symbolic representation then becomes relevant.

Phillips cites three closely related arguments supporting this point of view. The first is that those representatives who share the social characteristics of their disadvantaged constituents are likely to be better advocates on their behalf, particularly under conditions of deliberation in which delegative mandates are weak or inoperative. The second is that such representatives are also needed to see beyond the limitations of the present political agenda, by raising issues that are not salient to those who are used to exercising political power. And the third is that groups need to be explicitly represented because the coalition of groups within political parties may form around clusters of opinions that are only partial.

An example may illustrate this last point. Suppose working men and women as a group share an interest in high standards of working conditions. They would naturally then support a political party that campaigned on that issue. However, they might not share opinions on another set of issues (say, abortion). Since a political party will only be built on a subset of opinions of its supporters, there will be issues that some supporters would like pursued but which will be marginalized or ignored by the party in question. Thus, any party mandate is partial, and group representatives are necessary to put forward the claims that would otherwise be ignored.

The logic here is that parties have to campaign on combinations of issues. But since there are many issues, and only few parties, the combinations of issues that are actually represented in the political system at any one time will only be a small subset of all the issues that could be represented. Political parties, even in representational systems where they may be present in relatively large numbers, will substantially narrow down the range of views represented, since political parties may be regarded as organized bodies of opinion. The only way to overcome this organizational bias, it is said, is to have broader group representation within political parties, say by a system of quotas.

Notice, however, that, though the above are arguments for a politics of presence, they are arguments for there being some representatives who share the social characteristics of the previously disadvantaged, not an arguments for statistical representation in the sense we have previously discussed. Indeed, as Phillips (1995, p. 67) points out, the upshot of these arguments may well involve non-proportional representation in the statistical sense. Certain groups may be underrepresented statistically in the population, but may still need to have threshold representation in the political process if the need for symbolic representation and associated advantages is to be addressed.

If these arguments are accepted, they become reasons for favouring certain practices in the selection of representatives, most notably the use of quotas for women and ethnic minority groups in the selection of parliamentary candidates and the arrangement of districts in single-member constituency systems that ensure certain designated groups are able to elect members who represent them in certain respects (on this see Rogowski, 1981).

The problem with these conclusions, as Phillips herself notes, is that such practices appear to cut across the formal principle of political equality, to the effect that members of all groups should compete for political office on the same terms. If political equality is to be taken seriously as a value, how is it possible to allow one group or set of groups an advantage in the selection of members? For example, if quotas for women are used in the selection of parliamentary candidates, does this not mean that men are placed at a disadvantage when they run for office, and, if so, is this unfair? In reply to these sorts of questions, Phillips argues that we ought not to take the principle of equality in an abstract way and that we cannot deduce a politics of presence directly from the principle of equality. Instead, 'the core of the argument lies in a more historically specific analysis of existing structures of exclusion and existing arrangements for representation' (Phillips, 1995, p. 31).

Let us agree that the formal interpretation of the equality principle is not much help here, as it is often not much help in many situations in which original disadvantage has to be overcome. Even treated as a procedural notion, the rule that everyone should be treated the same is at best a defeasible concept, which can easily be shown to be inappropriate given some initial inequality (Weale, 1978, pp. 16–17). Where there is no clean sheet, clean sheet non-arbitrariness is not applicable. However, it is not clear that the relevant alternative is to place so much weight on the notion of 'an historically specific analysis', not least because no matter how historically specific one is, this will not decide the principles that should determine choice.

Suppose someone were to say that the objection to the practices implied by a politics of presence was that it violated a principle of impartial or non-arbitrary treatment. What could be the reply to this question? One obvious reply is that the practices were necessary to overcome existing discrimination or disadvantage. But another reply in turn to this view is that part of the lack of representation may arise from the failure of members of certain groups to put themselves forward, and that empirical research shows that there is less discrimination in, say, party selection procedures than the assumption appears to warrant. For example, Norris and Lovenduski (1993) show that it is supply-side factors (the absence of women putting themselves forward) rather than demand-side factors (prejudice and bias on the part of selectors) that account for the low number of women party candidates.

Would it follow from this observation that arguments from presence had no force? Arguably not. One could still hold that systems that promoted presence had advantages over systems that did not. To see how this might work, consider the following. Suppose we say that, for all the reasons that we have already considered, arguments connected with the politics of presence have force. This means that if a purely formal application of the equality principle was consistent with an adequate representation of some group, then we would count this a better situation than if application of the same principle led to less representation. But if representation of this sort has independent value, might it not lead us to modify the application of the purely formal equality test? Even if underrepresentation does not arise from discrimination, we could still judge it to be worth some sacrifice of the formal equality principle to achieve greater representation.

Why favour the representation of certain sections of the population over the proportionate representation of views that would be implied by a system that dispensed with any quotas or other special arrangements? One answer here is that it is people with interests who need the protection of the political system, not any particular set of political opinions. Indeed, if certain opinions were associated with certain groups, one would be concerned, according to the principle of equality, with the exclusion of that opinion, but this would logically seem to arise from a concern lest the interests of that group were being neglected.

Social disadvantage may be the relevant test here, but it does not have to be. One argument that bothers Phillips is what we might term the 'open-list' argument. If we make efforts to ensure that certain groups, such as women and ethnic minorities, are included in the process of representation, what is there to stop us saying that people with red hair or blue eyes ought to be represented in their own right? But the answer to this question is that there is no plausible basis of interest on which such groups would organize politically, whereas the characteristics that have been picked out in quota systems for European political parties or applied in the case of congressional districting in the US do reflect clear sections of organized interests.

What is clear is that there is no single criterion of the form 'this group is identifiable by this test, therefore it ought to be represented', but this is true given the nature of the argument. Consider a parallel case. Suppose we thought that there was a public interest in having more people with training in the natural sciences in the legislature. We might have a number of reasons for thinking this, and we might also note that at present natural scientists are underrepresented. Should we be worried by the thought that someone else might point out that water engineers, rat catchers and dentists were also underrepresented? After all, there is no general criterion that distinguishes the one group from the others, except a substantive judgement in each case about the contribution to public deliberation that each group could make.

Moreover, the argument about the representation of specific groups is as much related to concerns about diversity as it is to concerns about disadvantage. One reason for this is that the disadvantage argument would seem to imply only a limited period of time within which rectificatory measures should be taken. If the presence of certain types of representatives is justified in terms of overcoming historic disadvantage, then after a period, which may extend over some time of course, it would seem logical to remove the policy of preference as the legacy of disadvantage is worked out of the system. However, where there are distinct social groups, whatever their relative position in relation to others, then there appears to be a case for a policy of distinct representation.

One objection that has been raised to a politics of presence is simply the problem of multiplying diversity to the point where it becomes impossible to represent each element of the diversity in its own right (Goodin, 2004). As Goodin points out, this may arise from a variety of causes. There may be too many groups, a problem that arises the more sensitive we become to the difficulties of bringing different social groups under the same label. At one point in the UK, for example, people might have thought of the representation of ethnic minorities, without thinking too closely about the differences among those whose family origins were in the Indian subcontinent. That, clearly, was too simple a view. Even within a well-defined group, there may be too much heterogeneity of individual opinion and interest. And, there may be too many cross-cutting groups, particularly as individuals with similar backgrounds nonetheless construct their identities in very different ways, associating themselves with diverse movements. Given the practical limitations of size in the design of any legislative chamber, it might seem that the ambition to be representative of diversity in all its richness is unattainable. Goodin's own solution is to say that the requirement for the legislative chamber to have a diverse body of representatives ought to be understood as representing the sheer fact of diversity, so that legislators are reminded that when they make laws, they are making laws for people who differ from one another in a variety of ways.

This solution is a neat one to the dilemma as posed, but it will not work unless the legislators are conceived as having some deliberative autonomy. That is to say, their judgement about the merits of legislation cannot just be derived from a reading of the perspective and point of view of their own group background and identification. Rather it has to come from a willingness to engage with the points of view of others to whom one will have to give an account and with whom one has to engage in a process of evidence, argument and persuasion. Paradoxical as it may sound, the common interest in such a situation is the acknowledgement of difference.

A system of representation?

Where do these arguments leave us in terms of the competing theories of representative government with which I started this chapter? I have argued that a theory of representation cannot simply be based on the notion that key political decision makers should be statistically representative of the community of which they are a part. Political representatives must also stand in a relationship of accountability to those whom they represent, as well as exercising deliberative skills and engaging in the development of political principles and policy positions with one another. They also need to be authorized to enter into agreements if those agreements are necessary to achieve the public interest. Moreover, although simple statistical representation is not enough, too narrow a social composition among representatives is unjustified. In part, this is for protective reasons: members of unrepresented groups have their interests undervalued or ignored. Just as important, however, is the symbolic affirmation of political equality that a system of representation that is not exclusive comprises.

As noted at the beginning of this chapter, comparative political science has been traditionally concerned with the nature of the electoral connection between citizens and politicians, and the extent to which that influences the quality of representation. In particular, it has been argued that electoral systems based upon proportional representation provide for a wider range of representation, both of opinions and of social characteristics, than Westminster systems do. The claim that a wider range of opinions is represented in such systems is almost true by definition; to the extent to which PR systems of voting encourage multi-party, rather than two-party, competition, they will by that token foster a wider range of views. The broader representation of social characteristics is a purely empirical relationship, but it too might be thought to be built into the logic of PR systems, at least in so far as those systems have low electoral thresholds. Because it is easier for small parties to gain legislative representation with a low threshold, candidate selection occurs in a larger number of parties, and so biases in selection procedure can be evened out.

The normative argument suggests another criterion of evaluation, however, namely the deliberative quality of different representative systems. Since a requirement of representation is that representatives be able to engage one another in deliberative exchange, it would be interesting to know the extent to which different types of system enabled or discouraged high-quality deliberation. Political science has only just begun to analyse the content of discourse and there is not a body of findings to anything like the same degree that we find in studies of voting. However, in a pioneering volume, Steiner *et al.* (2004) aim to test the quality of deliberation in different types of parliaments. Their conclusions suggest that representational systems achieve a higher quality of deliberation than Westminster systems. Moreover, since the US in its first-past-the-post electoral system resembles the UK, in that respect if not in others, it is not surprising to find that it too does not fare well on the deliberative quality index. Given the difficulties of doing such innovative work, no definitive weight can be assigned to the conclusions. However, they would be consistent with the greater powers possessed by parliaments relative to the executive in representational systems compared to Westminster systems. If legislators have little to do that is independent, it is perhaps not surprising that when they debate, they manage less good-quality work.

However, it is possible to argue that representation is best achieved not through the detailed specification of any one part of the system of representation, but through the operation of the whole system. Pitkin (1967, pp. 221–5) mentions this idea in passing, but does not discuss in detail the level of analysis at which the discussion of representation should take place. Her general analysis of the different sense of representation is largely undertaken at the level of individual representatives within the political system. However, in an important, but brief, discussion towards the end of the book, Pitkin herself notes that political representation may occur in a community not because of what any particular people do, for example elected representatives, but because the whole system functions to supply representation. As she writes: 'Representation may emerge from a political system in which many individuals, both voters and legislators, are pursuing quite other goals' (Pitkin, 1967, p. 224). This suggests the possibility of a normative theory of representation being consistent with an invisible hand explanation of how representative systems work. Such an invisible hand explanation would accept representation could take place even if the motives of political actors were purely selfish. Private vices may conduce to public benefit.

The most famous example of a democratic theory that tries to model democracy on the pattern of private vices and public virtues is that of Downs (1957). In his economic theory of democracy, politicians are viewed as being motivated by the search for office, and they locate their party positions on a left–right ideological spectrum in such a way as to be closest in terms of their programme to the views of those electors whose votes they are seeking. Consistent with the results in the theory of voting first established by Black (1958), Downs was able to show that it was possible to construct a hypothetical world of party competition in which such behaviour would lead to politicians of different parties, under a plausible range of circumstances, converging on the ideological position of median voters, that is to say those voters located at the centre of the spectrum of public opinion. But is the centre of the spectrum of public opinion the right place for representatives to be? To answer that question we need a theory of aggregation.

7 Aggregation, Unanimity and Majority Rule

Political action is collective action. This is especially so in a democracy in which the pursuit of common purposes is important. Collective action by definition involves choices binding on all citizens. However, under the circumstances of politics I identified in Chapter 1 (partial cooperation and conflict in situations of confined generosity and bounded rationality), these choices will exhibit difference and diversity. Fallibility of judgement is one aspect of these circumstances. Even with goodwill and social awareness, citizens are likely to disagree in their political opinions and judgements. Differences of interest as well as of perception and values will lead the citizens to divergent views about how to direct and use the organized political power of the community in order to promote and protect common interests. If political representatives reflect this diversity, then there will be as much disagreement in the legislature as there is in the population. Inevitably, then, both at the level of citizens and of their representatives there is the problem of how disparate views are to be aggregated into the single choice that democratic governments must make.

It is common among a number of democratic theorists to call such differences of view 'preferences'. In many ways, this is an unfortunate term. It suggests that the problem of aggregation is one about how to satisfy conflicting wants, or perhaps even rather whimsical tastes. In some social situations, thinking about the problem of aggregation as one about satisfying wants makes a great deal of sense. If you and I are going out together to eat, and I know you like traditional food but hate nouvelle cuisine, whereas I am happy with either, then there is a clear case for giving you a veto on where we go, because your want satisfaction would be much lower than mine if the wrong choice were made. As Peter Jones (1988) has pointed out, however, it is a mistake to regard political choice in this way. Political choice is more like a jury deciding whether the verdict should be innocent or guilty than it is like satisfying competing wants within a group. Certainly within a theory within which citizens are thought of as having to make decisions on matters of common interests, we are better thinking of their views or opinions as judgements rather than as the expression of their own wants (compare Sunstein, 1991, pp. 6–14).

Yet the notion of citizen preferences as being the basis for democracy has found a place in the literature on aggregation. One reason for this is that public policy typically involves the making of choices among alternatives, and it therefore involves ranking those alternatives according to some scale of value. The most developed account of rank ordering comes from the economic theory of consumer preferences, which has found its way into the political science literature on aggregation. Hence, in what follows, the term 'preferences' is being used to indicate a ranking of alternatives by citizens or their representatives, without that carrying any connotation that these preferences are ill thought out or matters of merely subjective desire. The notion of preference and a preference ranking in this chapter is to be thought of as a judgement expressed as a ranking, perhaps only partial, of a set of possibilities. I am not saying that preferences in this sense are the only sort of raw material of choice in democratic politics, but I am presupposing that they are both typical and important.

When trying to aggregate different views or opinions expressed as preferences, the most common rule used is majority rule, which makes the collective choice depend upon the agreed view of a majority of those voting. However, many forms of political and non-political associations use other rules of collective choice. In some political systems a super-majoritarian principle is used for constitutional amendments requiring more than a majority to agree to a change. It is also possible to weight votes, so that some voters are given more influence than others. For example, in the EU's Council of Ministers, the votes of each minister are weighted by a formula related to the population size of each member state. Another variant is to use super-majorities, in which the criterion is not a simple majority of those voting but some specified proportion above the simple majority. The European Union's Council of Ministers also incorporates this modification by requiring a super-majority of the weighted votes to adopt a policy. Finally, among the many possibilities, a rule of unanimity can be required, so that all those affected by a policy would have to agree to its implementation before it were adopted. This is the rule adopted by some religious groups in the making of decisions as well as by many radical communitarian groups. It is also, in effect, the rule at work in the standard form of international agreements. The unanimity rule is thus invoked in a variety of circumstances, and, as Mansbridge (1980, pp. 252–69) has pointed out, it can thus be an expression of social unity or a device of self-protection.

The normative issues raised by the problem of aggregation are essentially concerned with assessing the relative merits of the various rules that can be used in moving from a statement of individual preferences to a statement of a collective choice. However, answering the normative questions about merits involves being clear on certain basic conceptual questions, for example whether we can meaningfully speak of a 'popular will' or the 'will of the people'. Since, on some theories of democratic government, the function of government is to enact the popular will, such conceptual questions are central. For example, the concept of a popular will is at the heart not only of direct accounts of democracy but also of the representational and Westminster models. So, in order to understand the logic of these models, we need to have a clear idea of what might be involved in the claim that aggregation should involve the construction of a popular will.

Of course, the claim that democracy requires a notion of the popular will has not gone unchallenged. In a famous passage Schumpeter wrote in criticism of what he termed the classical doctrine of democracy:

> There is, first, no such thing as a uniquely determined common good that all people could agree on or be made to agree on by the force of rational argument. This is due not primarily to the fact that some people may want things other than the common good but to the much more fundamental fact that to different individuals and groups the common good is bound to mean different things.

(Schumpeter, 1954, p. 251)

Schumpeter went on to argue that in the absence of a definite determination of the idea of the common good, the notion of a general will collapses and that though we may detect a common will or expression of public opinion 'from the infinitely complex jumble of individual and group-wise situations, volitions, influences, actions, reactions of the "democratic process," the result lacks not only rational unity but also rational sanction' (Schumpeter, 1954, p. 253). The inference was clear. We cannot use the idea of the popular will to form the basis for government action and public policy. A theory of democracy should therefore fulfil the negative function of protecting citizens from the tyranny of government abuses of power through the mechanism of political competition, and not the positive function of implementing or responding to popular opinion. In such protective theories of democracy there is typically a great emphasis upon what we can call counter-majoritarian constitutional mechanisms (for example, constitutional restrictions on legislative decisions) that limit or slow down the implementation of majority views. In this way, questions of aggregation immediately lead to questions concerned with the justification of alternative models of democracy, and in particular the possible merits of a liberal constitutionalist model of democracy, to be discussed in the next chapter.

The principle of unanimity

Some theories of constitutional government urge very strict limits on the operation of the majority principle. The worry is that majorities represent only sectional interests, and will pursue policies at odds with the public interest. Using super-majoritarian devices is seen as a way of constraining this sectional interest. For authors such as Buchanan and Tullock, the principle of unanimity is the obvious way of preserving individual freedom from majority coercion: in one sense it makes the collective choice voluntary (Buchanan and Tullock, 1962, p. 90). Unanimity can thus be urged as a principle of collective choice on grounds of freedom. The fundamental idea is that if decisions are taken according to the principle of unanimity, then individuals will not be coerced into public policies with which they fundamentally disagree or which impose disproportionate costs on them.

  Despite this rationale, there are some obvious problems with using unanimity as a principle of decision, which include the following: it is time-consuming to implement, thus raising the transaction costs associated with decision making; it privileges the status quo; and it is difficult to believe that preference convergence will take place, so that everyone will agree after discussion (compare Rae, 1975). Buchanan and Tullock (1962, pp. 97–116) acknowledge the problems of decision costs associated with this position, and argue in favour of various super-majoritarian rules as a second-best. But it is clear from their discussion that the unanimity principle is still the position that is normatively the ideal. The problem with the line of argument is a familiar one, however, namely that super-majoritarian systems create their own decision-making pathologies. The most important of these is a tendency towards 'pork barrel' allocations in public finance, by which spending is concentrated upon certain groups in the population above some notional optimal level, because that group can veto any change. Tax loopholes, subsidies to 'strategic' industries and price supports to farmers provide examples of such pork barrel expenditures.

In their discussion Buchanan and Tullock confuse this issue by suggesting the opposite, arguing that the pork barrel is a phenomenon of majoritarian politics. The plausibility of the argument was not helped by the fact that such empirical support as Buchanan and Tullock bothered to muster came from the United States, which is hardly a paradigmatic example of a majoritarian system. However, more important than this point is the fact that on theoretical grounds the expectation that majoritarian systems will produce the pork barrel seem ill-founded, as Brian Barry pointed out many years ago: 'The nearer a system comes to requiring unanimity for decisions, the more prevalent we may expect to find the "pork barrel" phenomenon' (Barry, 1965, p. 317). The argument here is that, with perfect information and low transaction costs, rational egoists have an incentive to misrepresent their preferences to get the bribe of coming in late, and, under imperfect information, log-rolling will produce specific and visible benefits since these are the items that are traded.

Inductive support for this general theoretical line comes from Scharpf's (1988) analysis of the 'joint decision trap'. The joint decision trap arises when there have to be a range of different actors, amounting to more than a majority, to agree to a measure in order for it to pass. Buchanan and Tullock's expectation that such super-majoritarianism will reduce exploitation and over-expenditure ignores the fact that there may already be a built-in dynamic towards certain forms of expenditure within the political system. As Scharpf points out, an example of just such a built-in dynamic is provided by the Common Agricultural Policy of the European Union. The virtual unanimity rule that has operated in this area has made it extremely difficult to reform the system, even when it was clear to informed observers that it was producing unwanted surpluses at high prices. As long as a minority of countries could use their effective veto to block reform, the pork barrel could not be eliminated.

Super-majoritarian justifications have not always turned on questions of public expenditure, however. The most notorious case is the case for super-majoritarianism to protect the 'peculiar institution' of slavery in the southern states of the *ante-bellum* US. In this case, Calhoun (1853) argued for a system of 'concurrent majorities', by which a majority of every state in the union would have to vote in favour of a constitutional change for it to be legitimately adopted. There is no argument in democratic theory for such a proposition within a system like that of the US in which the federal government has direct powers over citizens. True, such arrangements may protect historically negotiated compromises in the formation of federal unions, but the proposal for such protection is simply a way of preventing a change that is not only called for by considerations of justice, but also poses a direct challenge to democratic values.

Majority rule: the axiomatic defence

Of the conceptions of democracy I identified in Chapter 2, all but the liberal constitutionalists suppose that the proper principle of collective choice is that the will of the majority should prevail on matters of public policy, usually across a wide range of issues. Moreover, once we see the difficulties of unanimity, there seems to be a common-sense quality about majority rule. If the members of a group are divided about a common course of action, then to take the majority opinion seems fair. To base the common decision upon the views of a minority appears to put them in a privileged position, and even to allow a minority to block a decision – which is in effect what a super-majority requirement does – bestows upon them disproportionate power that is at odds with the ethos of political equality. But can these intuitions about the fairness of majority rule and its rootedness in the principle of political equality be given a sound intellectual basis?

One approach that has sometimes been used in democratic theory is the axiomatic one. This involves considering values like political equality as formal logical conditions to be imposed upon any method for aggregating preferences or opinions. For example, we may wish to impose the requirement that no one person's vote is to be given any more weight than the vote of anyone else. Similarly, we might say that if voters change their mind in favour of a particular alternative, then voting should reflect that change, or at least not more perversely in the opposite direction. Formal social choice theory is the study of the definition and implications of such requirements.

Within the field of formal social choice theory Kenneth May (1952) has shown that the simple majority principle can be characterized in terms of its logical properties. It is the only principle of collective choice to be simultaneously universal, positively responsive, anonymous and issue-neutral. A universal rule is one that is able to deal with all preference orderings. A positively responsive one is one that makes a collective choice in favour of an alternative more likely as opinion moves in favour of that alternative. An anonymous rule is insensitive to whoever is casting the vote. And a neutral rule uses the same procedure whatever the issues are that are being voted upon. These conditions together are sufficient to define majority rule and majority rule is the only decision procedure to satisfy these conditions. So, to take a simple example, if a group of friends together on holiday have to decide one day whether to go to the sea or the mountains for a trip, if they use majority rule to make the choice they will be using the only rule that gives them each an equal say, does not depend upon the particularities of the issues and is responsive to the balance of views.

May's result is both a uniqueness and an existence theorem. Existence theorems are very rare in social choice theory, so this fact alone gives a special quality to May's result. Perhaps because of this quality, the result has been invoked by a number of political theorists as a way of justifying the majority principle. For example, within Ackerman's (1980, pp. 277–89) liberal theory of justice, the May axioms are seen to embody the fundamental requirement of liberalism that no one citizen's view about the good life is to be taken as intrinsically superior to that of any other citizen and to be responsive to citizen preferences. Similarly, Waldron (1999b, p. 148) argues that in the absence of a superhuman repository of knowledge, the members of a community would agree that collective decisions are to be taken with reference to nothing other than the views of members, and that only a principle will do that gives no greater weight to the views of some members than others. Using May's theorem, Waldron claims that majority rule satisfies these conditions. In other words, these approaches see the May axioms as embodying substantive political values. What then might be those values? To answer this question, we need to consider the axioms one by one.

Of the four conditions, that of universal domain, comes closest to a purely technical requirement, which says that a decision procedure must provide an answer for the individual preferences registered by voters. It is uncontroversial in value terms, provided one is prepared to accept the assumption that political choices involve ranking alternatives. There are conceptions of political values that deny this assumption, but I have already suggested that there are some important political choices where ranking alternatives is necessary, and in terms of democratic choices in public policy the assumption can be granted.

Similarly, for the reasons that Waldron gives, it is hard to say that social decision rules should not be positively responsive in a democracy, and some, like Dahl (1998, p. 38), have argued that one criterion of whether an association is democratic is that the 'policies of the association are always open to change by the members, if they so choose'. Though there is much more to be said about each of these conditions, they do not seem so controversial as to be problematic for the axiomatic argument.

Issue neutrality means that no one person's conception of the good weighs more heavily in the balance than any other person's. If I favour the public subsidy of pushpin over poetry for low-minded reasons of the fun that pushpin gives, and you favour the public subsidy of poetry over pushpin for the high-minded reasons of the qualitatively superior pleasures that poetry prompts, our preferences will be counted equally. More importantly, majority rule will operate in exactly the same way no matter what the type of issue that is being considered. The counting of votes in a referendum over whether or not to require dog owners to hold dog licences will be exactly the same as the counting of votes in a referendum as to whether or not to phase out nuclear power, despite the obviously greater significance of the latter vote. Hence, when we are using majority rule, we are prepared to accept that the decision could go either way and that we do not think of it as an issue that raises problems about the basic human rights of minorities or other fundamental questions of constitutional justice.

In terms of the ideal of political equality, the property of anonymity is even more important, however. Anonymity means that no one person's preferences weigh more heavily in the balance because of who that person is. In other words, if we simply swap the names of individuals leaving the preferences intact, then the collective choice will remain unaffected. The views of dockers and dustmen thus count the same as those of dukes and directors. In a sense, we can say that anonymity embodies the principle of democratic equality, at least if that means everyone should count for one and no one for more than one. Since the majority principle is the only decision rule to satisfy all four conditions, including anonymity, we seem to have some ground for saying that its widespread adoption in different conceptions of democracy is more than an accident.

It can be argued, however, that thinking about majority voting as an expression of the principle of equality is misleading, because it ignores what can happen over a sequence of votes. Peter Jones (1988) asks us to consider three votes on three issues, where in each case the same two-thirds majority lines up against the same one third minority. Considerations of fairness and equality in such cases might suggest a proportionality principle, by which the one-third minority secured its preference in one third of the votes. Suppose, for example, within a political community there is a one-third conservationist minority and a two-thirds non-conservationist majority. Suppose within this community that there are three issues to be decided: the restoration or not of historic monuments; a decision on whether power lines should be above or below ground; and a decision on the preservation or not of a wilderness area. The conservationists, or their representatives, would presumably vote for the restoration of the monuments, in favour of the power lines being below ground and in favour of the preservation of the wilderness. The non-conservationists would presumably vote the opposite way on all three issues. In these sorts of circumstances, it is at least possible to argue that the principle of equality would require, or at least permit, the conservationist minority to have its way on one third of the issues in proportion to its numbers within the overall population.

This example is of course merely a special case of the more general problem of permanent majorities within a democracy. While the principle of majority rule might seem unexceptionable when applied to any one issue of public policy, it may become problematic when applied to a sequence of issues in which a minority is steadily opposed to the majority. Yet, application of the principle of neutrality will force the issues always to be resolved in favour of the majority, even when that majority is constant over a sequence of issues. Another way of putting this point is to say that Lipset's (1963) condition of cross-cutting cleavages, originally deployed in stating a condition for the stability of democracy, can also be interpreted as stating a condition for the legitimate application of the neutrality condition. Conversely, in cases where the social conditions for cross-cutting cleavages do not exist, then a widely canvassed set of institutional prescriptions takes us beyond majority rule, to super-majoritarian, consociational arrangements (Lijphart, 1968, p. 1977). In such cases, the proportionality principle seems unassailable, from the viewpoint of fairness, and indeed in consociational systems it is often implemented either in the way that resources are allocated or in terms of the rotation of office holders (compare Steiner, 1971).

What this line of argument shows is that the axiomatic approach is limited by its exclusive focus upon the formal properties of decision procedures, without considering the social and political circumstances within which such decision procedures are implemented. In itself, this would not be a criticism of the axiomatic defence of majority rule, merely an indication of its limitations of scope. Even to have an argument that worked under a wide, if not universal, range of circumstances would be impressive. However, there is one important reason why the limitation of scope is tighter than these sociological conditions suggest, and that is the difficulties that majority rule encounters when we move from considering decisions on pairs of alternatives to considering three or more alternatives.

It has been known since the eighteenth century, when Condorcet discovered the problem that majority voting over three or more alternatives may create cyclical majorities, that is to say majority votes in which no one alternative can command a majority against all other alternatives (see McLean and Hewitt, 1994, pp. 40–2). It is in fact easy to construct examples where the introduction of a third alternative disrupts an otherwise dominant majority. Consider the example portrayed in Table 7.1. In the first panel, we display the preferences of nine people together on holiday who have to decide where to go for the day. Persons 1 to 2 want to go to the sea, but persons 3 to 9 want to go to the mountains. Application of the principle of majority rule is quite straightforward in this case: there is a clear majority for the mountains, and a majoritarian ought to favour that as the decision.

Now suppose, however, that a third alternative is introduced, for example the possibility of going to the forest. A possible pattern of preferences is portrayed in the second panel of Table 7.1. The forest is the second preference for 1 and 2, but the former majority group is divided on the matter. For three of them it is their least preferred option; for the remaining four of the original majority it is their most preferred option. The problem comes when we apply the principle of majority rule as a decision-making device in a series of pair-wise votes. If the friends sincerely vote on the choice of mountains versus sea, they will still register the original majority of seven to two. But if they vote on mountains versus forest, the forest option will defeat the mountain option by six votes to three. Since mountains beat sea, and forest beats mountains, it would seem that forest should beat sea. However, if a pair-wise vote is taken between forest and sea, it can easily be verified that with the supposed preferences, sea will beat forest. In other words, there is a majority in favour of forest versus mountains, mountains versus sea, but sea versus forest. The collective choice is intransitive. The application of the majority principle leads to a cycle and it ceases to be clear what majority rule actually means.

Table 7.1   The choice for a day out

Panel (1) The binary situation

Person	First preference	Second preference
1	Sea	Mountains
2	Sea	Mountains
3	Mountains	Sea
4	Mountains	Sea
5	Mountains	Sea
6	Mountains	Sea
7	Mountains	Sea
8	Mountains	Sea
9	Mountains	Sea

Panel (2) The ternary situation

Person	First preference	Second preference	Third preference
1	Sea	Forest	Mountains
2	Sea	Forest	Mountains
3	Mountains	Sea	Forest
4	Mountains	Sea	Forest
5	Mountains	Sea	Forest
6	Forest	Mountains	Sea
7	Forest	Mountains	Sea
8	Forest	Mountains	Sea
9	Forest	Mountains	Sea

An important feature of majority rule cycles is that the collective intransitivity arises from a situation in which each individual's preferences are transitive. Each individual prefers their first preference to their third preference as well as their second preference, but the cycling of majority rule means that a seemingly third-ranking choice defeats a first-ranking choice, and to many this appears to be irrational. It is this potential of a move from individual rationality to collective irrationality that has led some theorists to reject the majority principle altogether, saying that if it is compatible with there being no Condorcet-winner, we really cannot attach any sense to the idea that majority collective preference should have any sway over us. For example, Robert Paul Wolff writes in the light of the paradox that 'majority rule is fatally flawed by an internal inconsistency which ought to disqualify it from consideration in any political community whatsoever' (Wolff, 1970, p. 59). Individuals might be willing to sacrifice their autonomy if there was a clear idea of the collective interest to which they should subject their judgement, but the paradox of voting shows that no real meaning can be attached to the idea of collective preference or choice. From another point of view, we seem to be back to Schumpeter's claim that the result of populism 'lacks not only rational unity but also rational sanction'.

Someone might argue that these problems merely reflected the logical peculiarities of the majority principle. If majority rule works so well in the case of two alternatives, does it just not have to be slightly modified when there are more than two alternatives in order to get round the problem of intransitivity? However, in a justly famous result, Kenneth Arrow (1963) showed that this was not true. There was no way of making social choices that could avoid the paradox of voting and satisfy otherwise intuitively attractive conditions, most notably that social choices should not simply track the preferences of one particular individual in society. Indeed, Arrow's theorem is even more powerful in the present context. The conditions that Arrow showed could not be simultaneously satisfied can be interpreted as weakened versions of May's axioms. In other words, Arrow's theorem can be understood as follows. Given that with three alternatives the principle of majority rule can produce intransitive outcomes, can we take less-demanding requirements of those that May imposed in the case of three alternatives and so produce transitive rankings? Table 7.2 shows the relations between the conditions, and Arrow's theorem says that the question has to be answered in the negative.

Arrow published the original version of his result in 1951 and almost ever since then theorists have thought it carried a pessimistic message for the value of democracy. Dahl (1956, pp. 42–3) noted that it was a 'brilliantly developed and quite startling argument' and bemoaned the fact that it had been ignored by political scientists. Runciman (1969, p. 133) declared bluntly that what Arrow had done was 'to show that strict democracy is impossible'. Building on a whole raft of social choice impossibility theorems following Arrow's, Riker (1982, p. 239) echoed this thought with the words: 'If the people speak in meaningless tongues, they cannot utter the law that makes them free.' In short, Wolff's pessimism about democratic authority in the light of Condorcet's paradox is strengthened among those who have examined its generalization in Arrow's theorem.

Table 7.2 Relation of May to Arrow conditions

Arrow's conditions	May's conditions
Collective rationality	Not a required condition
Universal domain	Universal domain
Pareto consistent	Positive responsiveness
Independence of irrelevant alternatives	Issue neutrality
Non-dictatorship	Anonymity

One possible line of reply to this pessimism is to say that, although logically interesting, the problem of cyclical majorities is not as serious in practice as one might think. Arrow's theorem does not show that cyclical majorities will always arise, merely that they cannot be guaranteed not to arise for all possible profiles of preferences. The logically devastating may not happen. A more robust view is that political preferences and contestation are essentially binary, so that third alternatives do not occur or if they do will be eliminated as discussion and choice progress over an issue. Politics always has a 'for or against' structure. Complications introduced by a 'third way' do not arise. Indeed, there is a long line of political analysis that has viewed politics as binary almost by definition. Aristotle (*Politics*, Book V. 1 and 2) saw the struggle over property between rich and poor as generally at the bottom of warfare within states. Marx and Engels (1848) echoed this thought in the *Communist Manifesto*, seeing bipolar class struggle as the key to history. Macaulay (1906, p. 82) traced the origins of the two parties in the Westminster system back to opposing tendencies in human nature, one favouring change and innovation and the other favouring conservatism. Schattschneider (1960) thought that the tendency of people to gather round one of two parties was quite natural, just as it was natural for people to take sides in a fight. And realists such as Waltz (1979) have argued for an underlying bipolar logic to the international order.

Yet, despite this impressive support, it is clear that there are often choices in politics that cannot be represented in a simple binary way. Third-way traditions of political thinking extend back through revisionist socialism in the 1950s (Crosland, 1956), Macmillan's (1938) middle way, Bernstein's (1899) reformism, liberal idealism of the late nineteenth century to Halifax's (1699, p. 50) trimmer, who when in a boat with one group of passengers, some of whom would weigh it down on one side and others who would weigh it to the contrary, conceives 'it would do as well, if the boat went even, without endangering the passengers'. Indeed, this evocation of a middle way suggests one possible route to escape the difficulties of aggregation suggested by social choice theory, namely to think about the alternatives in spatial terms, where the alternatives can be arrayed along an agreed dimension of evaluation. As we shall see in the next section, this does get us some distance with the problem, though not as far as its proponents might have hoped.

The spatial defence

A common way of thinking about politics is in terms of the contest between left and right. We may, as the authors that I quoted in the previous section did, think of that as a bipolar contest, with one group facing another. However, we may also think about left and right as a spectrum, containing a number of positions, each different from the other but each assessable in terms of how far it is on the right or on the left. For example, we can think about the left–right spectrum as running from 0 to100, with the most left-wing position at 0 and the most right-wing position at 100. Then for each position we should be able to judge where between 0 and 100 it falls.

Suppose a group of voters, whether citizens or parliamentary representatives, think in this way, so that they know where they stand in left–right terms and where each proposal that comes before them can be assigned in the left–right spectrum. Then each voter will have an 'ideal point', namely support for that proposal that coincides with his or her position on the spectrum. Proposals that differ from a voter's ideal point will be ranked lower than proposals on the ideal point. If all voters rank proposals at their ideal point most highly and then rank other proposals in descending order of value as they depart from their ideal points, then the voters will have single-peaked preferences. The closer a proposal is to their ideal points, the higher it will be ranked; the further away it is, the lower it will be ranked.

In the modern theory of rational choice, there is nothing in the concept of rationality that requires voters to have single-peaked preferences. A liking for extremes is not in itself irrational. However, single-peakedness does correspond to the idea that half a loaf is better than none. In some sense it is more rational to prefer those alternatives closer to our ideal than alternatives further away. Moreover, representing political differences as a spectrum implies that, though the voters may not agree on their positions, they do all agree on the criteria by which those positions are to be judged. Thus, they may recognize one another as being more or less to the right or more or less to the left, and so acknowledge their differences. Yet they at least agree on how proposals and positions are to be classified in terms of left and right.

Within this spatial framework, there is one central result of importance, namely the median voter theorem (Black, 1958). The median voter is defined as that voter that occupies the position 50 per cent up the distribution and 50 per cent down the distribution of voters. According to the median voter theorem, if all voters can be arrayed in a one-dimensional space and all have single-peaked preferences and none abstain from voting, then the winning alternative will be that alternative that coincides with the preferences of the median voter. In short, the voter with preferences mid-way between the most left-wing and the most right-wing voters will get his or her way. This does not mean that median voters always favour centrist policies. If the distribution of voters is skewed to the left or to the right, then the ideal position of the median voter may be someway to the left or to the right of the left–right ideological spectrum. However, it does mean that that median voter is in the middle of the distribution of voters, however they may be distributed along the ideological spectrum.

The logic lying behind the median voter theorem is reasonably straightforward. If all voters are voting and their preferences are single-peaked, then they will by definition vote for proposals that are closer to them over proposals that are further away. A voter at the mid-point of the distribution can make a proposal that coincides with his or her ideal preference and can know that this proposal will beat any proposal to the left or to the right. If the proposal is further to the left, then all voters right of the median position will prefer the median position. If the proposal is further to the right, then all voters left of the median position will prefer the median. Since the median position commands a majority over these other positions, it is in fact a Condorcet-winner. That is to say, it is that alternative that can beat any other alternative when pitched against it in pair-wise competition.

An ideological spectrum potentially contains a large number of positions and so the winning median position will always defeat a large number of alternatives. It may seem strange that this is so, when we saw in the earlier section that cyclical (that is to say non-Condorcet-winning) majorities could be generated with just three alternatives. How does it come about that in spatial accounts of voting we can identify the conditions for a Condorcet-winner even where there are potentially many alternatives? The answer is that the assumption of single-peakedness violates Arrow's condition of unrestricted domain. If voters were given no restriction on how they ordered alternatives, then there would be no guaranteed Condorcet-winner. This underlines how economical Arrow's theorem is, as Sen (1970, p. 49) pointed out many years ago. Drop just one of the conditions and things look very different. (Indeed, strictly speaking, a condition only slightly less strong than single-peakedness is necessary, see Sen, 1970, ch. 5*.)

The median voter theorem applies whether we are thinking about voters in relatively small committees voting on particular measures (cabinets, parliamentary chambers, party caucuses or international bodies) or mass electorates where citizens may be voting either on policy measures in referendums or for candidates in elections. Of course, the realism of the conditions it assumes will vary between these cases. Voters are much less likely to abstain in small committees than they are in mass electorates, but even in the latter case it can be shown that, provided abstention is random, it will not affect the dominant position of the median voter. Moreover, because the median position is unique and cannot be defeated by any other position, it has a claim to give a definite meaning to the notion of the popular will. If the will of the people is the majority position, then we can interpret that to mean the position of the median voter when we have more than two alternatives to consider.

It is crucial to the median voter theorem that competition takes place only in one dimension. Once this condition is no longer satisfied, then the claim that we can identify a popular will becomes more tenuous, and we are back to some of the problems highlighted by the Arrow theorem. To see the problem here suppose that instead of one dimension of ideological competition in a community there are two. The first is represented by the left–right spectrum and second by the green–brown spectrum. Voters and parties are therefore distinguished by their attitudes to property and redistribution on one side and their attitudes to conservation and pollution on the other. To make these distinctions a little more concrete I shall suppose that the members of a community are divided over two sets of issues. One set of issues concerns the extent of government intervention in society and the economy to maintain a 'welfare state', where some people are in favour of an extensive welfare state whilst others are against. The second set of issues concern nuclear power. Here too people can be grouped into two broad camps: those who favour nuclear power and those who do not.

Table 7.3 Two-dimensional political choice

		Welfare state		
		For	*Against*	
Nuclear power	*For*	w	y	
		(25)	(40)	65
	Against	x	z	
		(30)	(5)	35
		55	45	100

Party A (25 per cent): *w x y z*
Party B (30 per cent): *x w z y*
Party C (40 per cent): *y w z x*
Party D (5 per cent): *z x y w*

Suppose, then, for the sake of simplicity, that the members of society can either be for or against a 'welfare state' or for or against 'nuclear power'. Suppose also that opinions on these two sets of issues are not perfectly correlated, so that, for example, some who are in favour of the welfare state are also in favour of nuclear power, whilst others who are in favour of the welfare state are opposed to nuclear power. Similarly, some who are in favour of nuclear power are also in favour of the welfare state, whereas some of those opposed to nuclear power are also opposed to the welfare state. There are thus four logically possible political positions that members of the community can adopt: pro-nuclear power and pro-welfare state; anti-nuclear power and pro-welfare state; pro-nuclear power and anti-welfare state; and anti-nuclear power and anti-welfare state. Imagine, for the sake of the example, that the members of the community are divided among these alternatives according to the distribution of their first or ideal preferences as given in the matrix in Table 7.3. We can think of the cell entries either as party positions in a legislature or as the proportions of the electorate who support each of the positions.

We can also suppose that members of a political community can identify not only their first preference for public policy measures but also second and subsequent preferences. These lower-ranked preferences become important, for example, when parties are contemplating with whom they might form parliamentary coalitions, or voters are wondering whom to vote for when a candidate of their first preference party is not standing in an election. In Table 7.3, in addition to the matrix of ideal positions, I have also set out one hypothetical set of preference orderings (there are potentially many more) over the alternative policy positions for all four imagined political groupings.

Note that for each of the dimensions taken individually there is a clear majority winner, as can be seen from the marginal figures. For example, there is a majority of 55 per cent to 45 per cent in favour of the welfare state, if we just consider that dimension on its own. Since, by definition, the median voter is part of the 55 per cent, it is also clear that this is the position that coincides with the ideal preferences of the median voters. Similarly, there is a 65 per cent to 35 per cent majority in favour of nuclear power. There is, however, no group as large as 50 per cent plus one that is in favour of any combination of policies. The largest group, represented by party C, contains only 40 per cent of the population and so there is no majority position across both dimensions taken together. Can we in these circumstances make sense of the idea of majority rule in terms of the Condorcet criterion?

With the preference profiles suggested in Table 7.3, we can still find a Condorcet-winner, even though there is no absolute majority across the combination of alternatives. A majority prefers w to x, y, and z. Moreover, if voters or their representatives vote in sequence on the two sets of issues, then the combined consequences of that vote (known technically as the issue-by-issue median, see Ordeshook, 1986, pp. 245–57) will coincide with the Condorcet-winner. Thus, in Table 7.3, 65 per cent of those voting are pro- rather than anti-nuclear power, so that taking a majority on the nuclear power issue alone will lead to a collective preference in favour of nuclear power. On the second dimension, since 55 per cent are in favour of the welfare state, that too would be the majority outcome. Putting both these votes together to form the issue-by-issue median will lead to w (the alternative that combines nuclear power and a strong welfare state), which is of course the Condorcet-winner. Hence, the Condorcet-winner will be chosen by the issue-by-issue median, which may be defined as that alternative that would be chosen by a sequence of votes on the majority principle in each of the relevant dimensions of choice.

This association between the issue-by-issue median and the Condorcet-winner is not accidental: indeed, there is a logical connection between them. A Condorcet-winner is defined as that alternative that can beat all others when pitched against them in pair-wise comparison. If the issue-by-issue median did not coincide with the Condorcet-winner, that would mean that, in some dimension of collective choice, a majority of voters would prefer an alternative which lacked one of the essential properties of the Condorcet-winner. But, if that were to happen, the putative Condorcet-winner would no longer be able to beat it, and so it would not be the Condorcet-winner. Hence, there is a contradiction in supposing that the issue-by-issue median and the Condorcet-winner do not coincide. Put another way, issue-by-issue voting separates all the alternatives into sets by reference to whether their distinctive features (for example, attitudes on nuclear power or the welfare state) are preferred by a majority or not. The intersection of these majority preferred sets defines the issue-by-issue median.

Implicit in this coincidence of the issue-by-issue and the Condorcet-winner is the requirement that the different dimensions of each alternative are separable from each other. Separability here means that the choice in one dimension does not depend upon the choice made in another dimension. A simple example with which to illustrate this condition is provided by slightly altering the dimensions of choice in Table 7.3. Suppose that one dimension remained the welfare state, but the other dimension involved not nuclear power policy but a choice between high and low taxation. It is quite possible that issue-by-issue voting would lead to that alternative representing the combination of a strong welfare state and low taxation. Although not contradictory in strict logic (since someone might hold that public expenditure savings to maintain low taxation could be secured from elsewhere – perhaps nuclear power), there is clearly a pragmatic contradiction between these two positions. Each choice has in practice implications for the other, so that treating them separately neither makes sense in itself nor could it be expected to lead to an alternative preferred by a majority when placed against all others in pair-wise comparison (compare Robertson, 2006).

Subject to these qualifications we have shown that in a spatial context we can make sense of the majority principle in terms of the Condorcet criterion. In one dimension, with single-peaked preferences, there will always be a majority winner, which will be the position of the median voter, and which will also be a Condorcet-winner. With two dimensions of political competition we can extend this idea to the issue-by-issue median, which is a position consistent with the Condorcet-winner, if such a winner exists. But does such a winner always exist? The answer is 'no' and I explore the implications of this in the next section.

Two dimensions with no Condorcet-winner

Consider the example shown in Table 7.4. This adapts the example from Table 7.3, but assumes that there is a different distribution of

Table 7.4   Two-dimensional political choice without a Condorcet-winner

		Welfare state		
		For	*Against*	
Nuclear power	*For*	w (40)	y (20)	60
	Against	x (20) 60	z (20) 40	40 100

Party A (40 per cent): $w\,x\,y\,z$
Party B (20 per cent): $x\,z\,w\,y$
Party C (20 per cent): $y\,z\,w\,x$
Party D (20 per cent): $z\,x\,y\,w$

preferences. With this preference profile there is no Condorcet-winner. This can be checked by considering a sequence of pair-wise votes: w will be preferred by a majority to both x and y, but it will not be preferred by a majority to z, even though both x and y are also preferred by a majority to z. Hence, the outcome of a sequence of pair-wise votes is not a unique winner but a cycle, as w beats x, which in turn beats y, which in turn beats z, which then beats w. Put another way, for any alternative that may be selected, there is bound to be some other alternative that beats it in a pair-wise comparison. If there are good reasons, as I argued in the previous section, for taking the issue-by-issue median as the second-best to the straight application of the majority principle where there was no outright winner, then they seem entirely to lose their force in the present case, since the phenomenon of majority rule cycling undermines any sense of what the majority collective preference might be. In any particular case where one would take a vote, the outcome seems only to depend on the arbitrary fact of the point at which the voting stops.

It is worth noting in this connection that the preferences of individuals may be perfectly coherent, even when there is cycling at the collective level. Looking at the ideal preferences of individuals in Table 7.4, it is easy to see how the individuals holding those ideal preferences would have the preference orderings that they do. In particular, we may note that there is no 'extremism' in the individual preference orderings. In each case the individual starts with an ideal preference, and then chooses second or third preferences by holding on to a dimension that is more important, placing last the alternative that fails in both dimensions. Thus, we seem to have a case where the 'irrationality' resides not in the individuals who compose society but in the way that their individually rational preferences are amalgamated. We seem to be back to Riker's claim that if the people speak in meaningless tongues, they cannot utter the law to make them free.

This stress on the meaninglessness of popular rule might seem to echo familiar conservative objections against democracy, going back to Plato's *Republic* or Thucydides' *Peloponnesian War*, and invoked subsequently by the *Federalist Papers*, that popular passions were unstable and shifted in unpredictable ways, so that no coherence could be expected from popular participation. But the elegance of formal social choice theory is that it does not depend upon these contentious empirical premises. Arguments about the difficulties of aggregation have been built up on the assumption that popular preferences remain constant and the emphasis of the analysis has been upon the different, and inconsistent, ways in which a given body of preferences can be aggregated into a collective choice. Thus, someone arguing an anti-majoritarian case on the basis of social choice theory is potentially on strong grounds, since it can be said that an assumption relatively favourable to majoritarianism is being taken and shown to yield inconsistencies or incoherence, even in the case – spatial voting theory – where we seem to have a *prima facie* interpretation of the majority principle. If this line of argument can be made to work, it thus promises to be a powerful one.

One central issue in this debate concerns the extent to which intransitive outcomes are likely to arise. Riker argued, on the basis of a series of formal results in spatial voting theory, that once political competition took place over two dimensions, the conditions for there being a Condorcet-winner were so stringent that for practical purposes we could suppose that they did not exist. He thought that whenever we observed a winner emerging from a process of voting, it did not represent a stable balance of the political preferences that the voting system was processing so much as an artefact of the process itself together with the rhetorical and manipulative skills of the proponents of that alternative. In particular, since dimensionality was so important, a great deal of rhetorical effort went into manipulating the dimensionality of political competition, with winners typically seeking to maintain the saliency of the dimension on which they won and losers searching for new issues. He sought to illustrate this view with a series of interpretations of key historical episodes (Riker, 1982, 1986) supposedly illustrating how political actors could exploit situations in which there was no Condorcet-winner.

Mackie (2003) has challenged Riker's account of a number of these episodes, arguing that Riker was wrong to think in many cases that there was an opportunity to exploit an underlying cyclical preference profile, and in some cases Mackie's counter-interpretations are hard to dispute. How far, then, should we be worried in practice by the theoretical possibility of cyclical preferences in more than one dimension? Here I suggest that we distinguish the issues arising from dimensionality from those arising from cycling. Although an increase in dimensionality will often produce cycling, it will not do so invariably, as my running example illustrates. However, increasing dimensionality may well be the precipitant of political change. Thus, in the archetypical majoritarian system (Lijphart, 1984), namely New Zealand before its electoral reforms, one finds long periods of one-party dominance, in large part associated with the dominance of the left–right ideological dimension (Nagel, 1993, 1998). When a new issue dimension started to intrude upon New Zealand politics, the conditions were created for rapid and extensive public policy change, associated with the ending of New Zealand's traditional protectionist stance. Hence, if we wish to understand why neo-liberalism went further and faster in New Zealand than anywhere else in the developed world, the answer is intrinsically associated with the pattern of preferences that is established when a new dimension of political cleavage is superimposed upon an existing one.

But ideological complexity is not likely to produce cyclical preferences, since ideologies have certain logical constraints built into them that will prevent political entrepreneurs from exploiting particular combinations of issues. Cycling is more likely to be associated with party systems in which ideological differences between parties are less important in political manoeuvring than the aspirations of party leaders. Thus, in a fluid party system such as that of the Third and Fourth French Republics (Williams, 1964, pp. 428–43), in which parties served as the vehicles for the political ambitions of leaders, cycling is more likely, since the search for political power is a zero-sum game in these circumstances and it is well known that there is no stability in such games. In short, the potential for chaos suggested by the development of social choice and spatial theories of democracy should be used to distinguish different types of democratic system rather than provide an argument in favour of constraining the institutions of democracy, however well or badly they are functioning.

This conclusion is reinforced when we consider that, even if there is no Condorcet-winner, the workings of decision procedures within political institutions will typically produce an outcome. The significance of this is sometimes missed because social choice theorists have argued that a good decision procedure should be consistent with certain conditions, and that accidental features of decision making, for example the order in which issues are processed, should not make a difference to the outcome. Outcomes should not be 'path-dependent' (Arrow, 1963, p. 120). The obvious question to ask at this point is whether this attempt to detach outcomes from the processes that led to them is so important. In fact, in a number of social choice processes, this requirement is regularly violated. The obvious example is the market. Traders in a market will typically have divergent views about which of the various equilibrium outcomes they would most prefer. Which view predominates in practice will depend on the initial endowments that each brings to the market. Markets therefore do not meet the condition that the final choice is independent of the path to it. This is partly because all social institutions work by establishing pathways of choice and then processing decisions according to those established pathways. Indeed, the dependence of the final choice upon those pathways is what gives many institutions their legitimacy.

Within voting systems the relevant pathways of choice function in part by breaking down complex alternatives into their component parts. To illustrate this point consider the choice between policies in the running example of this chapter. The combinations of alternative welfare state and nuclear power policies represent descriptions of four possible social alternatives. Treated as a whole that alternative might be vulnerable, under majority rule, to some other combination of policies. But how would we know whether there was some other combination of policies that would defeat it? The examples I have been considering are highly simplified. We are only looking at two dimensions of policy and two possible stances within each dimension. In practice, there is likely to be so much complexity that it is impossible to look at whole alternative sets of policies pitched against one another. Thus, in practice, even if a society were confronted by a pattern of cyclical majorities along the lines of that presented in Table 7.4, it would be extremely unlikely to know that this was the case.

As well as these cognitive and ideological constraints on political competition, there are also strong institutional pressures to prevent a synoptic evaluation of alternative policy combinations. The principal means by which this is accomplished in functioning democracies is by political parties, which reduce the many dimensions of potential competition down to two or three. Moreover, policy making is in practice highly sectorized. Policy communities are an established feature of different fields of policy, forming intellectual and political reference-groups for different issues. Of course, this can lead to a lack of coordination on problems where actors need to cooperate across sectors. But even with greater coordination across three or four policy sectors, we would still be a long way short of the synoptic rationality implicit in Arrow's condition that the final choice should be independent of the path to it.

Suppose we acknowledge that democratic decision making typically does not take place over complete combinations of policies, and that instead representatives compete on a subset of issues in indirect democracies and electorates decide questions issue by issue in a direct democracy. Then we are saying that the final choice of policy is not independent of the pathway to that choice.

In the first place, if political questions are decided issue by issue, in accordance with the principle of majority rule, then, if there is a Condorcet-winner, issue–by-issue majoritarianism will select it. Since, as I have argued earlier, the criterion of the Condorcet-winner yielded the most acceptable interpretation of the majority principle when no one alternative commanded a simple numerical majority, this tendency of issue-by-issue decision making is to be welcomed.

Secondly, there may be no Condorcet-winner among a set of alternatives given the preference profile of those voting. In these circumstances, issue–by-issue decision making will still yield a result. Moreover, provided that the issues are separable, in the sense that voters' preferences on one issue do not depend on how the voting turns out on another issue, then the outcome of the issue-by-issue voting will be stable, with no voters having any rational incentive to unpick the final result (see Ordeshook, 1986, pp. 245–57, for this result). This is sometimes known as a structure-induced equilibrium (Shepsle, 1979), and the essential point about it is that the pattern of institutional decision making fixes the outcome in such a way that there is no tendency for a political community deciding issues in sequence to go round in circles. Thus, issue-by-issue majoritarianism will never from choice eliminate a Condorcet-winner if there is one, but it will produce a definite answer when there is no Condorcet-winner to be found.

Of course, where there is no Condorcet-winner, the issue-by-issue median is vulnerable to defeat by at least one alternative when the situation is viewed from a synoptic point of view. Institutional and procedural constraints will inhibit the identification of that alternative and may not be reached by sequential voting. Nonetheless, there is in theory a combination of policies that a majority would prefer (this simply follows logically from the definition of a Condorcet-winner). But there should not be a normative worry about selecting the issue-by-issue median in this case. Although the community has chosen an alternative that is less preferred than another alternative, the problem is generated by the cyclical structure of the preferences. Since one alternative has to be selected, there is bound to be one alternative that will defeat it.

In terms of the alternative conceptualizations that I identified in chapter 2, arguments surrounding the problem of aggregation go only a little way towards helping us with an intellectually defensible evaluation. I have tried to show that the paradoxes of social choice need not incline us towards the anti-majoritarian liberal end of the spectrum in the way that Dahl, Riker and Runciman suggest. In one sense, no doubt, Riker was right: it is not possible to identify the popular will with confidence as it is revealed in the selection of one alternative outcome rather than another. But this is partly because the demands of synoptic rationality involved in a comparison of alternative policy packages cannot be met in any but the most simple of worlds. Outside very constrained situations citizens do not choose over logically integrated political programmes. Issue by issue we may know what the majority wants, but there is typically no way of knowing whether the intersection of these majorities, in relation to all issues, expresses a popular will. Nevertheless, the issue-by-issue median is the best approximation we shall have to a popular will.

Empirical aspects

In mass electorates, how likely is it that political parties will reflect the views of the median voter? Much of the basic work here has been done by the Comparative Manifestos Project (CMP). This account shares the assumption of economic theories of democracy, like those of Downs (1957), that parties compete with one another in elections in order to win votes. However, unlike Downsian theory, parties are not seen as pure office-seekers, who set their agendas competitively and are willing to shift their policy positions purely in response to the prospect of electoral advantage. Rather, according to the CMP view, parties maintain distinct ideologically informed policy positions, seeking support from the electorate by stressing the extent to which their own policy stance accords with widely shared values. Thus, in the choice between guns and butter, the proponents of guns will stress the importance of national defence and security in the international order, whereas the proponents of butter will stress peace, prosperity and plenty (compare Budge *et al.*, 2001).

Moreover, according to the CMP findings, the system of party competition performs the function of political representation, through a correspondence between the expressed preferences of voters and the governments that were formed after the election (McDonald, Mendes and Budge, 2004; McDonald and Budge, 2005). There is a high degree of correspondence between median voters and median parties in parliaments, and also a high degree of correspondence between median parties and participation in government. To be sure, the degree of correspondence varies across political systems, and PR systems to a better job than those based on first-past-the-post in translating popular preferences into political representation. But the main result is that elected governments do typically contain parties whose policy positions coincide with those of the median voter on the left–right spectrum. In that sense, at least, such governments are representative. They have a median mandate bestowed upon them.

Some may find this a rather surprising result, since there is a great deal written and said about the discontents of democracy. If the will of the majority is so prominent, how does it come about that so many are dissatisfied? One answer to this question is that such dissatisfaction is just what we should expect in the light of the median voter theorem. After all, if median voters get their way, no other voters will, and it is typically the case that there are many more non-median voters than there are median voters. So it is hardly surprising if there is widespread dissatisfaction. There would of course be even more widespread dissatisfaction if non-median voters got their way, but that comparison is not one that it is possible for voters to make. However, the other part of the answer concerns the dimensionality of political competition (see McLean, 2006; Nagel, 2006). Where there is more than one dimension that is salient to political choice in mass electorates, then even if parties are responsive to the median voter in one dimension, they could be far away from the median in other dimensions.

Despite these complications, the median voter result makes sense, both empirically and logically, if we can accept that majority preferences have a special status. However, worries about the tyranny of the majority question that claim. So, to that issue we now turn.

8 Democracy, Rights and Constitutionalism

Modern democracies are properly thought of as constitutional democracies. One of the many consequences of this is that they appear to contain an ambiguity in their institutional structure and principled rationale. On the one hand, as democracies, they are said to provide the means by which the people govern, or at least elect the representatives who are to govern. On the other hand, as embodying constitutional values, they involve institutional arrangements, such as the separation of powers or a system of checks and balances, limiting the powers of government. Thus, constitutional democracies are typically governed according to two sets of principles: constitutionalism, which prescribes that governments should conduct their business according to rules that limit their freedom of action, and the democratic principle, which prescribes that governments should implement the will of the people, as determined by voting.

We have seen in the previous chapter that one liberal constitutionalist argument, drawn from social choice theory, seeks to undermine the principle of popular rule by questioning its very meaning. We have also seen that no strong attack on majoritarianism can succeed, since there is a coherent meaning that can be given to the notion of a popular will, namely the choice that would result from the application of the principle of majority rule understood as the preference of the median voter in any particular dimension, institutionally constrained if need be. However, the proponent of constitutional values might still challenge the idea of popular government, not on the grounds that it was meaningless but on the grounds that the application of the principle of popular sovereignty would violate the principles of limited government. Neil MacCormick once formulated this potential conflict with his customary clarity:

Democracy says the people should be sovereign; constitutionalism denies that any sovereignty should be absolute and free of restraints

181

or limits. Rather than plainly asserting the will of the people, it says that even the will of the people will not exercise power wisely or justly save under acknowledged limits. Constitutionalist governments are carefully respectful of the limits on state power. (MacCormick, 1989, p. 101)

Such a distinction of principles is particularly important for the theory of democracy. If democracy is a political system for achieving certain purposes that cannot be achieved within a political regime that sees government purely as a means for imposing constraints on individuals' interaction, then a significant stress upon constitutional principles would seem to undermine this rationale. If common purposes and the common interests that they serve are so important in a democracy, how can democrats accept the idea that there should be principled limits to the scope of public power, if that power is needed to secure those common interests?

The conflict between constitutionalism and democracy is not purely theoretical, however. In some political systems where there is a clear separation of powers, constitutional courts have the power to challenge legislation on the grounds that it violates constitutionally prescribed rights. For example, the US constitution in its first amendment protects freedom of speech by imposing on the federal legislature a constraint on its powers of legislation: 'Congress shall make no law … abridging the freedom of speech, or of the press.' Of course, this prohibition is not self-evident in scope or effect. Does it protect the publication of pornography? Or the burning of the US flag as an act of protest? Or the encouragement of sedition? These are all questions that the US Supreme Court has had to decide at various times in its history. Yet that is precisely the point. It is up to the Court, not Congress, to determine the powers of congressional legislation. In other words, the separation of powers means that the Court takes priority in determining the limits of what elected representatives in the legislature can do.

In this respect, the US constitution comes closest among modern democracies to the ideal of constitutional government, in which a system of checks and balances and the separation of powers impose restrictions on the scope of legislation that popular majorities can adopt. For example, the first amendment to the US constitution would almost certainly mean that some forms of legislation, intended to prevent 'hate speech', would be declared unconstitutional. By contrast, in other democracies, the constraints are not so tight. In the UK, for instance, it is a legal offence to incite racial hatred through speech or publications, a provision that would not be permissible according to the US constitution, even if there were a large majority of the population in favour of such a measure (Dworkin, 1985, p. 335). In this respect, the institutional power and position of the US Supreme Court embodies the idea of constitutional government as proposed by the tradition of liberal constitutionalism.

However, although distinctive in extent, the separation of powers is not unique to the US nor is the constitutional model of government generally. That the separation of powers has to be considered along with popular sovereignty is a view that is to be found in virtually all the models of democracy that we are considering. Within representational systems both consociational democracies and the Nordic democracies accept the need for some separation of powers, and in the case of consociational democracies there are various restrictions built into political practice that limit how governments behave. Ian Budge (1996) is also quite happy to accept, in respect to his populist electronic democracy, that the normal constitutional protections on citizens' rights would exist, so that a commitment to constitutionalism does not vary directly with a commitment to participation. Historically, Westminster systems have been the most resistant to incorporating formal constitutional devices for the separation of powers explicitly into their political arrangements. Yet, in 1982 Canada amended its constitution to include the Canadian Charter of Rights and Freedoms, in 1990 New Zealand passed its Bill of Rights Act and in 2000 the Human Rights Act came into effect in the UK (Hiebert, 2005). In all of the cases, the effect of the constitutional change was to limit the freedom of the legislature to pass measures of which a majority of representatives approved.

Why should we find this mixture of constitutional and popular principles within the institutions of modern democracies? One possible answer to this question is that most modern democracies are the heirs of the liberal political theories originating in the seventeenth century, which favoured an account of limited but non-democratic government. When the societies in which these liberal principles were prevalent democratized, there was an ideological and institutional legacy of liberal constitutionalism that was in conflict with democratic values. This legacy is expressed in the conflict between limited government and popular government that MacCormick identified. In particular, where liberalism has left the legacy of a strong doctrine of human rights, we should expect to see a tension between advocates of limited government and advocates of democracy.

A second view, however, denies this interpretation, and argues that limited government is consistent with the ideals of democracy once we understand the need to regulate political competition among different political movements and bodies of opinion and interest. This view is closer to a republican conception of democracy in which the separation of powers and the system of checks and balances are seen as devices for ensuring that popular power is not usurped by special interests and in which there is no domination by one group over another (Bellamy, 1999, pp. 119–23).

Practically and conceptually, therefore, there is a complex set of relationships between the principles of popular government on the one hand and those of limited government on the other. These relationships involve questions both of the logic of the relevant concepts and the values that different political traditions assert. In order to assess these varying relationships, I shall begin at the conceptual level, and consider what constitutional presuppositions are involved in the idea of popular government itself. Although the issues of value cannot be resolved by conceptual analysis alone, understanding how in the most general case the idea of popular government is related to that of a constitution will help focus attention on where choices among political values are at stake.

The constitutional basis for popular government

One common way of speaking about democracy is to think of it as a system of popular sovereignty. This was the way that MacCormick formulated the problem in the quotation I gave at the beginning of this chapter. Such an approach attaches the idea of the rightful ruler to the idea of the people. Can this conjunction of ideas be made intelligible, however? To answer this question, we need to consider what is involved in the idea of sovereignty.

The traditional doctrine of sovereignty, as formulated by Austin (1832) in the tradition of Hobbes (1651) and Bentham (1780, p. 200; and 1782, p. 1), made the sovereign that agent to whom the bulk of the population was in the habit of obedience, but who was not himself in the habit of obedience to anyone else. The key attribute of sovereignty on this account was the acceptance by the subjects of a political order of the ability of the sovereign to determine those rules to which they were subject to the exclusion of any other source for determining those rules. Austinian sovereigns were at the pinnacle of a hierarchy of agents with the power to fix rules, and were the only agents at that pinnacle. It looks at first sight as though this is an account of monarchical sovereignty, but Austin himself thought that it could be applied quite easily to the case of democracies (compare MacCormick, 1999, p. 67). If we make the people sovereign, then they delegate their authority to parliament. They may make the delegation subject to conditions or they may give a high degree of discretion to their political representatives, but the basic idea is that they retain their sovereignty that is exercised in their capacity as electors.

The notion of the sovereign having the final decision seems to make intuitive sense, and if we think that in a democracy we have popular rule, then it seems natural enough to think that the sovereign will be the people. However, as Hart (1961, pp. 72–5) pointed out a number of years ago, such an account of democracy and sovereignty is far from clear conceptually, and it is impossible to make sense of democratic rule-making authority on this basis. Hart's critique of the Austinian model of democratic sovereignty rests upon a contrast between the notion of sovereignty in a monarchical society and the notion of sovereignty within a democratic society. In a monarchical society, we can think of society as being divided into two segments, the sovereign who gives orders and the bulk of the people who obey those orders. However, in a democratic society, such a separation is not possible, since the source of laws and policies is to be found in the people itself. How can we speak of people obeying orders that they give to themselves? When this is not merely a metaphor, we have clearly transformed the notions of orders and obedience. Moreover, as Hart also pointed out, we cannot separate the notion of the people into one capacity in which it issues orders and another capacity in which it follows those orders without making implicit reference to a body of power-conferring rules, which seems to make the rules, not the people itself, the basis of political authority.

To illustrate this argument, consider a simple contrast between a stylized absolute monarchy of early modern Europe and a contemporary democracy. In the stylized monarchy, the law-giver makes law, in the form of orders, and the people follow those laws (to some degree at least if the authority of the monarch is intact). In such a situation there is a distinction between the law-giver and those subject to the law, since the two roles are filled by different actors. Whatever institutional procedure is used by the law-giver to announce rules, it is clear that the source of the laws is to be found in the person of the monarch. No such distinction can be said to apply in a contemporary democracy. If the people are the final source of political authority, then if they are an Austinian sovereign, the people have to be conceived as giving a law to themselves. Yet, the notion that this issuing of a command that those subject to authority have to obey describes what is happening in a modern democracy stretches the normal meaning of words. In particular, to the extent to which the people or their representatives do make laws, they do so collectively. Yet, citizens obey or disobey the law as individuals.

The fundamental point of Hart's critique is that, for a democracy at least (and he also thought more generally), the picture of sovereignty residing in a relation between a law-giver and subjects was faulty. The conceptual apparatus is simply the wrong one in terms of which to characterize the authority to make rules. It is transferring to a democratic society a picture of relations of authority that might conceivably have applied to a monarchical society. Instead, what we need to substitute is the idea of the electorate as making the law according to an established body of *constitutive* rules. The notion of the authority to make laws has to reside in an account of rules for making rules (second-order rules) and the role of the electorate and their representatives, according to these power-conferring rules, to make primary legislation. Such constitutive rules are the essence of a political constitution.

To highlight the way in which this account avoids muddle, consider the case of a constituent assembly, that is to say a body of representatives who assemble to establish the basis of a political order. If we locate the authority of a constitutive assembly in the electorate who select the representatives, we have to ask how it comes about that the people have any authority to elect a constituent assembly. We seem to be in the situation in which this can only be the case if the authority is somehow self-constituting. But what does it mean to say that authority is self-constituting? Of course, groups of people claim to be able to constitute their own political authority, but the claim is nugatory unless that claim is recognized by others. Merely making a claim to self-constituting authority will not suffice. That claim has to be recognized by others and this amounts to their recognizing some institutionalized procedure, or some body of rules. Democratic sovereignty thus means that a group of people is governed by institutionalized procedures that are recognized by those with some relevant capacity to be authoritative in respect of that group of people.

The older Austinian conception of sovereignty had the notion of a 'habit of obedience', but it is clear that, in relation to a body of rules, the foundational notion is not that of obedience but recognition, for unless there were recognition there could not be any conformity to the rules and hence obedience in that sense. We can, however, still preserve the truth in the Austinian notion of 'habit' if we take this in the sense not of what has customarily happened in the past, but in the sense of a disposition to recognize. To be sure, a disposition to recognize may well arise as a matter of custom and practice, since there are sometimes good reasons to accept past practice as definitive of current authority. But the key to the authority of the rules lies in the disposition to recognize rather than in the practice of past obedience, even though past obedience may be a prompt to present recognition.

The concept of rule-recognition is important because it raises the issue of what is reasonable recognition rather than rational obedience. The traditional Austinian notion of sovereignty was tied to the notion of the will of the sovereign, where the concept of the will was understood as a specific event of the mind. The sovereign could move subjects because the movement of the sovereign's will issued in changes in the world that produced obedience. Armies and police forces could embody threats that would make it rational to obey. By contrast, for a body of rules to be recognized as authoritative depersonalizes authority and detaches the recognition from the will of another.

By means of this argument we can see how constitutionalism in one of its many senses is presupposed in any account of democratic authority. First, in order to make sense of how law-making authority arises, we need to have the concept of a set of constitutive rules, according to which powers are allocated to agents entitled to make laws. Popular government on this account is government that is responsive to expressions of popular preferences in some systematic way. We cannot see law as just the imposition of the will of an individual, as we might have done under an absolute monarch. Secondly, and related to the first point, such a system of constitutive rules depersonalizes the notion of authority. But how does this conceptual analysis relate to the substantive question about the conflict between democratic and constitutional values?

To move towards an answer to this question, recall Rousseau's concept of popular sovereignty as one in which the body of citizens constructs a general will. In order for this to happen, all citizens have to be present and willing at the moment of legislation. If this were all that was involved in democratic government, then little or nothing would be needed by way of a set of constitutive rules. All that need be known is what the majority thought on any matter of policy as the expression of the general will. Yet, as Rousseau himself recognized, government involves more than this. It involves applying the laws determined by the general will and interpreting their meaning in particular cases. Even in the Rousseauian scheme, there has to be some transfer of authority from the people, as sovereign, to bodies exercising political power.

In circumstances in which legislative authority is exercised by representatives, rather than the body of citizens themselves, there is an even greater transfer of authority.

One reason for the notion of constitutionalism, therefore, is that any system in which authority is exercised on behalf of citizens, rather than being exercised through their direct willing, is liable to a distortion of purpose. If political institutions are bestowed with powers for the purpose of benefiting the body of citizens, then some means is necessary to ensure that this purpose is fulfilled. In other words, once we see that sovereignty is conceptually linked to the idea of a body of constitutive rules, then the question inevitably arises as to the extent to which these rules are suited to a justifiable purpose. How might we judge what is an acceptable purpose? The obvious way to do this is to refer back to the general justifying strategy, according to which democracy is justified as a means to promote common interests among political equals who recognize their fallibility. Since the creation of political capacity involves the creation of potentially powerful agents, who can distort the purposes for which they were established, we might think of constitutional principles as dealing with the way to control this power in the public interest.

Moreover, the common interest in question is that of members of the political community considered as equals. As I have argued, this requirement of political equality has a number of dimensions, but a central feature is that the political system does not privilege a particular group of people within society. This requirement may be directly linked to the notion of constitutional government, since as Sidgwick (1891, p. 535) once pointed out, constitutional governments carry out their work according to certain fundamental laws. The implicit contrast here is with government by arbitrary decree; but government by arbitrary decree would be inconsistent with the demands of political equality.

So far I have argued that certain rights that may appear to have a basis in some independent idea of constitutional government can in fact be provided with a rationale in terms of democratic practice. It is sensible to establish these rights as constitutional rights, because by doing so we best achieve the underlying goal of advancing the common interest of the members of a society who regard themselves as equals. However, this coincidence between the principles of constitutionalism and democracy does not mean that the two sets of principles are entirely the same. More precisely, we may say that to provide a democratic rationale for certain constitutional principles is also to provide an interpretation of the scope and significance of those principles, and to indicate what their limits are.

The argument so far is that we can find a rationale for constitutional principles of the separation of powers, but the grounds for such a rationale are located in concerns for the public interest and the extent to which institutions under a constitutive set of rules need to be guarded from distortions in the exercise of authority. However, although a possible line of argument, this does not get us as far as liberal ideas about the role of constitutional governments in protecting individual rights. To be sure, any set of rules will contain the notion of a right in the sense of someone being the subject of rightful authority under a power-conferring rule, but this is hardly the same as a right in the liberal sense. For although liberal rights confer powers on individuals, not all rights that confer powers are liberal in character. To understand the issues around constitutionalism and majority rule under a properly constituted political authority, we need to move from the logic of constitutive rules to a consideration of substantive claims to rights and the liberties of citizens.

Rights-based constitutionalism?

Consider the way in which Schumpeter expressed the conflict between democracy and the protection of individual liberties:

> Let us transport ourselves into a hypothetical country that, in a democratic way, practices the persecution of Christians, the burning of witches, and the slaughtering of Jews. We should certainly not approve of these practices on the ground that they have been decided on according to the rules of democratic procedure. But the crucial question is: would we approve the democratic constitution itself that produced such results in preference to a non-democratic one that would avoid them? (Schumpeter, 1954, p. 242)

Here there is a clear statement of the view that popular government may conflict with the protection of individual freedoms and legitimate interests. A similar point about the contingency of the connection was made by Sir Isaiah Berlin some years ago, in his remark that 'men of imagination, originality and creative genius, and, indeed, minorities of all kinds, were less persecuted' in the Prussia of Frederick the Great or the Austria of Josef II than in many an earlier or later democracy (Berlin, 1969, pp. 129–30). Whether this is historically accurate or not is a moot point. The conceptual point is, however, surely correct. The degree of limitation upon the scope of the operation of power is logically distinct from the source of that power, and if there is a relationship it is a contingent, empirical one, rather than a definitional one.

The freedoms and interests about which Schumpeter and Berlin write are often thought of as 'rights', and the importance of rights is that, according to some conceptions at least, they specify limits on what one person can do to another. As Nozick (1974, p. ix) once put it stating the classical liberal view: 'individuals have rights, and there are things no person or group may do to them (without violating their rights)'. If no person or group may violate rights, then no democratic authority should do so, and the ideal of limited government trumps that of representative government. Obviously such a challenge to democratic authority requires an account of the status and force of the notion of a moral right, and the notion of such a right is a complex one, to which I cannot do justice in a brief space (for an excellent discussion, see Jones, 1994). All I can do here is offer some interpretation about two crucial matters relevant to the present discussion and use these interpretations to carry the weight of the rest of the argument.

The first point concerns the distinction between rights understood as features of the way in which institutions work and rights understood as moral claims, independently of any institution. For example, in an institutional sense, citizens may have rights not to be persecuted, burnt or slaughtered, in the sense that these interests are protected by government and they are generally respected. However, there is another, purely moral, sense in which people can have rights, even if certain freedoms are not generally respected. Thus, we may say, in the moral sense of the term, that people have the right not to be persecuted, burnt and slaughtered, even if in practice that is what is happening to them. Obviously, the moral sense of rights may be used to criticize the functioning and performance of any set of institutions to the extent to which they do not recognize or respect these rights. It is oversimplifying, but helpful, to think of institutional rights as legal rights and moral rights as human rights. It is of course by appeal to the notion of moral or human rights that Nozick was able to say that because people have rights, there are things that no person or group, including governments, can permissibly do to them.

The second point about rights concerns their logical structure, and is applicable to rights in general whether they are understood as legal or human rights. Rights can be thought of as claims, as when people fleeing persecution claim the right to asylum or when the parties to a contract claim the fulfilment of its terms. However, they also function in other ways, of which the best account is given in Hohfeld's (1923) classification. Hohfeld thought of rights not only as claims but also as liberties, powers and immunities. Any particular right can be thought of as exemplifying one of more of these different elements. For example, treasure-seekers looking for marine salvage are at liberty to take what they find, but they have no claim against other treasure-seekers that they be allowed to take the prize first. Other rights can be thought of in different ways, including as combining elements of Hohfeld's categories. For example, the right to vote may be regarded as a mixture of powers (the ability to cast a ballot) and claims (that the public administration provide the facilities). Similarly, freedom from arbitrary arrest can be thought of as in part an immunity and in part a claim. Any particular right typically exhibits features drawn from one or more of these categories.

Why might rights be thought valuable in any of the senses in which they can be characterized? After all, rights even when they are thought of in moral terms do not exhaust all that is morally important in human and political relationships. There are virtues of charity, benevolence, courage and honesty that people may not have a right to expect others to show but which they would admire them for showing. What is so special about the category of rights? Joel Feinberg (1970) once offered an interesting reply to this question. To think of moral relations in terms of rights, he suggested, meant that people could insist on what was due to them and stand up for what was properly owed them. Being able to insist in this way made for self-respect, respect from others and gave a sense of personal worth and dignity. We can illustrate this point with an example taken from Sidgwick (1891, p. 28), although he puts it to a different use. Under the nineteenth-century English Poor Law, the guardians had a duty to provide relief for the poor, but no poor person could sue for relief. Therein, of course, lay just the assault on dignity.

The other main reason why rights may be thought important morally is connected with the claim that without rights we should not be acknowledging the 'distinction between persons' (Rawls, 1999a, p. 24). This is a way of expressing an interesting feature of rights, namely that they can act as a counterweight to claims of the public interest or the common good. Suppose, to take a frequently used example, punishing someone who was innocent was publicly beneficial in the sense that it provided the community with a scapegoat and so reduced resentment in the population at large. It would still be wrong to do this, according to a believer in rights, because it would be using that person for ends that were not those of the person concerned purely for the benefit of other people. This would amount to not acknowledging the separateness and integrity of persons. The claim that someone has a right not to be punished if they are innocent is intended to stop such instrumental use of persons, and in that sense to recognize their separateness.

With this understanding of the concept of a right, how are we to evaluate Schumpeter's claim about the solely empirical connection between the protection of rights and the practices of democracy? To say that a relationship is a contingent one is not to say that it is negative. Although democracy practice could, under certain circumstances, lead to rights violations, this is not to say that it will or that there are alternative forms of political arrangements that would do better by the same measure. Empirical studies of the relationship between democracy and human rights show a strong, positive correlation. Summarizing the relevant literature, Landman writes:

> results demonstrate that democracies (or those countries moving towards more democratic forms), wealthy countries, and those that have become developed are less likely to violate personal integrity rights. On the other hand, those countries involved in international and civil warfare, countries with a large population, the presence of an authoritarian regime, previous levels of repression, and those that have undergone a transition to either 'anocracy' or autocracy are more likely to violate personal integrity rights. One study shows that the benefits of democracy with respect to the protection of personal integrity rights come into effect with the first year of the democratic transition. (Landman, 2005, pp. 557–8)

In short, those political regimes that embody democracy are also those political regimes that are best in terms of protecting human rights. To be sure, the correlation is not perfect, and human rights abuses are found in democracies, so that there is a possibility for human rights violations. Moreover, though the relationship between democracy and human rights is strong and positive, it is possible to argue that it reflects the experience of democracies at only a certain stage of their development. Perhaps the positive relationship owes more to coincidence than one would like to think.

One way of responding to this scepticism is to show that rights are more closely related to democracy in terms of guiding values than is presupposed in the Schumpeter/Berlin critique. To do this, I shall divide the relevant rights into three categories – political, civil and economic – and look at each in turn.

Political rights

Schumpeter's argument is little more than a statement of logical possibility as it stands, which is not easily supported by empirical evidence. But, even considered as a statement of bare logical possibility, it has problems, for we cannot simply identify democracy with the principle of majority rule. We also have to consider the underlying principle of political equality, which provides a principal part of the rationale of democratic government. Looked at from this point of view, there may well be rights that are constitutive of democratic practice (compare Ely, 1981).

If there are rights that are constitutive of democratic practice itself, they will include such rights as freedom of assembly and association, freedom to debate matters of public concern and to criticize the government of the day, freedom from arbitrary arrest and imprisonment, freedom from political obligations, such as taxes and conscription, that have not been the subject of democratic decision as well as equality before the law, so that there are no privileged classes in terms of the scope of legal rights and duties. To say that these rights have a democratic character is not to say that any one of them, if breached, would turn a democracy into an authoritarian form of government. It is to say, however, that, in the absence of such rights, temporary minorities would always have the temptation to turn themselves into privileged groups that would be more capable of resisting the attempt of a minority to turn itself into a majority.

Does this mean that we have a reconciliation between the principle of limited government and the principle of popular government? Not necessarily. Consider a right such as the freedom to communicate political information. If this is treated as a free-standing constitutional right, without taking into account its democratic rationale, then it would appear to prohibit a government from controlling the content and manner of political information. However, there may be good democratic reasons why there should be such control. In a world where the media of communication are owned by private individuals, unfettered freedom of political communication might result in minority points of view being driven out from public debate and the propagation of opinions favoured largely by the rich and powerful. This would be contrary both to the cause of the common interest and to the principle of political equality.

Empirical evidence suggests that these media effects exist. Cronin (1989, pp. 116–24) cites examples where the results of state referendums in the US have been affected by the amount of public broadcast time that one side of the debate has been willing and able to buy. These effects, moreover, arise despite federal regulations that require broadcasters to provide fair access to competing points of view in public debate. In fact, as Cronin (1989, p. 121) points out, no broadcaster ever lost a licence due to violations of the fairness doctrine, even when the violation occurred over a number of years. Similar worries have been raised in Italy by Berlusconi's ownership of the media when he was prime minister (Lane, 2005). Application of some principle of rough equality of representation in politics could require significant government control in order to uphold a central principle of democratic practice. So, rather than simply placing limits upon government, as traditional constitutional theory would do, the democratic rationale for constitutional political rights might imply vigorous government action.

I have argued that the fundamental rationale for a system of democratic decision making is the advancement of certain common interests given the circumstances of politics. If this is so, then the chief common interest that the members of a political community will have is in the rights and powers vested in the political institutions that protect and advance those common interests. It should be clear that these interests may not be identical with the interests of the government of the day or even the popular majority on which the government of the day is based. As Holmes (1988, p. 29) points out, protection of the minority is a common good, both for the minority and for the majority. In particular, where there are subgroups, the compromise embodied in constitutional restrictions can secure the cooperation necessary for economic prosperity and military independence. To impose no constraints on what majorities can do is to undermine the compromise between subgroups on which any complex political order needs to be based. For example, it can be imprudent to allow majority governments to draw electoral boundaries to their own advantage as the Stormont government was allowed to do in Northern Ireland for fifty years. The build-up of resentment in the minority community can hardly be said to be in the common interest.

Conversely, even a democratic rationale of constitutional political rights can be consistent with removing powers from elected representatives and placing those powers in independent hands. Consider, for example, the issues associated with the drawing of constituency boundaries or the financing of political parties. It would simply be unrealistic to think that these matters could be left to elected representatives, since at any one time the parties in power have too great an interest in the outcome to be able to make impartial decisions. Hence, in this sort of case, we might imagine not vigorous action by government to police the operation of constitutional rights, but the appointment of independent bodies, created to serve a longer-term public interest, by controlling the operation of the political system.

The way of reconciling democracy and constitutionalism in this case is to say that democratic practice needs to be orderly practice if it is to serve the purposes for which it is justified, and at any one time central democratic institutions, such as political parties, would be prone to distort the order on which that practice is based. The obvious analogy is also the most telling. Democratic deliberation does not consist in everyone trying to have their say at the same time, but in an orderly proceeding, with a neutral person in the chair, according to rules understood by all participants. By contrast, if everyone tries to speak at once, no one will be heard. In so far as constitutional rules and convention secure the conditions of democratic practice, there is no theoretical conflict involved, though of course there may be practical conflicts from time to time, just as there are when people from the floor challenge the ruling of the chair.

Democracy and civil rights

Aside from these rights, however, there will clearly also be rights that, though they may be associated with democracy in practice, will be logically distinct from any definition of democracy that we can offer. Thus, a second set of principles concerns rights that are essential to the idea of constitutional government, independently of the idea of democracy. This set is formed by what may be termed civil rights, such as freedom of religion, freedom of conscience, freedom of non-political speech or freedom of sexual behaviour. Unlike the first set of rights, these civil rights do not seem to be tied essentially to the notion of democratic government. Whilst it would seem to be inconsistent to imagine a democratic government that prohibited a group of citizens from organizing peacefully to change public policy, it would not be incoherent to suppose a democratic government imposing restrictions or privileges in respect of civil rights. For example, both Sweden and Norway, which many might regard as archetypical egalitarian democracies, have established churches and levy taxes for their upkeep. If freedom of religion means complete separation of church and state, which arguably it does, then there is no reason to suppose that this separation would be respected within functioning democracies.

Consider one particular civil right, namely that of liberty of conscience. I take this as an example in part because it can be seen as a
principle that lies behind a number of civil liberties, for example priv-
acy and freedom of religion, as well as other liberties such as exemp-
tion from military service. It is also a fairly strong claim, which means
that if it can be made compatible with the principle of majority rule,
then other, perhaps less stringent freedoms, are also likely to be compatible. Finally, there is also an argument in the history of political
thought that it is a culturally distinct idea. Indeed, John Plamenatz
(1963, p. 46) makes the striking claim that of the traditional freedoms
it is the only one that can claim to be distinctively European. This cultural distinctiveness will turn out to be important in the development
of the subsequent argument.

Suppose then that a society has a constitutional arrangement in
which liberty of conscience is guaranteed, and this is an operative
right in the society. By saying that it is an operative right, I mean that
it is upheld against the pressures of the elected government in a significant number of cases. For example, I imagine that the courts may
uphold exemptions from military service for individuals who would
otherwise be conscripted into the army, or they grant charitable status
to certain religious groups, giving them tax advantages, which they
would otherwise be denied by public policy. How far is freedom of
conscience as it operates under constitutional protection in this sort
of way compatible with the principles of democracy?

Following the example of the democratic rights I shall make the test
of compatibility consistency, not with any majoritarian decision whatsoever, but only with those forms of majority decision making that
can be shown to be compatible with the underlying rationale of democratic institutions. In other words, the principle of liberty of conscience
has to be compatible with protecting or advancing the common interests of the members of society where they wish to treat one another as
political equals.

If this is the test, then there is an inconsistency at the theoretical level
between democratic practice and freedom of conscience. This is not
to say that the conflict arises all the time or is invariable. Yet it is to say
that there is no way in which the conflict can be avoided in principle.
In some cases, there will be a clash. Such a conflict would not arise had
John Stuart Mill been successful in *On Liberty* in showing that personal freedom had a tendency to serve the public good (Mill, 1859).
But it is a commonplace of commentaries on Mill that he fails in his
consequentialist justification of freedom, at least in showing that others

derive a benefit – even indirectly – from the exercise of freedom by minorities. To make the argument for the protection of freedom complete, Mill has to appeal to the idea that freedom is somehow an intrinsic good for creatures who wish to transcend the 'ape-like' faculty of imitation. Such freedom can certainly be an interest of individuals, perhaps even their primary interest, but that does not show that there is a public interest in protecting and advancing such freedom. For there may be other public concerns, for example public order or protection from offence, that are harmed by the exercise of individual liberty, and a consequentialist argument will leave open how these interests balance in any particular case.

Consider the case of military conscription. Suppose that a community is fighting a just war to protect its territorial integrity. It may be simply too costly, in terms of the protection of the country, to allow the exercise of a right of freedom of conscience, since that would undermine the fighting power of the armed forces. In making this decision, there may well be concerns of course about dishonesty in the presentation of particular cases. But, even abstracting from that worry, the price of freedom of conscience may well seem too high for members of the political community. Here considerations of individual freedom and the public interest appear to be in direct conflict.

It will not do at this point to invoke the principle of political equality. That principle is compatible with taking a rather hard-nosed view of the rights arising from the principle of freedom of conscience. To the argument that it is contrary to the principle of equality to override conscientiously held objections to a course of action, defenders of the action in question could well say that they would be prepared to have their rights of conscience overridden in similar circumstances. The principle of political equality requires that restrictions on freedom of conscience be even-handed; it does not require that they be generous, which is what a principle of liberty of conscience would require.

To be sure, there can be public interest reasons for favouring freedom of conscience as a principle in many cases. For example, on one account, the origins of the idea in Europe are rooted in the experience of religious wars in the sixteenth and seventeenth centuries. Toleration on this view arises because it is preferable to civil or international war (Rawls, 1996, pp. 148–9), although Skinner (1978, pp. 244–9) has noted how there were also principled arguments available at the time. As an account of the origin of the practice of toleration this has much to commend it, but the practice to which it gave rise falls significantly short of the practice that would be implied by adoption of the principle of liberty of conscience in its full sense. One way in which this can be seen is in the fact that religious toleration was typically only extended to limited groups, roughly speaking those whose dissent could kick up enough fuss to disrupt the political order, and whose interests therefore had to be accommodated within the political system. In England, for example, the eventual seventeenth-century settlement extended full religious liberty to Protestant groups but not to Jews and Catholics.

The upshot of this is that, though it is possible to advance reasons of public interest for a practice that often resembles respect for liberty of conscience, the justification of toleration in the former case falls short of what would be required in the latter. There certainly is not an extensional equivalence between the principle of liberty of conscience and a public interest-based rationale, in the sense that the practical implications of the two principles are distinct in a number of cases.

It would be possible to square the circle if we could provide an account of democracy in terms of autonomy. But I argued in Chapter 5 that this was not possible in any strong sense of the notion of autonomy. Democracy certainly has to be compatible with the notion that individuals are capable of reflection and choice, and that they are the best judges of their own welfare in general terms, but that is such a minimally demanding sense of the term that it requires us merely to hold that citizens can make morally significant choices in their decision making. It does not tell us anything about the priority to be accorded to individual liberty against other values such as public order or the protection of collective interests. Moreover, as I also argued in Chapter 5, once we assert that human autonomy gives rise to some moral priority to be accorded to individual liberty, we are likely to want a libertarian political system rather than a democratic one.

A similar point can be made if we conceive constitutional restrictions as 'gagging' clauses or ways of keeping certain contentious issues out of democratic politics. Holmes (1988) draws attention to the arguments for constitutionalizing certain issues on the grounds that making them the subject of political discussion raises the temperature too much for all the participants. Just as friends might agree among themselves not to bring up certain topics in conversation, so members of a polity might benefit from having certain issues remitted to the judiciary. Holmes himself shows how the issues of both slavery in the US in the nineteenth century and abortion in the twentieth have been kept out of politics for fear of disrupting the political relations among important groups. However, as Holmes (1988, p. 56) himself notes, such evasiveness can have serious disadvantages. It gives a premium to those willing to raise the political stakes by threatening disruption, violence and, in the limit, civil war.

A gap seems to open up, therefore, between the principles of democratic choice and a commitment to a strong principle of liberty of conscience. This gap of principle is institutionally represented in the political conflict that can exist between the decisions of a majoritarian political system and the constitutional protection that might be accorded to the conscientiously held practices of individuals and groups. The reason for this theoretical discrepancy is to be found in John Plamenatz's insight, I conjecture. Freedom of conscience is a culturally specific value. It is the political expression of a certain sort of individualism. A community may choose to acknowledge such a value, but that would be the result of a democratic choice.

Despite the lack of theoretical affinity between the practice of democracy and the principle of freedom of conscience, it is still possible that there is an empirical relation between them. This is, indeed, my own view. By and large, and despite Isaiah Berlin's examples to the contrary, it is democratic regimes that seem to provide the conditions within which liberty of conscience is respected rather than authoritarian ones. The reason for this, I imagine, is that, although political equality does not require citizens to take a generous view of the conscientious claims of others, it provides the political conditions within which tolerant attitudes are promoted. Having to negotiate with the interests of others and come to some compromise is one way in which people can come to see that there are points of view other than their own, and it is in just such contexts that an attitude of toleration is likely to be developed.

Thus, in acknowledging the equal place of others to determine the common interest we necessarily recognize that we should be willing to compromise in the pursuit of our own interests. Compromise goes beyond justification, since the latter is compatible with using the procedures of the political process to your own ends, when this is possible, provided you have the power and you have explained what you are doing. Compromise, by contrast, will sometimes enjoin actors not to use their legitimate power to its full extent, even when they are able to do so, if by another course of action they can meet an opponent part of the way. Compromise, in this sense, is not an attempt to stand in a neutral position but to stand in a context-bound common position (Bellamy, 1994, pp. 436–41 and Bellamy, 1999, chapter 4). But the principle of political equality may push people at times beyond compromise to what we may call a sense of accommodation. This is stronger than compromise in the sense that it involves a willingness to take fewer advantages for oneself in the interest of getting as many people on board as possible. One of the ways in which it is manifest is in the 'politics of accommodation' as described by Lijphart (1968). The aim here then is not simply to get one's own way with some concessions to those who have competing interests, but instead to enlarge the sense of interests operative in a political situation, so as to incorporate the interests of others.

Democracy and property rights

A third set of rights, sometimes connected by theorists to rights to freedom but in fact logically distinct, are property rights. In one form or another property rights are often made a matter of constitutional provision. For example, the German Basic Law secures a right to private property for citizens, although it also prescribes (in a rather typical social Catholic way) that property has duties as well as rights. As Buchanan (1986, pp. 255–6) has noted, this is an area that tends to divide libertarians or classical liberals on the one side from social democrats on the other. Both may agree that there should be clear restrictions upon governments to interfere with the civil liberties of citizens, but they disagree on the protection that should be afforded to property rights. Whereas social democrats see property rights as institutional devices by which control of productive assets is assigned to individuals, the assignment to be judged on the consequences it produces, libertarians and classical liberals typically wish to assimilate property to the list of 'natural' rights, and to say that a person's entitlement to property depends upon their ability justly to acquire or receive property from others.

Again, the question at this stage is not whether either side in this dispute is right, but what such an example tells us about the relationship between constitutionalism and democracy. Although the social democratic account of property would not seem to present any serious problems for democratic theory (as I shall argue later), classical liberal accounts are a different matter. If the right to property is a natural right, and constitutional government aims to protect natural rights, then there could quite easily develop a conflict between the protection of property rights and democratic decision making. The areas of policy where one would most expect this conflict to emerge would be over such matters as the state's right to take property into public ownership, the taxing of property for the purposes of redistribution or the imposition of limits upon the uses that owners made of their property rights. So, here again, we seem to have a clear case, at least under the classical liberal account of property, of the conflict between constitutional government and democratic government.

Should there be constitutional limits on a democracy's right to legislate on matters of property? As I have already noted, this is an issue that divides classical liberals from social democrats, with the former wishing typically to impose only procedural limits – for example that the treatment of property be even-handed between different groups – whilst the latter wish for stronger constitutional protection for private property in particular. A decision of this matter has considerable implications for the scope of public policy and the ability of collective mechanisms of choice to deal with the cumulative and unintended consequences of individual interaction. Stringent limits on the ability of a democracy to control and regulate the use of private property would limit measures that could be adopted in environmental policy, anti-monopoly policy, health and safety legislation, the control of pension fund investments, the relief of poverty or the adoption of measures of consumer protection.

In the US the tension between democracy and constitutionalism in this respect was manifest during the so-called 'Lochner era', after the decision in *Lochner v. New York*. In that case the Supreme Court ruled that minimum wage and maximum hour laws were a transfer of property from employers to employees and as such were prohibited under the constitution (Sunstein, 1988, pp. 342–3). The point about this judgement was that it went beyond simply stating that measures for worker protection had to be adopted with due process and applied according to the principle of equality before the law to a position in which the range of permissible democratic purposes was restricted. It thus conflated a constitutionalist position on the way in which the exercise of political power was to be conducted with a libertarian view of property rights.

Measures adopted by democracies to deal with the use of property will typically be forward-looking, that is to say they will seek to regulate the use of property so as to achieve a stated purpose. Libertarian accounts of property are typically backward-looking, however. That is, they ascribe ownership and entitlement in terms of the transactions that have taken place between individuals within a social order. Thus, one way in which the libertarian or classical liberal position could be made good would be in terms of a theory that showed how the existing body of property rights grew legitimately from a historically given set of transactions. But libertarian theories of property, which have normally been based on some variant of Locke's (1690, pp. 327–44) account, have proved notoriously weak in this respect. They cannot deal with the problem of how to justify initial acquisition, moving too easily to the conclusion that the existing distribution arose through a series of transactions that were either just, or should be treated as though they were just. And they presuppose what Honoré (1961) has termed 'full liberal ownership' rather than the more complex bundles of rights that in fact make up property rights in modern societies (compare Reeve, 1986, pp. 94–100).

Moreover, it seems simply a historical mistake to ignore the fact that certain forms of property have had their origin in legislative decision. The most important of these forms has been the creation of limited liability for commercial enterprises, which restricts the debt liability of owners in the event of bankruptcy, and without which the modern corporation would not exist. In Britain during the 1840s the matter was debated extensively, and it is clear that forward-looking arguments about the social benefits that might be thought to flow from the greater willingess to take risks allowed by adoption of the principle of limited liability were decisive in the passage of the legislation (Atiyah, 1979, pp. 564–7).

It does not seem, therefore, that there are strong reasons for imposing stronger constitutional restrictions upon the majority's right to legislate in matters of property than are implied by the principles of the rule of law in any case. The means employed should be proportional to the goal being sought and there should be no arbitrary discrimination in the treatment of different sorts of property owners. To entrench a right to private property in a constitution that would make it unconstitutional for a duly elected government to control and regulate property in the public good would seem to go further than is warranted by any persuasive argument.

Courts or legislatures?

So far I have argued that there has to be a constitutional basis for democracy. Assigning authority to chambers of elected representatives or citizens in a referendum can only be done through a framework of constitutive rules (such rules may of course take only the form of accepted conventions). Moreover, democracy is linked to but not identical with ideas of constitutional protection. The values of democracy and constitutional protection are not always consistent with one another, as the example of freedom of conscience shows, and constitutionalist attempts to make a natural rights theory of property trump democratic determination will not work. Yet, without the idea of a set of constitutional rules, through which sources of authority are defined, we could not have the idea of a democratic order.

However, even if these conclusions are granted, there will still be difficult issues of institutional choice, over which there are deep divisions of political principle. Constitutive rules are second-order rules: they are rules for determining the first-order rules that comprise the way in which citizens relate to one another. This means that the constitutive rules define which institutions have a say in the determination of primary rules such as whether abortion is to be permitted, whether blasphemy should be a crime or whether a certain class of citizens, say prisoners, should have the vote. More specifically, the constitutive rules can give authority in some of these cases for a constitutional court, interpreting the constitution, to override the elected legislature if it judges that the elected legislature has passed a law in violation of a basic constitutional principle. This is the power of judicial review in the strong sense. Its paradigm expression is in the constitution of the US, though to a lesser degree it is also found in Germany in its Basic Law. By contrast, in many democracies, though the courts may have powers to prevent governments breaking rules that governments themselves have declared that they will abide by (as with the traditional UK doctrine of *ultra vires* under which the courts could negative some government action), they do not have the power to declare statutes unconstitutional if duly passed by the legislature. It is this issue of who can determine the content of laws when courts and legislatures clash that defines for most people the controversy between constitutionalism and democracy.

If the account of constitutive rules given earlier is correct, there are proposed ways of dealing with this conflict that will not work. One of these is Ackerman's (1991, 1998) theory embodied in the idea of 'we, the people'. Taking the US as his reference point, Ackerman argues that there are certain moments of constitutional politics in which previous political principles are redefined and which then define a subsequent era of politics stretching over decades. In the US these were the Federalist founding regime, the Republican reconstruction regime and the Democrat New Deal regime. All these changes of regime are democratic in character, in the sense that they are collective popular transformations in which majorities are mobilized. On this account, when the Supreme Court remakes law in a fundamental way, as it did when it declared school segregation unconstitutional in *Brown v. Board of Education* in 1954, it is not asserting its own authority, but rather interpreting and applying the authority of the people. As Ackerman puts it:

> It is not the special province of the judges to lead the People onward and upward to new and higher values … What the judges are especially equipped to do is preserve the achievements of popular sovereignty during the long periods of our public existence when the citizenry is not mobilized for great constitutional achievements. (Ackerman, 1991, p. 139).

The courts do not usurp the proper role of the legislature; they work out the consequences and implications of political revolutions in which legislatures, and all other major political actors, are involved.

Whether the separation between constitutional politics and normal politics, which this theory requires, can be maintained is a moot point, particularly in view of doubt that Mayhew (2002) has cast on the idea of 'critical elections' in the US. However, the problem is as much conceptual as historical. What the theory requires is a collective performative, through which the people, as a whole, wills itself into a new mode of being. But this is to place the emphasis upon the act of willing, rather than the acceptance and recognition by those subject to the law of the need for change. To be sure Roosevelt accomplished great and lasting legislative change, but the 'switch in time that saved nine', when the Supreme Court accepted his labour legislation, meant that it was achieved through established, though strained, constitutional procedures.

By the same token, there is another familiar resolution of the courts/legislature conflict in the idea that what happens when courts are given the power to determine the constitutionality of legislation is that the people are engaged in an act of self-binding, akin to the way in which Ulysses was strapped to the mast (for an excellent review of the arguments, see Holmes, 1988). On this view, the constitutional powers of the courts derive from the willingness of the people in its better moments to guard itself against temptation in its weaker moments. Here again, however, there is simply metaphor rather than conceptual clarification. The argument requires the uneasy postulate of a collective popular self. Perhaps a single monarch could institute constitutional restrictions in this way, but no collective entity could do so without either a background set of constitutive rules – in which case the conventional meaning of sovereignty has gone – or a revolution in habits of obedience. The contest between courts and legislatures, in those jurisdictions in which there is strong judicial review, seems as clear as ever.

Dworkin (1996), however, has claimed that there is no contest between democracy and constitutional protection, arguing that a strong doctrine of the separation of powers is one way in which popular government can be realized. The essential premise of this argument is that the judiciary is often in a significantly better position than elected representatives to give expression to the democratic value of equality, and in particular the principle that all citizens should be treated with equal concern and respect. The difficulty with this view, however, is that it draws too sharp a distinction between the courts as deliberative institutions, guided by an ideal of equal respect, and legislatures as aggregating institutions, responding to the weight of votes. Once we see that legislatures are necessarily deliberative institutions in their own right, the necessary contrast fades. Once we also see that certain political rights, for example the right to petition the legislature, are ways in which social groups can participate in the shaping and interpretation of a society's morality, the contrast ceases to exist at all.

There is, incidentally in this context, an interesting question about the extent to which the US Supreme Court has functioned as a counter-majoritarian institution. Empirical analyses suggests that its decisions track with fair accuracy the movement of public opinion over time (Mishler and Sheehan, 1993; Stimson, MacKuen and Erikson, 1995). As public opinion became more liberal in the 1950s and 1960s over such issues as ethnic minority interests or abortion, so the Supreme Court became more liberal, and as public opinion began to turn more conservative, so the Supreme Court followed, so that in practice the Court may not have been such a counter-majoritarian institution as theory might suggest. The mechanism by which this tracking took place was the appointment process which allows the president the right of nomination. And, despite some spectacular 'wrong' nominations by presidents (Eisenhower is alleged to have said of Earl Warren, thought to be a safe conservative on appointment, that his nomination was 'the damndest fool thing I ever did'), it is clear that presidents seek to sense the mood of the country when making appointments.

However, even with this acknowledgement of the role of responsiveness to popular opinion in the judgements of the US Supreme Court, it is impossible to avoid the conclusion that a political willingness to invest a constitution with reverence and to allow a court to determine policy must spring from a distrust of popular government, at least at the national level. The Supreme Court is not the agent of popular revolutions in political principle, nor is it a device by which the people binds itself. Rather it is an expression of the belief that citizens acting collectively through their representatives cannot be trusted with the interests of minorities. Jeremy Waldon (1999a, p. 222) has noted how odd this belief is when set against the belief in human rights, since the latter belief is an expression of a sense of the dignity of persons. It may also be a self-frustrating belief. If government action is needed to deal with collectively shared problems, then if that action is declared unconstitutional the prospects are poor. For, when ambition is set against ambition who knows what stasis may follow?

9 The Boundaries of Inclusion

So far we have defined democracies as political systems in which important decisions of public policy depend, even if only indirectly and at one remove, on public opinion. However, this definition implicitly leaves one major question unanswered. How should we define the relevant public? Clearly, it is possible to define the public narrowly or broadly, with quite different implications for our understanding of the character of the political system. This is the problem of inclusion. Robert Dahl (1989, p. 119), who more than any democratic theorist has drawn attention to this problem, points out both that the issue of inclusion is central to our understanding of democracy and that relatively little attention has been paid to it. Thus, ancient Athens is typically called a democracy, but women, slaves and metics (resident aliens) were excluded from the rights of citizenship. The exclusion of such a large proportion of the population might lead someone, with good reason, to withhold the name of democracy from the system. Similarly, up to the time that Switzerland gave the vote to women in 1971, we might want to say that it was not a democracy, despite its extensive participationist practices and system of proportional representation.

How does it come about that political systems, which looked at from the point of view of their participatory practices would be regarded as paradigm cases of democracy, are less than democratic when looked at from the point of view of their exclusiveness in terms of political rights? One possible answer turns on an ambiguity in the notion of 'the people'. As Maragaret Canovan (2005) has pointed out, the concept of the people is ambiguous, since it can be taken in at least two different senses. It can be treated as a collective noun, in which case it refers to a collection of individuals regarded as a single entity, as we might say that a people has inhabited a territory for centuries, without meaning that any individual has lived a long time. On the other hand, it can refer to a collection of individuals in respect of a set of persons sharing some common characteristic, as we might say of a particular set of people that they have each just moved into a locality. This ambiguity of meaning is marked by logicians in the distinction between distributed and non-distributed properties. Thus, to say of a group of people that they have moved to a locality recently is to speak of some feature they have in common that can be taken in a distributed sense. It is true of each and every one of them. To say of a people that it has lived in a territory for centuries is to speak of a property that cannot be distributed among the individuals.

It is important when speaking about popular rule to be clear when one is using the term of a non-distributed collective entity and when one is using it distributively. Athens and Switzerland could be regarded as democracies, despite their highly exclusionary practices, if the body of citizens were understood collectively, as a singular group whose members governed their own affairs. Once one asks how that membership is defined, however, and so raises the question of whom membership is distributed to, one is looking at the question from an individualist point of view, and this immediately raises the question of how it is that some individuals gain membership and others do not.

If we take the criterion of individual inclusion into account, a democracy is not simply a political system in which public choice depends upon public opinion, but is also a system in which the public is defined on an inclusive basis. In this sense, the notion of inclusion can be said to be central to the definition of democracy. A democracy, on this definition, seeks to accommodate the interests and opinions of a wide range of individuals and allows competition for power and influence on an inclusive basis. A narrow basis for citizenship means that a political system in some sense fails to be democratic, no matter how much political participation by eligible citizens it allowed in the making of decisions.

Yet, if inclusion is important in the definition of democracy, it is impossible to imagine a democratic system without practices of exclusion, and these are widespread in democracies, including those that take political equality seriously. For example, even when citizenship is not a necessary condition for securing political rights such as the right to vote (as is true in the UK, for example, where resident Irish and Commonwealth citizens can vote), it is invariably the principal basis. All democracies implement an age test on the right to vote so that those below a certain age are excluded, as are most foreign residents, some citizens who live abroad and, in some jurisdictions, those found guilty of certain crimes. More importantly, one can argue that democracy itself requires some distinction between 'self' and 'other', for if democracy is about determining a common choice for a group of people, there needs to be some specification of those people for whom the choice is to be common and binding.

How, then, are we to determine the principles that enable us to settle problems about exactly how inclusive or exclusive the definition of citizenship should be? After all, we cannot simply say that the public should itself decide who is a member, because, as Robert Dahl (1989, p. 121) has pointed out, this would give a licence to narrowly elite bodies of citizens to define citizenship in exclusive terms. Under apartheid in South Africa the majority of white citizens denied the political rights of citizenship to black members of society for decades. If we were simply to say that any body of citizens was entitled to define its own membership, this would produce the absurd result that apartheid South Africa was a democracy. The test of inclusion cannot therefore be the product of a decision-rule used within a political system. Rather the decision-rules that are used must presuppose that issues of inclusion have already been settled.

The discussion is also complicated by the fact that the term 'inclusion' has become fashionable among political theorists and policy makers in recent years, so that it has collected to itself a number of quite distinct and discrete problems. Robert Goodin (1996) has pointed out, for example, that the notions of inclusion are used to discuss problems of political participation, problems of poverty and problems of free movement, as well as issues connected with the definition of citizenship. In what follows, I shall seek to avoid the complications of these multiple, and not always related, issues, by focusing on a limited number of quite specific questions arising from three issues.

The first of these can be put as follows. Given that we think that the members of a political community should be allowed to govern themselves democratically, which members of that community should be qualified to participate in the decision-making process? This question focuses upon principles for determining what qualification members need to have in order to possess and exercise political rights. The second question can be expressed as follows. Even when we have defined political rights of citizenship within a community, does it follow that all qualified members of the political community should be entitled to a voice on everything? After all, in most democracies there are systems of local government, the effect of which is to exclude citizens, who otherwise have full political rights, from participating in the making of some decisions affecting particular localities. I shall refer to this as the problem of partitioning. Thirdly, there is the question of whether we should confine political representation solely to human interests or whether there is a case for 'enfranchising nature'. This is the problem of extension beyond current human interests.

The problem of qualification

Even if we accept, as I have suggested we must, that democracy is to be defined as a political system in which there is a high degree of inclusiveness in the rights of citizenship, it is still plausible to think that there ought to be some exclusions from political rights. Some political rights are denied to children below a certain age, serving prisoners in many countries or temporary visitors from one country to another. But, unless these are to be ad hoc exclusions without any justification, we ought to seek for principles which would enable us to see why certain categories of those affected by political decisions ought to be excluded from influence in the making of those decisions.

In looking at this issue, I shall take the right to vote as my primary example. This is sometimes regarded as a purely formal right, which does not give an accurate account of the power, or lack of power, that citizens are capable of exercising in a democracy. However, it would be a mistake to think of the right to vote in this way, and it is striking how in political systems in which one group seeks to dominate the political process, restriction of the franchise is a crucial instrument of control. For example, under segregation in the southern states of the USA before the 1960s, exclusion of African-Americans from the vote was widely practised, usually through the imposition of maladministered literacy tests. Not only did it deprive African-American citizens of such political influence as comes with the vote, but it had the further effect of keeping them off juries, thus leading to all-white juries in lynching trials who would acquit obviously guilty whites accused of the murder (Caro, 2003). Similarly, in many political systems gerrymandering of constituencies and corrupt electoral practices are important means by which elite control is maintained, so that the right to cast a meaningful vote is important, if not the sole political right of importance. Moreover, because voting rights have a relatively determinable character, discussion of their distribution can stand proxy for the other political rights of citizenship such as the right to free association or the right to petition the government.

The assumption that the right to vote should be widely distributed is so common that it can be difficult to understand its principled rationale. To overcome this problem it is useful to consider an explicit argument from another age for exclusion on a large scale, and to see where it goes wrong. One such argument is to be found in James Mill's *Essay on Government* (1820, p. 27), where Mill makes the case for excluding from the right to vote all but men over forty. Thus, all women and men under the age of forty are excluded. This argument is particularly striking coming from someone who in many respects was radical in his political opinion. However, besides its historical interest, I take it that the conclusion James Mill wishes to establish is unjustifiable to modern intuitions. So where does it go wrong?

Mill's argument rests upon the twin assumptions that political participation is a cost and that the heads of households can represent the interests of other members of the household. If we grant the assumption that political participation is pure cost, it follows that if individuals can have their interests represented adequately by someone else, for example the head of their household, then it would be to their advantage to do so. One way of protecting yourself from the predatory political ambitions of others is to ensure that they do not have the capacity to engage in politics to your disadvantage. Hence, a rule that limited the right to vote to the minimum necessary to protect people from government tyranny would be a prudent rule for the members of a community to follow, even from the point of view of those who would be excluded.

Notice that, as Mill states it, this argument comes very close to validity in the sense in which logicians speak about an argument's being valid. In logic, as distinct from common usage, an argument is regarded as valid if it takes a form in which false conclusions cannot be derived from true premises (Salmon, 1973, pp. 1–7). Mill's argument is almost valid in this sense. Where it slips up is to assume that if political participation is a cost, and if households are the unit of representation, then it is the head of the household who needs to have the right to vote. Political participation being a cost, it follows that it would be best if as few people as possible bear that cost, but in principle this could be *any* person in the household.

Logical validity is quite a weak requirement, however. Logically valid arguments do not require true premises, merely that the chain of reasoning should not lead from true premises to false conclusions. Logical validity does not prevent false conclusions being derived from false premises. (After all, the following is a valid argument in logic: 'If the moon is made of cheese, it can be eaten. The moon is made of cheese. Therefore it can be eaten.') In this context, the significance of Mill's slip can be seen. The assumption that he really needs to deliver his conclusion is that male heads of households are the best members of the household to represent its members' interests. Yet, laid out in this way, the false premise contained in the argument is pretty easy to spot: generational and gender conflicts mean that male heads of households are not invariably the best, or even good, representatives either for young men or for women. Indeed, it may be that one of the reasons why the principle of inclusion is so widespread these days is that people are now (rightly) sceptical of the thought that one segment of the population can be as strongly committed to the interests of another segment of the population as they are to their own.

One speculative possibility here is that once individualism has entered a political culture, it becomes very difficult intellectually to base the franchise on a narrowly exclusive basis. One striking feature of franchise reform in late nineteenth- and early twentieth-century Britain, for example, is how rapidly it expanded given that for centuries it had been so exclusive. Before the 1867 reform of franchise fewer than one in five men had the vote (Woodward, 1962, p. 182). By 1900 nearly three in five men had the vote. By 1929, following the extension of the vote to women in 1918 and then women under thirty in 1928, some 90 per cent of the adult population over the age of twenty-one had the vote (Butler and Butler, 1994, p. 240). Within two generations, therefore, the right to vote had been extended from less than 10 per cent of the adult population to the vast bulk of adults. Of course, seen from the viewpoint of those agitating for the vote, this would seem a long time, but in the context of the centuries that had gone before, the transition is remarkably quick.

If we were looking for something to account for this shift, then the obvious explanation is the sheer intellectual difficulty of defending any particular point of demarcation between those who should get the vote and those who should not, once individual interests and opinions are taken to be the reference point for representation. This is an intriguing feature of James Mill's argument. It looks an out-of-date argument if the extension of the franchise is taken to be the goal, but what is interesting about the argument is that it assumes that if someone can show a distinct personal interest that would be protected by political inclusion, then that person should be given the right to vote. It suggests that the test of qualification should be merely that one has an interest in the outcome of a political process. In this respect, it lets the individualist cat out of the bag.

Yet, if James Mill's original formulation of the argument seemed too narrow and to lead to a mistaken conclusion, the revision – requiring merely ability to demonstrate an interest – seems too broad. Consider the following example. As a short-term foreign visitor to a country, I may well have an interest in the result of the election. For example, I may be drawing my income from abroad, and know that if one party is elected to government currency fluctuations will move in my favour, whereas if another party is elected the fluctuations will be to my disadvantage. Moreover, if I have a large income, the degree of my interest in the result might be considerable. Despite these conditions, it seems implausible to say that as a foreign visitor I should be given the vote. Yet, that conclusion would be warranted if the sole test for the vote were the fact that someone has an interest affected by the outcome of an election.

Is there any other test, apart from that of possessing an interest, which can be brought in to narrow down the range of inclusion to something that seems to make more intuitive sense? At this point it is useful to consider John Stuart Mill's position on the franchise. The son was in general more radical than the father, but on the franchise the son's position ends up being potentially more restrictive. For John Stuart Mill, acquiring the right to vote depended on a test of both interest and competence, the test of competence taking the form of literacy and mathematical tests (Mill, 1861a, pp. 329–31). Moreover, Mill took the test of competence to imply that there should be more votes given to those who were judged more competent. For example, he favoured giving university graduates more votes than non-graduates, and indeed in the UK some university graduates in effect had two votes, since they could vote both in the constituency in which they resided and for members of parliament representing university constituencies.

We have already touched on some of these issues in discussing the principle of political equality, but it is useful to consider this implication explicitly in the present context. There are many reasons, of course, why the J.S. Mill inference should be resisted. There is the doubt about the extent to which any group (including university graduates) can internalize a strong sense of competing interests. There is the historical experience of societies, for example the southern states of the USA before desegregation, where literacy tests have been misused by ruling groups to exclude challenges to political power (see the cases reported in Tribe, 1988, pp. 1092–4, as well as the examples cited in Caro, 2003). And there is doubt about whether the various dimensions of intelligence actually hang together in predictable ways. We probably all know highly intelligent people who could not be trusted to buy a railway ticket, and people with lots of practical good sense who are not good at algebra. If intelligence is not homogenous, it is difficult to see how we could construct a non-contentious test of political competence.

This is not to say that competence is irrelevant, however. The sole ground for excluding children from the vote has presumably to be the fact that they are thought to lack the competence to make the relevant decisions. This is, of course, a rough–and-ready assumption. There are some bright ten-year-olds who could give their elders a good run for their money in any test of political knowledge. On the other hand, it would not be practicable to discriminate in favour of politically bright children as a general practice, and any injustice that might be thought to be done to the precocious is offset by the fact that the disqualification is only temporary. As Rawls (1999a, p. 196) puts it, such a restriction does not discriminate unfairly among persons or groups, since it falls evenly on everyone in the normal course of life. In this sense it is compatible with the requirements of political equality.

What about the case of those with learning disabilities? It might seem that any test of qualification will exclude at least some people with severe learning difficulties. Yet people with learning difficulties are some of the most vulnerable people in society, and therefore count among those who have an interest to be protected. Moreover, one of the forms of discrimination they typically suffer is an underestimation of their potential. For example, in the first deliberative poll that was ever conducted, a participant who characterized herself as having learning disabilities pretty effectively routed a senior Conservative MP on the question of legislation that was then going through parliament. For these reasons, and given that we are here talking not about a clearly identifiable group, but a spectrum of abilities that is distributed across a population, it seems just as easy not to try to make a categorically separate caste of one group. This may seem anomalous if we make the comparison with children, but it is not. Although those with significant learning disabilities can be regarded as adult children from the point of view of competence, they are distinguished from children in the sense that they cannot be so easily identified. In part, not excluding them formally from political rights stems from this practical circumstance.

With these qualifications in mind, it would seem that we now have the potential to establish a principle in terms of which we could allocate the political rights of citizenship. If we combine the interest test with the qualification test, does that give us a criterion that is meaningful? Here again the case of the temporary resident poses a difficulty. Many temporary residents will be able to pass both a competence and an interest test. Yet, can it really be right that, say, academic visitors spending a few months abroad should be able to vote in elections in the country in which they are temporarily living?

Putting the question in this way might suggest that the real issue is one of temporary versus long-term residence. However, not even this will quite do, for it might imply that citizens ought to be deprived of the vote once they reach a certain age. After all, it could be argued that people above a certain age have no interest in making present sacrifices to some future good of the sort that might be involved in, say, reducing consumption now in order to prevent climate change taking place over a number of decades. Moreover, if everyone above a certain age, say eighty-five, were deprived of the right to vote, such a restriction would pass the Rawlsian test of fairness: it would fall evenly on everyone in the normal course of life.

Such a possibility shows that the granting of the political rights of citizenship is not simply an instrumental device to protect one's interests within a community (though it is certainly that); it also shows it to be a symbolic acknowledgement of civic dignity. To deprive the old of the right to vote would be an assault on dignity for which there is no justification. Moreover, on a more mundane level, quite apart from the fact that long-sightedness does not seem to be uniquely associated with youth, the debarring of the elderly from political citizenship would seem to indicate a defective understanding of the basis on which political rights are awarded.

In particular, what the example shows, I suggest, is that the interests underlying the granting of the right of citizenship must not only presuppose competence and be serious. They must also be tied to a commitment that the person has to the political society in question. Tribe (1988, p. 1084) puts this well in his principle that 'even though anyone in the world might have some interest in any given election's outcome, a community should be empowered to exclude from its elections persons with no real nexus to the community as such'. Such a nexus need not be a subjective one, based on attitude, but one rooted in the circumstances of the lives of individuals. Compare, for example, the temporary visitor and the indefinitely resident guest worker. After a while, the interests of the guest worker become closely bound up with those of the society in which he or she lives. It is not simply that guest workers pay taxes – after all so do short-term visitors – it is also that certain matters of collective concern (the state of public transport, the quality of the housing stock, policies on crime, decisions about economic management, and so on) are also relevant to them. However, even this is to put the case too narrowly. Political rights may be important in enabling a group to express its own interests in relation to matters of collective concern. However, such groups typically develop their own associations and forms of political culture that enable them to make a contribution to the collective culture of the society to which they belong. In so far as debates about the balance of collective interests lead to debates about political ideals, migrant groups are in a position to make a unique contribution to that debate.

If we say the relevant criterion is in terms of a nexus between the individual and the political society of which he or she is a member, we can find the rational kernel of the old property test for the right to vote. In societies in which the most important economic asset is physical property, a clear way of evidencing commitment to one's own polity is the possession of property. Hence, there is some sense in requiring the possession of property as a qualification for the franchise. It betokens a commitment to the political society in which one lives. In a modern economy the primary source of economic value is the skills and talents of workers. The commitment of human capital – one's willingness to work and participate in the collective life of the society – then becomes a way of demonstrating commitment. Once one has worked for some time, that commitment is demonstrated.

One way of stating the underlying principle of this approach is to say that the granting of political rights can be seen to be contingent on already existing practices within a certain society, and in this sense the basis of political inclusion is a sort of consistency test. There is nothing in this theory of political rights that says that rights ought to be granted in an absolute sense. It may well be, for example, that certain societies at certain times are entitled to restrict the free movement of labour, so that outsiders cannot enter and form an economic and social nexus. The development of commitment by outsiders to a society presupposes the free movement of labour, and there is considerable disagreement as to whether there is any general human right to free movement (see Barry and Goodin, 1992). The approach I have outlined merely says that if a society does allow the free movement of labour, such that a number of guest workers have come to live in that society, there must come a point where they are no longer denied political rights. It should also be noted that in making the test one of an objective nexus of interest, I have not supposed any test of cultural compatibility. To say that guest workers and others should culturally identify with the society in which they live seems to overemphasize the cultural homogeneity of any reasonably large society, but also to put up an unjustifiable barrier to citizenship.

What of those who have by one means or another cut their nexus with society? There are a number of ways in which this can occur, for example crime, residence abroad or as victims of social exclusion. On the topic of crime, there are probably as many arguments against depriving prisoners of the right to vote as there are in favour. To be sure, convicted criminals have in some sense voluntarily cut their nexus with society by taking unfair advantage of the compliance of others with the law to their own benefit, and the loss of political rights, along with civil rights, might well seem an appropriate social response. On the other hand, someone could well argue that the responsibility of exercising the vote was an important part of the process of rehabilitation.

The person who emigrates from a society to live abroad seems, after a while, to fall into a different category. It seems unduly harsh to deprive someone of the vote who, say, goes to live abroad for three to four, or perhaps even five, years. On the other hand, it seems unduly generous to extend the same privilege for those who have been out of the community for up to twenty years, as was done with UK legislation passed in 1989 (Blackburn, 1995, pp. 78–80). Indeed, so generous is it that some of a cynical turn of mind might suppose that the motive was party advantage rather than a desire to be fair. Of course, there is no theoretical principle to which appeal can be made in determining the exact cut-off point, but any plausible decision would have to strike a balance between the need to ensure that people were not deprived of a voice where there was some uncertainty about their nexus with the community being restored through return as contrasted with the extension of a right where there was no prospect of return.

That leaves the category of the socially excluded, who may – say because they have no permanent place of residence – find themselves deprived of political rights as well as economic security. Here I am inclined to say that, although in one sense the nexus with the community has been broken, there is another sense in which such persons are even more dependent upon public choices and collective decision making than the run of more fortunate citizens. For this reason, whatever the practical difficulties, it does not seem fair that such people should automatically be deprived of the right to vote.

The general principles of interest, qualification and commitment through a nexus to the community therefore provide a basis for the allocation of the franchise. Of course, the detailed institutional and practical recommendations that follow from these general principles are subject to particular circumstances. There is no general theory that will say that six years as a guest worker should entitle someone to the franchise whereas four years do not. Similarly, there is no way in which the age at which citizens should acquire the right to vote can be determined theoretically. However, despite these limitations, it is possible to say that the principles of political inclusion are not entirely arbitrary.

The problem of partitioning

If we assume that we have principles that enable us to decide who should be entitled to citizenship, we also have to consider what the scope of those citizenship entitlements should be. In particular, we should note that not all citizens in well-functioning democracies have a say in everything that passes in their society that is made a subject of political decision. For example, both local government and federalism are ways of saying that some subset of a people should have more say over particular issues than some other subset. Both presuppose that there are some issues that should be decided by local, not larger, majorities. But how can we decide the proper decision-making powers of these local majorities? Where local identities are very strong for cultural or other reasons, there seems to be a clear *prima facie* case for respecting, as much as possible, the collective preferences of those who live in the locality. However, as a general answer, this seems to me to be insufficient for a number of reasons.

First, although local government may rest upon clearly identifiable and historically given identities, it need not do so, and in many areas of a modern society typically will not do so. Hence we need some principles for the case where clear identities are not given. Secondly, political cooperation among established political units may mean the transfer of powers from one level of government to another level. Clear examples of these trends at work are provided by the way in which the powers of the European Union have grown in the last thirty years. But unless we say that there can be no principled appraisal of these transfers of powers, it seems as though it ought to be possible at least to state a criterion in terms of which the allocation of powers can be appraised.

John Stuart Mill offers one possible principle in his discussion of the basis upon which powers should be assigned to local government:

> after subtracting from the functions performed by most European governments, those which ought not to be undertaken by public authorities at all, there still remains so great and various aggregate of duties, that, if only on the principle of the division of labour, it is

indispensable to share them between central and local authorities. Not only are separate executive officers required for purely local duties (an amount of separation that exists under all governments), but the popular control over those officers can only advantageously be exerted through a separate organ. Their original appointment, the function of watching and checking them, the duty of providing, or the discretion of withholding, the supplies necessary for their operations, should rest, not with the national Parliament or the national executive, but with the people of the locality. (Mill, 1861a, pp. 411–12)

In this passage Mill locates the rationale of local government within his broader democratic principles, and in particular within an account of how the members of a community can best act together to promote their common advantage. How then, on this basis, can we approach the problem of partition?

For Mill the basic test to establish whether functions should be carried on at a higher level than a given locality is whether citizens in other localities can be said to be personally indifferent or not in how the locality treats the matter. His own examples concern law and order, and he argues that it cannot be a matter of personal indifference to the members of a country if one particular locality became a 'nest of robbers or a focus of demoralization, owing to the maladministration of its police' (Mill, 1861a, p. 420).

This test of personal indifference thus asserts that where potential causes of concern are so remote that they do not affect the personal interests of the rest of a political society, then there should be a presumption of the devolution of political power to the locality in which there is a personal interest. It is important here that the test is that of personal interest. The test implicitly relies upon a distinction between what affects the personal interests of citizens and what affects their interests in so far as those interests are constituted by a disinterested concern for the well-being of the community at large.

An example can illustrate how this test might work. Suppose a town has to make a decision whether to build a swimming pool or a theatre. The test of personal indifference says that I am entitled to be part of that decision (and more generally the class of decisions of which this is an instance), provided that the decision is of some personal relevance to me. This need not require that I shall actually use either of the facilities in question, though it will involve changing the options that are available to me in my daily life. Thus, the decision has to affect me personally, either by the new options it presents or by virtue of the increased tax-burden that I might expect to bear. However, I do not get a say in the decision merely because I take an interest in such questions, in the sense that I have an opinion that it is generally good or bad whether people swim regularly or go to the theatre. Thus, neither the distant aesthete, who thinks the theatre an improving experience for people, nor the distant swimming champion, who likes the thought of a swimming pool full of people doing their lengths, is qualified by their interest to have a say in the decision.

Why should this notion of personal interests be so central to the test of right to a say, and political and personal ideals be excluded in the test? One possibility is that the test of personal interest is tied conceptually in one respect at least to the notion of harm. Joel Feinberg (1984, pp. 33–4) has pointed to a sense of harm in which the potential for harm is to be understood as a setback to one's interests, where one's interests are things in which one has a stake. Thus, if I own shares in a company I have a stake in its performance and its fortunes, and my interests are advanced or set back depending upon how well the company does. I do not have a stake in this sense if I merely follow in a disinterested way the fortunes of the company, say out of curiosity or an academic concern with how a particular sector of the economy is doing.

The right to have a say in political decision making follows this logic of stakeholding and of one's own interests being bound up with how well the local community is doing. It can be regarded as a special case of the idea that persons should have a nexus with the political community in which they claim a right of political participation. In this sense it follows the logic of responsibility. When you are responsible for something, you are liable in some way for its performance, and in particular you bear a cost if it goes wrong. Merely having views about an institution, no matter how idealistic or well motivated those views are, is not the same as having an interest in that institution in the sense that you assume liability for its performance. The principle of 'no taxation without representation' clearly follows this logic.

The test of personal indifference might seem to invert the logic of interests in democratic participation in the following way, however. A common assumption in relation to democratic participation is that political agents have to cast their arguments in terms of conduciveness to the public advantage if they are going to call upon the power of the state. From this point of view, absence of personal interest is the test that has to be passed before one can engage in public arguments about the general interest. Thus, we expect our political representatives to exclude themselves from participating in the vote on a certain question if they personally stand to gain or lose by the result. How can we square these practices with the applicability of the personal interests test? Part of the answer concerns the extent to which the decision affects an interest that is *purely* personal. Consider, once again, the decision about the swimming pool versus the theatre. If I am an affected party, I stand to gain or lose by the decision that is taken. However, I stand to gain or lose along with others. The interest is personal in the sense that it has some effect on me personally, but it is not personal in the sense that I am the only person with a stake in the matter. Clearly we should exclude people from decision making who do have a distinctive stake in the matter at hand that may prevent their weighing the claims of others properly, but this does not imply that we should exclude those who share a stake with others. Moreover, the exclusion of those without interests applies only in the test of inclusion. It does not follow that considerations have to be excluded in the discussion and decision on matters of public choice once the relevant constituency has been determined.

It might be thought that the test of personal indifference implies a bias towards the local, in the sense that it suggests that as many matters as possible should be devolved to local level. Such a bias towards the local is a feature of the principle of subsidiarity (Føllesdal, 1998), which can be given a rationale in terms that might seem close to the test of personal interest. John Finnis has expressed this line of reasoning with great clarity:

It [subsidiarity] affirms that the proper function of association is to help the participants in the association to help themselves or, more precisely, to constitute themselves through the individual initiatives of choosing commitments (including commitments to friendship and other forms of association) and of realizing these commitments through personal inventiveness and effort in projects (many of which will, of course, be co-operative in execution and even communal in purpose). And since in large organizations the process of decision-making is more remote from the initiative of most of those many members who will carry out the decision, the same principle requires that larger associations should not assume functions which can be performed efficiently by smaller associations. (Finnis, 1980, pp. 146–7)

In short, since persons constitute themselves through the processes of choice and making commitments, it is wrong for a higher body to usurp the choices that could be made at a lower level. Personal development, and the interests associated with it, imply political organization on as small a scale as possible.

The problem with this argument, however, is that it is possible to endorse the premise without inferring the conclusion. That is to say, it is perfectly possible to hold that personal development is best realized through the free exercise of choice without thereby thinking that political authority is always best lodged at the lowest level possible. The tacit, but crucial, premise in the argument for lodging power at the lowest level is that the threats to the free exercise of choice come exclusively from political sources rather than from, say, private corporate institutions or governments at the lower level. It is certainly true that states, traditionally holding the legitimate monopoly of coercion, are likely to be powerful sources of control. States control armies and large bureaucracies. They have tax-raising powers and they can command land and property. But it is also true that economic corporations can monopolize employment opportunities in specific localities, and they too have considerable resources at their disposal. Moreover, their power can be exercised through routine operating procedures in ways that it can be difficult to detect, so that discrimination in hiring and promotion are not easily identified, let alone controlled.

Similarly, it is perfectly possible for local elites to use the authority of subnational government to achieve their purposes, thus limiting the freedom and dignity of others. Indeed, one of the arguments that James Madison (1787), in *The Federalist Papers*, used for having a strong federal tier of government was the need to avoid the danger from local tyrannous majorities. If we wish to avoid unfairness in the distribution of the costs of political cooperation, then we shall have to have a system which prevents local majorities from tyrannizing over local minorities and one of the ways of doing this is to enlarge the scope of government. Enlargement of scope might also be the way to prevent entrenched rent-seeking groups from dominating the decision-making processes of national policy making.

So far, I have considered the question of partitioning in terms of territorial units. However, one question we can ask is whether the subunits have to be territorial, or whether they can be organized on some other basis. Some theorists argue for the importance of devolving power to functional, and not just territorial, groups. But if there is to be functional partitioning of decision-making responsibility, on what basis should it be assigned? The answer here is surely that the test of personal indifference is also the right one to apply. For example, if a religious group is given control of schooling, then it ought not to make any personal difference to me how they resolve any disagreements they might have within the group about what orthodoxy should be taught. However, the extent of such devolution of decision making is not always uncontentious. For example, Young once argued that there is a case for public recognition and support for the self-organization of oppressed groups, a commitment to take into account group-generated policy proposals and a willingness to grant veto power over issues that affect them directly, for example by giving women veto power over issues to do with reproductive rights (Young, 1989, p. 184). If we ask how such a set of recommendations differs from the sort of practices that are implied by the politics of presence discussed in Chapter 6, then one important difference concerns the assumptions that need to be made about the relationship between group membership and wider citizenship. For Young, there is not a strong argument for transcending group differences in order to achieve the perspective of citizenship. Indeed, in some respects, she presents the perspective of citizenship as a totalizing category that threatens to eliminate difference.

Can we entirely repress the thought, however, that the partitioning of decisions should be located in a conception of the interests of citizens as a whole, as distinct from the interests of groups that might make up a society? It is useful here to consider the case of the consociational democracies, such as the Netherlands, which Young clearly thought offered parallels to her own way of thinking. One of the main features of consociational democracies like the Netherlands in the heyday of pillarization was the extent to which matters of public policy were devolved to associations representing the main social groups. Especially in areas of polity where cultural identity was important, such as education, representatives of Catholics and Protestants were given power and resources to shape policy in accordance with their own sentiments.

Such a devolution of power might seem to provide a glimpse of the sort of arrangements that Young had in mind. However, the example also provides an explanation of why simple devolution needs to be embedded in wider structures of representation. Even with certain matters of policy devolved to representatives of major groups, other important matters of society-wide interest (economic and monetary policy, foreign policy and defence policy) have to be dealt with at the highest collective level. Thus, in the Netherlands, even in the heyday of the politics of accommodation, there were elaborate devices of inclusion, involving balanced cabinets and a balance in the staffing of the public service. Indeed, it is a plausible hypothesis that no consociational arrangement can work without some overarching sense of identity enabling members of society to think as citizens and not merely as members of specific groups. If democratic politics is about the pursuit of common interests, and not simply the mutual adjustment of otherwise contending social forces, then it will not be possible to implement a pure politics of difference.

Extension beyond persons?

Even with these principles, we still have some troubling cases, in particular: what about future generations or the rest of nature? How are such interests to be included? Should we seek to enfranchise nature or future generations in various ways? After all, we can say that both nature and future generations have interests. It would seem logical to protect these interests by finding some way of including them within the processes of political decision making (the link between them being the assumption that short-termism in political democracy damages both). Terence Ball (2006) has pointed to the way in which couching the arguments for nature protection in terms of the interests of future generations and other species draws upon conventional protective accounts of democracy, whilst seeking to rectify the imbalance of political power between nature and humans.

One possibility that has been recently canvassed is that some forms of democracy are more likely to promote ecological interests than others. For example, both Goodin (1996a) and Bronwyn Hayward (1996) favour participatory, discursive forms of democracy on the grounds that these forms of democracy are more likely to be favourable to ecological concerns. Robyn Eckersley (2000) identifies a number of institutional devices of a deliberative democratic kind that would enhance the protection of nature, including mandatory reporting on the state of the environment, the constitutional entrenchment of the precautionary principle and ensuring diverse cultural representation in political decision making so that a wide range of perspectives is heard.

Another, and more radical, possibility discussed by Dobson (1997) is that there could be proxy electorates on behalf of future generations and other species. One obvious objection to this line of argument is to deny that having an interest alone is sufficient to constitute a ground for inclusion. This was in effect what I argued in the case of the right to vote more generally. Those who were incapable and those without a nexus to the community may properly be excluded. Yet, our natural world certainly passes the nexus test. Indeed, it would be difficult to think of a more appropriate candidate for passing that test. So, the claim of nature is not simply that there is an interest to be represented, but also that it is the sort of interest that is normally taken as grounds for inclusion.

If future generations and at least some other species pass the nexus test, this leaves the test of capacity. Here it might seem that there was a knock-down argument against the political inclusion of nature or future generations, since it would seem that neither can communicate their interests to us. However, among proponents of enfranchising nature, this is just the assumption that has been contested. Goodin (1996a, p. 841) for example cites Stone to the effect that it is a lot easier for my lawn to communicate to me that it needs watering than it is for the 'United States' to communicate to the Attorney General that it is in its interests for Al Capone to be prosecuted. Similarly, Dryzek (1996, pp. 20–1) has argued that we should treat signals emanating from the natural world with the same respect that we accord signals emanating from human subjects.

Clearly if these claims could be made good, then nature would have satisfied all the conditions that we have determined for inclusion in the franchise. Obviously there would be practical problems about how to arrange for such representation, but these would be subsidiary to the main point of principle. Can the point of principle be carried, however, and in particular can the assumption about the communicative capacities of nature be made good? The unwatered lawn provides a good test in this context. One reason for being sceptical about the communicative competence of nature is that the signals we receive are likely to be ambiguous. My grass is brown, but the dandelions, which have deeper roots, are flourishing. Is nature telling me to water the lawn or not? Any representatives trying to decode the message are likely to disagree. Nor can we solve the situation by importing some general principle asserting the importance of species flourishing. The conservation of certain species may well involve us inhibiting the colonization by another species of a particular piece of territory.

The point is not to question the claim that we can speak about nature doing well or badly, but rather to insist that any particular judgement is likely to be contested, and that representatives who were doing their job might be expected to disagree as much as anyone else. Moreover, in some ways, talk about giving nature the vote seems to be the wrong way to think about the issues. The sort of proposals that Eckersley advocates are ways of ensuring that in the process of democratic deliberation certain sorts of considerations, and the interests to which they point, are given a role in decision making. That role is, however, necessarily indirect in the sense that it must pass through the minds of citizens. To phrase the interests of nature in terms of enfranchisement, if taken literally, is to offer an institutional solution to what is a moral and cultural problem.

10 International Relations and Democratic Ideals

Democracy, as an ideal, involves the members of a political community participating in the government of that community. This is sometimes described in terms of 'self-government'. In ancient Athens, it took the form of citizens ruling and being ruled in turn. In the modern world, it takes the form of the people choosing those representatives who are to govern and whose tenure in office depends upon electoral accountability. These two conceptions of democracy – the ancient and the modern – differ from one another in many respects, but in both cases it is assumed that we can identify a body of persons, continuing over time and in a particular place, who constitute a people. Article 1 of the United Nations International Covenant on Economic, Social and Cultural Rights of 1966 asserted: 'All peoples have the right to self-determination. By virtue of that right they freely determine their political status and freely pursue their economic, social and cultural development.'

I argued in Chapter 8 that we could not properly understand democracy as a system of popular self-government in any literal sense. To do so would be to take an analogy from a society in which one person or group was sovereign (in the sense that they did not defer to anyone else) whilst another group was subordinate and subject to the will of the first. As Hart (1961, pp. 72–5) pointed out, such a model cannot fit the case of a political system in which virtually all adults participate. The only way we can understand a democratic political system is therefore in terms of a body of secondary rules that define powers of decision making in the public sphere. The notion of popular self-government needs to be demythologized together with the rhetoric of self-determination that goes with it.

How then can we understand in a non-metaphorical way the ideas of popular self-government and self-determination? The key concept in this connection is that of recognition. We can define a political society as consisting of those who recognize one another as entitled to participate in government according to some set of commonly recognized rules. There is in this definition a double process of recognition. The members of a political society have to recognize the rules and they also have to recognize one another under those rules. This does not mean that there cannot be disputes about the rules or that there cannot be questions raised about the admissibility of particular people to membership under the rules. However, there does have to be sufficient general recognition, otherwise we are faced with a situation of political break-up or secession. A political society in this sense is independent of other political societies when the commonly recognized rules define a scope of political decision making for a group of persons who recognize the standing of each other under those rules and where the decisions are sufficiently important for the members of the political society. (The concept of 'sufficient importance' is left at an intuitive level for the purposes of this discussion.)

One implication of this approach is that not all political societies can or need to be regarded as fully independent. For example, provinces in federal systems have their own distinctive secondary rules of decision making, and provincial authorities often decide matters of considerable importance. However, there are other matters of political importance – usually currency matters, foreign affairs and defence – that are decided at a higher level than the province. Since these are important matters, it follows that the province in a federal system is not a fully independent political society according to the definition, which, of course, is what we should expect. Within federations we have a collection of political societies, but they are not fully independent political societies.

I noted in Chapter 9 that the concept of 'the people' was ambiguous between an individualist and a collectivist interpretation. In the individualist sense, the boundaries of the people could be extended by bringing more members of the community into the sphere of political rights. If we consider the concept of a political community as I have defined it, then there is no reason why it need be democratic. All that the concept required was the idea of mutual recognition under a common set of secondary rules. However, such a political society will be democratic if there is a general recognition on the part of the overwhelming bulk of the adult population that the bulk of the adult members of that society are entitled to participate in government to a common and meaningful degree, of which the entitlement to vote is the most tangible expression.

In so far as we can meaningfully talk about popular self-government in a non-metaphorical way, we must have in mind some notion of a body of people making decisions according to a common set of rules in a situation where there is general recognition of the right of the bulk of adult persons to participate. To speak of collective entities like 'a people' having the right to self-determination is, then, an elliptical way of referring to a situation in which individuals typically have rights within a scheme of decision making. However, this internal aspect of popular self-government would have no importance if democracies were not also free of external control. Otherwise, they would be in the situation of provinces within a provincial federation – or perhaps in an even worse situation.

There are of course difficult questions involved in determining what is meant by a people being free of external control. It cannot mean free of external constraint, because that would be impossible, but it is difficult to say what sort of constraints are compatible with a valid claim to a people exercising self-government. Clearly, to take one obvious case in which self-government fails, if a people is subject to imperial rule by a foreign power, then it is not free of external control. However, a people may throw off the shackles of external political rule only to find itself subject to demanding economic or security constraints that limit severely what it can do, as many post-colonial regimes have found during the last fifty years. How tight these constraints can be before we say that popular self-rule is a sham is difficult to say, and different conceptions of collective independence will give different views of this question.

However, problems of international interdependence are not solely problems for former colonial peoples. Indeed, it is now commonplace for analysts to see societies, both democratic and non-democratic, being locked into complex forms of interdependence. There is much discussion as to exactly what this means, what its extent might be and what it involves for those countries whom it affects. For example, some think that international interdependence is so great that it constitutes a global system in which countries are caught up in a set of worldwide relations. Others see interdependence as intensifying relations between countries in specific regions, but not necessarily on a global scale, so that there is less national political control within regions such as Europe or east Asia and interdependence intensifies in these areas. Yet, however interdependence is conceptualized and measured, there is no doubt that countries can affect one another in complex and multiple ways. David Held has put this well when he says that overlapping 'spheres of influence, interference and interest create dilemmas at the centre of democratic thought' (Held, 1998, p. 22).

Democracy, I have argued, is founded on the idea that common interests need to be attended to in circumstances of political equality and fallibility. In conditions in which nations could plausibly be said to constitute a community of fate in the sense that those common interests are sufficiently important, there are established models of democratic organization and institutions, the main ones of which I have been discussing as the three chief variants of representative government. Of course, there are differing views about how well or badly these particular institutional arrangements perform when dealing with problems. No doubt in any particular case common interests will be handled well or badly depending upon circumstance and the competence of the actors involved. Yet, when thinking about institutional arrangements at the national level, there are models of democracy in terms of which we can envisage political authority being exercised.

In a period of international interdependence, how far is it possible to envisage democratic institutions operating at the international level? Many writers have seen the internationalization of political life, and the interdependence that goes with it, as one of the prime challenges to democratic theory. For example, Dahl (1989, pp. 318–19) identifies internationalization as a transition as important as the move from city-state to nation-state. According to Dahl, just as the move from political organization at the city level to organization at the national level reduced the intensity of democratic participation but increased its scope, so the internationalization of political life reduces national democratic control as an increasingly large number of decisions that affect citizens within democracies are made in locations outside the boundaries of those democracies. As Dahl also notes, in so far as this is happening, national governments are becoming local governments, but we have no clear idea of the sort of democratic structures that might be put in their place.

As a way of delineating this problem I suggest that the problem for democratic theory arises from the conjunction of four claims, each of which is plausible in itself, but the combination of which leads to an inconsistency. The four propositions may be stated as follows:

(1) Serious policy problems are increasingly international in scope.
(2) Some form of legitimate international government is needed to deal with these problems.
(3) International government cannot be democratic.
(4) Only democratic government is legitimate government.

The inconsistency can easily be seen. Legitimate international government is needed to deal with an increasing range of problems, but that form of government cannot be legitimate because only democratic government can be legitimate and international government cannot be democratic. The need for effective action is at odds with the requirement that the action also be democratically legitimate. We thus have a quartet of propositions, the conjunction of which leads to an inconsistency.

The contradiction is such that there is no inconsistency should someone deny any *one* of the four propositions. No three of the claims in any combination form an inconsistent triad. Indeed, the conjunction of any three of these claims characteristically defines a political position. Thus, the school of cosmopolitan democrats (for example Held, 1995) deny (3), but assert the other three propositions. In other words, they accept that in general international government is currently insufficiently democratic, but assert that it can be made more democratic by suitable institutional reforms, in order to deal on an international scale with problems of interdependence. Similarly, those in the anti-globalization movement, whilst acknowledging that there are powerful international institutions, assert that more issues can be brought under local democratic control than currently is allowed, and so implicitly deny (2).

Since we obtain a political position by conjoining any three of these claims, and any three claims together asserted as true implicitly deny the fourth, we can examine each of the political positions by examining what they deny. However, before embarking on this examination, one preliminary issue needs to be got out of the way. For some authors, there is a significant theoretical difference between 'government' on the one hand and 'governance' on the other. The term 'governance' is protean in connotation and like many terms in the social sciences has become stretched in its meanings (for a good discussion, see Kjær, 2004). However, one leading usage is to contrast the process of governance as the making of rules and policies with the institutions of government as the organization through which policies are made. Whereas 'government' refers to an institution that is identifiable as the centre of a hierarchy of authority, 'governance' refers to a process of rule-making that takes place in multiple locations through institutions and practices that interpenetrate at different levels of political organization, local, national and international.

If we relied heavily upon this distinction, then we might think that the contradiction implicit in our four propositions was dissolved. Someone might assert that, although the only form of government that could be legitimate was democratic government, international affairs were a matter of *governance* and there was no reason to expect legislative practices of international governance to conform to the same principles of justification as those of domestic *governments*. Governance and government simply referred to different things, and it would be confusing to bring them into the same discussion. Accepting this means that the paradox generated by our four propositions is easily dissolved, is this a way forward?

No one can be prevented from using words in whatever way they choose to define them, and if someone simply stipulates that 'government' and 'governance' are to be used in discrete and different ways, then that is the end of the matter as far as the meaning of terms is concerned. However, there are also substantive political and normative issues at play in the discussion, and it is difficult to see how these can be dealt with by a simple verbal manoeuvre. In fact, in even purely verbal terms, it is difficult to specify a clear distinction between 'government' and 'governance'. The term 'government' can be used to refer to a specific institution in the sense of that body of persons who comprise the government of the day or, more abstractly, as that institutional component of the state that undertakes executive functions. But the word 'government' can also be used to designate the process by which authority is exercised. For example, when Engels (1892, p. 424) wrote that under communism 'the administration of things' would replace 'the government of persons', he was using the term 'government' in the process sense, making it more or less identical with the way in which the term 'governance' has been used in recent discussions.

Moreover, there is no mileage to be gained in contrasting rule-making through centralized and hierarchical processes on the one hand, as the domain of government, with decentralized and multi-level processes on the other hand as the domain of governance. How far decision making at any level of political organization has become decentralized and less hierarchical in the last two or three decades is largely an empirical matter, and the empirical question is not addressed by a verbal distinction between 'government' and 'governance'. Rather what is needed is careful empirical analysis of the ways in which processes of government have adapted to the international challenges that they face. In what follows, then, I shall accept that there is a distinction between the institutions of government and the process of governing, and the latter may usefully be marked by terming it 'governance'. However, making this distinction does not dissolve the contradiction implicit in the four propositions that I have advanced.

Where there is governance, there is a process of authoritative rule-making and the claim that many democratic theorists wish to make is that no form of authoritative rule-making can be legitimate, in serious political matters at least, unless it is democratic. The question still has to be whether we can deny or modify any one of the propositions in order to avoid the contradiction.

Dropping one of the claims?

1. *Policy problems are increasingly international*

I have already suggested that this proposition has its origin in processes of interdependence. However, it might be claimed that the fact of interdependence, in and of itself, was not important. After all, in some respects, all political communities that have not been entirely autarchic have some degree of interdependence with one another, for example in respect of trade or migration. The mere fact of interdependence to some degree is not enough to show that policy problems are international, let alone that they are increasingly international.

The scepticism at this point is well motivated at least in the sense that doubts about the reach of democracy internationally presuppose a contrast between a time when collective self-government in all important issues was a plausible ambition and a time (now) when it is not. The concern about the threat to democracy from internationalization must rest on a presumed contrast between a period when democracy at the national level functioned reasonably well (say, for example, the period between 1945 and 1975 for the developed liberal democracies) and a subsequent period when increasing international interdependence weakened the autonomy of national democratic states. Clearly, there are two ways of challenging this contrast. The first is to show that national autonomy was lower in the period 1945–75 than is commonly assumed; the second is to show that there has not been the growth of interdependence that the argument requires.

The first of these moves in fact asserts a double-barrelled claim: there was less national autonomy and more international interdependence than is commonly assumed in talk of global interdependence *and* recognizing this would make no difference to our appraisal of the extent to which national political systems embodied the principles of democracy. It is possible to hold to this double-barrelled position, but it is difficult to do so without appearing Panglossian. Indeed during the period 1945–75 there were critics of liberal democracies who questioned the authenticity of those systems' democratic credentials by arguing the dependence of their governments on international forces and sources of control. It is of course a complex question as to how far their critique of the dependence of national governments on external forces was correct. But the logic of the position, if not unassailable, is at least plausible: if there was the degree of dependence that they asserted, then it would be difficult to say that government was democratic in the sense that decisions were responsive to popular opinion rather than the needs, say, of international bankers or hegemonic institutions.

In addition to the complex empirical questions in these debates there is also a tricky conceptual issue, namely that of when an external constraint becomes so tight that we can say that there is effectively no freedom of choice or manoeuvre. All choices are made under constraint, and so pointing to the existence of constraints or influences on decision making is insufficient to deny either individual or collective autonomy. Of course, under the constraints some decisions will involve most costs than others. For example, it is commonly assumed that in order to prosper in economic terms domestically it is necessary for countries to participate in international trade on broadly capitalistic terms. Some countries, North Korea and Albania being the most obvious examples, have resisted this policy over a long period of time, and their prosperity has suffered as a result. However, it might still be said that they were exercising their autonomy to have national autarchy at the expense of economic prosperity rather than prosperity at the expense of national autarchy, so that although the decision was constrained, it was also in a meaningful sense free.

Making the right judgement on these matters is not something that can be determined mechanistically, and it is related to the much-discussed question of when formal freedom is so constrained by material circumstances that it ceases to be freedom at all. There is no consensus on this either among political theorists or in the world at large. Except for those who wish to hold to the position that only the formal dimensions of freedom are relevant and that the material consequences of decision are irrelevant to our saying that a decision is free, there is the view that the reasonableness of the constraints is the relevant set of considerations. Unreasonable constraints on choice will render the choice unfree; reasonable constraints may make free choice more difficult but do not destroy its character as free.

Supposing that during the period 1945–75 most national democracies had enough reasonable freedom of manoeuvre for us to say that they had sufficient decision-making autonomy, is it plausible to say that increased international interdependence has weakened that autonomy to a degree sufficient to call into question the scope of domestic democratic control? There is no doubt that varying forms of international interdependence exist. For example, physical interdependence exists through the sharing of an environment that modern production methods have made common. Most of the major contemporary environmental problems – acid rain, ozone depletion, global warming, the transport of hazardous waste and deforestation – are international in character, and some of those that are not, for example urban air pollution, arise as a consequence of the international trade in vehicles. This international dimension means that the action of one national actor has implications for others, and often many others. Then there is economic interdependence. When price signals move around the world almost instantaneously, as happens with modern electronic stock markets, it becomes more difficult for governments to insulate their economies from the effects of large monetary and capital flows, unless they practise an economic autarchy that substantially reduces their country's standard of living. There is also demographic interdependence, since modern methods of transport make it much easier for individuals and households to move internationally, whilst wars and famines can displace large populations across national borders. All these forms of interdependence are, of course, mediated through increasingly global systems of communication and news reporting. The question, however, is not the fact of such interdependencies but their extent and significance.

David Held and his associates have been as assiduous as anybody in collecting and collating the data on this question, and – with all the scholarly caveats that one needs to put in place – their work does show increasing interdependence. They recognize that in the economic sphere increases in international trade and finance since 1945 can in part be interpreted as a return to the classical era of the Gold Standard in the late nineteenth and earlier twentieth centuries, and they are scrupulous in also recognizing previous waves of globalization in the pre-modern, early modern and modern periods. However, they conclude that in the contemporary period, there has been a distinctive form of globalization, marked by a unique clustering of patterns across different spheres, including migration, shared global environmental threats, and innovations in transport and communications (Held *et al.*, 1999, pp. 424–5).

As Held and his colleagues also point out, this distinctive pattern of globalization has occurred at a time when the nation-state has become the near-universal model of political organization. They suggest that this is a paradox. But is it? It does not follow from the fact that policy problems are increasingly international that some form of international government is necessary to deal with these problems. Perhaps they can be dealt with in another way, through the instruments available to nation-states and other forms of government. This possibility involves denying the second proposition.

2. *Legitimate international government is needed to deal with problems of international interdependence*

It might seem obvious that if there are policy problems that are generated from international sources, then some form of international governmental action is necessary to deal with those problems. However, it is possible to argue that this inference moves too quickly, and for some people international government is not part of the solution but part of the problem. How might this arise?

The obvious line of argument for someone who wished to argue this case would be to insist that the problems that need to be addressed are as much a consequence of big government as something that requires big government for its solution. In other words, the proponent of this position does not need to deny that there are problems on an international scale, but simply needs to assert that the right way to deal with these problems is by decentralization and creating smaller and more localized communities. This seems to me to be the position of certain strands of thinking within the green and anti-globalization movements. For example, in their critique of the Euro Lucas and Woodin (2000) accept that globalization is occurring, but stress its adverse effects in the form of growing inequalities, environmental damage, poverty in developing countries and the threat to democracy. The solution is not to advocate stronger forms of international organization, but to press for stronger and more diverse local economies, a shift of control from the boardroom to the community and a scaling down of economic activity. From this perspective, state actors are liable to overemphasize the problems that require international cooperation and design solutions that serve their own interests or the interests of elites rather than of general citizens.

It is, I think, possible to argue for this position, in the sense that there is strictly speaking no inconsistency involved, but it seems to me to be implausible. This is not to deny that sometimes governments do have an interest in talking up the scale of problems to give themselves some freedom of manoeuvre from their domestic constituents. However, one can argue that there is much more evidence for the contrary point of view. Governments may well have a strong interest in denying the international implications of their domestic policies. For example, the UK for a long time denied the problem of acid rain in Scandinavia (Weale, 1992, ch. 3), because to acknowledge the problem would have led to the need to change pollution control policy in a costly way. Even small communities can cause spillover problems for others if they are sufficiently numerous and their effects are aggregated.

3. *International government cannot be democratic*

The claim that international government cannot be democratic is hotly contested by cosmopolitan democrats. Cosmopolitan democracy is a school of thought rather than a single view, but for the purposes of the present argument, I shall treat it both as an ethical position and as an organizational prescription, the link between the two being an assertion about the need to deal with problems of interdependence.

Proponents of cosmopolitan democracy advance the claim that democratic values should apply at an international level, and not simply at the level of the nation-state. In the previous chapter, I noted how the movement within political systems had been one of inclusion in the sense that an increasing proportion of the adult population of a country gains political rights. This logic of inclusion is based upon the principle of political equality understood as the principle that all individuals are entitled to have their interests considered politically on a par with other individuals. The cosmopolitan turn extends this thought across national boundaries. Since, in an interdependent world, the choices that are made in one part of the globe will have effects in other parts of the globe, perhaps other very distant parts of the globe, there is no reason to preclude participation in those decisions by those who are affected.

It could be argued that the international state system does succeed in this inclusion, since states have formal equality in that system and conventional principles of international law would protect their territorial integrity. However, it is at this point that the radical edge of cosmopolitan democracy emerges, since the unit of inclusion is made the individual rather than the state to which that individual belongs. Cosmopolitan morality is universalist in this sense: if anyone is entitled to certain fundamental political rights, such as the right of participation, then all adults are entitled, at least in respect of decisions that affect their lives. On this basis, participation through the state system would not be adequate, since it would not recognize the equal rights of all given that states are unequal in power and influence. In other words, the cosmopolitan infers from an ethical claim about the equal importance of interests, wherever the bearer of those interests is located in the world, to a principle of political organization.

A clear statement of the fundamental political proposition involved here is given by Archibugi and Held:

> The term *cosmopolitan* is used to indicate a model of political organization in which citizens, wherever they are located in the world, have a voice, input and political representation in international affairs, in parallel with and independently of their own governments. (Archibugi and Held, 1995, p. 13)

The principal rationale for this position stems from the assumption that the citizens of national democracies no longer constitute a community of fate. Instead, we should think of the citizens of different democracies as being locked into a series of overlapping communities of fate.

It is, of course, not valid to infer simply from the existence of overlapping communities of fate that there should be a form of political organization in which citizens should have direct representation and voice independently of their governments. At present transnational problems are dealt with by a series of international regimes, of which governments are members. This is not to say that the way in which these problems are handled is adequate, but any qualification about adequacy is needed to be able to infer from international problems to the direct representation of individuals. So the crucial move in this form of cosmopolitanism is to reject international regimes as being adequate responses to transnational problems, on the grounds that such international agreements are not subject to norms of democratic accountability. According to this argument, if there is a case for representative democracy at the national level, there is just as strong a case for representative democracy at the international level, where individuals, and not simply governments, are the units of representation.

The force of this position can be seen if we consider what some of its leading proponents think are its institutional implications. Archibugi (1995), for example, endorses proposals along the lines originally put forward by the International Network for a UN Second Assembly. These proposals envisage an Assembly of Peoples, which would be constituted by directly elected representatives from each of the member states. This body would supplement rather than replace the General

Assembly made up of the representatives of governments. One advantage of the Assembly of Peoples, according to Archibugi, is that it would provide some means of providing democratic voice to those peoples whose governments were autocratic. The new Assembly would be elected on the basis of seats being proportional to population, so that the largest countries would have more representatives, but no country, not even the smallest, would be without one representative. If the new Assembly were an exclusively consultative body, as the European Parliament was up to 1979, it could be brought into existence by resolution of the existing General Assembly.

There are many other detailed institutional implications that cosmopolitan democrats have drawn from their general approach. However, without going into these details, it is pretty clear what the overall thrust of the position is. All nation-states face the challenge that the problems they seek to confront now often have sources beyond their borders, which the reach of their power cannot touch. Existing international organizations that have some capacity to deal with these problems are insufficiently democratic. Therefore the principles of representative democracy that have hitherto been applied at the national level now need to be applied at the international level. Just as democracy had to make the transition from the city-state to the nation-state, so it must now make the transition to the international global order.

However, we cannot assume that norms taken from democratic institutions at the national level can be transposed to the international level without there being some significant change in their mode of operation and effect. In particular, there are institutional and cultural preconditions for democracy at the national level that are not replicated at the international level. The pattern of historical development for most major stable democracies is one in which nation-building – in the form of territorial consolidation, administrative centralization and cultural homogenization – took place before democracy developed (Flora, Kuhnle and Urwin, 1999). Practices of party competition depend upon these consolidations having taken place. For example, although political parties compete with one another, they do so within a common political culture defining what issues are relevant to public debate, what processes are appropriate in dealing with those issues and what interests and opinions are to be represented. Of course, the boundaries of these understandings change over time, and at any one time may be contested in various ways, but the change is nonetheless embedded in historically given institutions and political cultures. Citizens in established democracies know which newspapers to write to when they are angry about some measure of policy, what to expect of their representatives and what other groups are likely to be sympathetic or unsympathetic to their cause.

These problems are distinct from the problems of scale that an international democratic order would raise. Dahl has argued that there is a problem of scale in democracy, suggesting that the scale is simply too large at the international level to make democracy feasible. Just what the relationship is among scale, a sense of political efficacy on the part of citizens and the functioning of democracy is difficult to say empirically. Dahl's own work with Tufte (Dahl and Tufte, 1972) did not present an entirely unambiguous set of conclusions on this matter, suggesting that there were some respects in which the smaller democracies of Europe worked better than the larger democracies, but without making out a clear-cut case that small is democratically beautiful.

There is, however, one aspect of cosmopolitan proposals that raises an interesting question of political principle and that suggests an unresolved theoretical puzzle pointing in an opposite direction to the one in which cosmopolitans themselves would wish to go. This concerns the dual representation of both governments and citizens as individuals in democratically reformed international organizations. For example, in the proposal for the second UN Assembly, cosmopolitan theorists accept that governments should be represented as well as individuals. Thus, Archibugi takes it for granted that states with a population of fewer than one million will gain a full representative, thus presumably acknowledging some collective entity – the peoples of such states – alongside the individual citizens of such states. Moreover, in both the proposals for the UN and the acceptance of the political institutions of the EU, there is no challenge to the rights of governments to be represented as the prime units in the decision-making process. The claim is simply that they should not be regarded as the sole representatives of their peoples. Yet, the status of this collective representation remains under-theorized by cosmopolitan democrats. To be sure, we can easily understand why it may be necessary from the point of view of *Realpolitik* or perhaps even from the point of view of international law. But why is the representation of states justified? Unless we can provide an account of why collective representation is justified, we have a lacuna in the theory.

One answer to this question picks up on a feature of representation that I identified in Chapter 6. The representation of states is necessary in international decision making because creating the sort of international agreements that are necessary to solve international problems requires a degree of mutual assurance among decision makers that can only be given when credible commitments can be made by those who are party to the agreements. Consider, as an example, a typical pollution control agreement. When there is an agreement to reduce pollution in the global commons of the oceans or the atmosphere, it is usually necessary for political representatives to make a promise that their domestic sources will reduce pollution. The joint commitment of a number of such representatives is normally necessary for such an agreement, because in the absence of such a commitment no one has an incentive to sign. The logic here is one of an assurance game, in which the willingness of others to commit themselves to an agreement increases the incentive for any one party to commit itself to the agreement.

Assurance, however, requires the commitment to be credible. It is not enough for parties to an agreement to say that they are going to implement pollution reductions. There must also be ways in which that commitment can be relied upon. Because of their distinctive authoritative powers, states are in the best position to be able to give make such commitments credible. This is not to say that whenever states commit themselves they always do what they say (or indeed mean what they say). It is to say, however, that it is rare for other institutions to be able to make commitments of the scale and kind that are necessary to secure worthwhile international agreements, and where this has occurred – for example as with the major international companies manufacturing ozone-depleting substances – it still required states also to be committed to the measures.

If this is a sound rationale for the representation of states in international organizations, it does not invalidate the argument for the representation of individuals, but it does call into question its relevance. If we add to this concern the difficulty of imagining how the usual practices of party competition would work in a meaningful way across national borders, then it is difficult to see how international organizations can be democratized in the way that proponents of cosmopolitan democracy suppose. There is no easy way out of the thought that international organizations cannot be democratic.

4. *Only democratic government is legitimate government*

It might seem obvious from the point of view of democratic theory that any form of government needs to be democratic, even if one can allow differences of view as to what varieties of institutional forms fit the relevant description. If there is a justification for the claim that the best form of government is democratic, does it not follow directly that international government should also be democratic? In fact, the answer to this question is far from obvious.

It does not follow from the claim that governments need to be democratic as a warrant for their political authority that all forms in which they exercise their political authority should take a democratic form. When anyone acts under delegated powers, for the exercise of which that person is accountable, there is no presumption that the form in which they exercise those delegated powers should conform to the way in which they account for the exercise of those powers. Suppose, for example, that a popular referendum is a constitutional requirement in a country when a major international treaty is signed. The government involved in the negotiation of that treaty will need to explain its content and rationale and should abide by the results of the referendum. However, it does not follow that the actions of the government negotiating the treaty have to be conducted by means of a series of referendums or even involve any public consultation during the course of the negotiations. The exercise of the powers may, indeed typically will, take a different form from the way in which that exercise is accounted for.

Some writers wish to go a stage further than this claim, however, and say that in international negotiations problems of democratic accountability do not arise because legitimacy need not be secured through the input of public opinion but only through the outputs of the effective delivery of goods and benefits. Scharpf (1999) in effect argues this case in respect of the EU. What matters to legitimacy, it may be argued from this perspective, is not that decisions are made with regard to some form of democratic accountability, even of the purely retrospective kind, but rather that benefits are secured through international action that could not otherwise be secured. For example, what will legitimate international action on the environment in democratic terms is that the citizens of various countries will be better off than they otherwise would have been without the action. It does not matter that they did not contribute to the formulation of the policy or have no say over it once it has been agreed. So long as the goods are delivered, legitimacy will be secured.

This move in effect denies the relevance of the protective argument for democratic institutions once we move from the domestic to the international level. However, the circumstances of politics that gave rise to the protective argument domestically also apply internationally.

That is to say, the diversity of interests and viewpoints that are necessarily involved in the making of any political decision mean that it will be important for people to be able to protect their interests. Indeed, it can be argued that the protective argument is even stronger in the case of international agreements than in domestic politics because the logic of such agreements creates a high degree of discretion for those involved in international negotiations. This is, in effect, the burden of Robert Putnam's account of two-level games in international negotiations (Putnam, 1988). On this view, international negotiators have two sets of actors to whose preferences they need to relate: the negotiating partners at the international level and their domestic constituents at the national level. This fact is important because it is the requirement *simultaneously* to satisfy the preferences of both sets of actors that is crucial to understanding the logic of international negotiation. Yet, this two-level feature can also account for the way in which negotiators, ostensibly acting as representatives of their domestic constituents, can secure increased independence of those constituents' interests.

To illustrate this possibility, consider a stylized international trade negotiation. Such negotiations typically involve the need for countries to grant economic concessions to one another in the form of opening markets, reducing tariffs, readjusting currency exchange rates or granting property rights. Citing international pressures to achieve an agreement that is beneficial all round, negotiators gain power relative to their domestic constituents by making the international agreement the occasion to rebalance interests using the argument that concessions are the necessary price of the agreement, for example in opening up a particular sector of commerce to international competition. In this way, the pattern of domestic interests is rebalanced under pressure from the international level. Conversely, and in parallel, negotiators gain bargaining advantages at the international level by stressing to their peers the extent to which their negotiating freedom is limited by the demands of their domestic constituents. This dual independence derives directly from the logic of two-level games.

It may of course be, on any one occasion, that the rebalancing of interests is justified by the broader public purpose that it serves. Yet, in terms of familiar protective considerations, there are arguments for making those involved in international negotiations accountable, at least in the sense that they should be able to offer an account *ex post* that provides some justification of the balance struck between competing demands, and of course the anticipation of having to give such a justification is itself a reason to constrain the way in which different interests may be played off against one another in the negotiation. In short, output effectiveness is not a substitute for some degree of input control. Such accountability does not require a wildly optimistic account of representation, but would be consistent with a form of Burkean Whig account of representation of the sort favoured by Schumpeter.

Another reason for denying the relevance of democratizing international organizations rests on the view that the issues involved in international negotiation are technical and therefore not of the sort that requires political accountability. This is one of the claims made by Moravcsik (2003) in his criticism of those who accuse the European Union of having a democratic deficit. Moravcsik argues that many of the issues dealt with in the EU typically concern technical matters such as product standards, which are matters of administrative regulation rather than the substance of democratic debate. If this is so in the EU, which of all international organizations is one of the deepest and more extensive regulation of member states, the same should hold *ex hypothesi* of other international organizations.

The problem of democratic accountability is not so easily dispensed with, however. Although a great number of decisions made in the EU are essentially matters of technical standards, not all of them are. More importantly, even technical matters can turn out to have broader, sometimes unforeseeable, political implications. Thus, the BSE crisis in the UK in the 1990s helped politicize the processes by which food safety standards were determined. More generally, it is a commonplace of risk regulation that the setting of acceptable risk standards is not simply a numerical exercise involving the calculation of relative frequencies, but it also requires attention to public values and public perceptions. Thus, the boundary between the technical and the political is not only shifting but is itself subject to contestation.

I conclude from the consideration of this proposition and the three others that none can plausibly be denied. Thus, the conflict between the demands of effective government at the international level and the demands for democratically legitimate government at that level are, in some deep sense, in conflict with one another. What then can be done?

Democratic values and international concerns

It might seem from the foregoing discussion that there is simply a contradiction involved in the need to combine effectiveness with democratic legitimacy and, if so, there is no sensible way forward. However, instead of thinking of the issue in terms of propositional contradictions, we can think about it as a practical dilemma. It is usually the case in the design of policies, practices and institutions that desiderata compete with one another. Tax systems that are simple will not be equitable; voting schemes that allow a wide diversity of political representation may not produce stable governments; schemes of social insurance that are highly redistributive may deter work effort; and so on. Looked at as a practical matter, the task of institutional evaluation or design is to combine the desiderata in a way that is feasible.

In thinking about the competing desiderata of democratic design, we should start not with institutions but with values. At the beginnings of representative democracy at the national level in the late nineteenth and early twentieth centuries, it was not possible to predict the institutional forms that mass democracy could and would take. This did not make democratic values less relevant. Rather it meant that their implications were difficult to identify and predict. One way forward then is to consider democratic values and their applicability to the international level of political organization. Whatever institutional implications such values may have or may be developed over time, it ought at least to be possible to identify the extent to which a value may be relevant or needs to be conceptualized in a new way once we move to the international level.

In a brief but important discussion in *The Law of Peoples* (Rawls, 1999b, pp. 23–30), Rawls argues that a normative theory of the international order should be constructed on the basis not of relationships among states but relationships among peoples. He suggested that one difficulty with making states the focus was that it allowed too much influence from realist ideas of international relations and, in particular, sanctioned the use of war as an instrument of policy. By contrast, he asserted, construing the relationship as one among peoples would not have these effects.

One difficulty with this suggestion is that it seems to suppose that peoples have a natural existence independently of the states of which they are a part, whereas there are good reasons for saying that no political peoples are natural or primordial (Smith, 2003, p. 32). Indeed, Rogers Smith goes on to argue that presuming the existence of peoples has the unfortunate consequence of facilitating support for divisive or exclusionary policies in matters of migration or ethnic identification (Smith, 2003, p. 140). Even if this were not true, however, it can still be argued that a focus on peoples to the exclusion of states was a mistake in an interdependent world. International relations depend upon there being agents who can enter into relationships with one another in a credible fashion. International relations are typically built upon inter-state relations because those are the only agents that have credibility for many of the serious global problems that countries face. Hence, there is an unavoidability about international relations depending upon interstate relations.

From the point of view of democratic principles, the task is not then to transcend or surpass interstate relations, but rather to ensure that when states negotiate with one another they faithfully represent the interests and the values of those in whose name they are acting. In part, this is to underline the importance of the principle of political accountability in relation to domestic constituents that I discussed in the previous section. The idea there was that improved political account-ability was necessary in, say, international agreements because of the logic of two-level games that would otherwise operate. However, it can also be argued that the democratic concern with international action implies more general obligations on states as the representa-tives of peoples who live according to democratic norms and values. This is not to replace the focus on states with a focus on peoples, but rather to draw out the implication of the fact that in their international dealings states are acting in a representative capacity.

Consider, then, the concern with the value of common interests. I have suggested that one fundamental element in the justification of democracy is a concern to protect and promote common interests. Public goods and the allocation of primary goods require a legislative capacity and we should not assume that their provision can be left to the sum of individual interactions and transactions that take place within civil society. There is a necessity for collective deliberation and deci-sion. This logic is one that applies to individuals and provides the ration-ale for there being a political authority with the capacity to advance the common interests of citizens. The same logic, however, applies to the relationship between states. States need to do more than simply interact with one another in pursuit of their own interests (though they do need to be prepared to defend their own legitimate interests if need be). But simply to stand in an interactive relationship with one another leaves states with no capacity to decide collectively on the circumstances and outcomes of their interactions. Under those conditions, we should expect there to be an under-supply of international public goods and a misallocation of the equivalent of primary goods for individuals.

This is not simply a matter of transcending the Hobbesian state of nature that is often said to characterize the international state system.

It is common in the literature on international relations to characterize the interaction of states without a common power in Hobbesian terms, in which there is a continual struggle for mastery and control by each state over others. There is, however, a different tradition going back to Grotius, which up to the end of the nineteenth century was the dominant one, and by which states in the international system owed duties of non-interference with one another. According to this tradition, states in the international system were to be treated as equals and should respect one another's territorial integrity as well as abide by the terms of treaties freely entered into. Sidgwick (1891, p. 230) offered the interesting suggestion that this account of the relationship among states in the international system was the equivalent of the account of the individualist minimum among individuals in society. That is to say, just as according to a libertarian account of society individuals owed one another duties of non-interference but not positive duties of mutual aid, so states should not be aggressive towards one another but had no duties to act for the benefit of others.

However, under even these conditions (benign by comparison with the Hobbesian picture), there would still be a need to deal with the collective international problems that arose as a result of the interaction of states. In other words, the common collective interest of states, as representatives of their peoples, would require the establishment of the equivalent of a legislative capacity at the individual level. By this logic, the development of regimes to ensure the supply of international public goods, such as environmental protection or the determination of the principles of international trade, is equivalent to the establishment of a legislative capacity at the domestic level. Just as in order to be able to overcome the deficiencies of the minimal state at the domestic level there is a need to construct institutions of common action, so the need to deal with international problems produces a need to go beyond the Grotian norms and the institutions they imply. This is not to say that the development of international regimes can be explained by the need to fulfil a role in an international system. Rather it is to say that, if we are looking for a rationale for international regimes, we should see them as playing a role analogous to the role of deliberated legislation in domestic societies. It follows from this that regime effectiveness is an important democratic value, since in the absence of regimes' being effective they cannot play the role of providing the conditions within which common interests can be served.

What would it mean to go beyond the Grotian norms? If we take the analogy between the Grotian norms and the individualistic minimum seriously, then it would mean adopting principles of international behaviour that involved a positive commitment to international co-operation and not simply an instrumental attitude that saw international action as a convenient way to advance national self-interest. This would involve active support for multilateral institutions constructed to deal with international and global problems, a willingness to volunteer to play one's collective part in fair schemes of international cooperation, and a disposition to share burdens where this was necessary to solve common problems. These would be collective responsibilities that a democratic community could take on as a community.

By a parallel line of argument, deliberative accountability is import-ant in international regimes, since in circumstances of general falli-bility the decision premises of policy choices within regimes are likely to be faulty. Of course, the fact that international agreements involve conflicts of interest as well as convergence of interests among nations means that there is a built-in incentive in negotiations for controver-sial proposals to be challenged. However, the implications of fallibil-ity for the practice of regimes goes beyond the fact that states have reasons to challenge one another's evidence and arguments. Regimes need to be constructed in such a way that there is clarity in the evi-dence upon which decisions are made, including clarity about lack of evidence. When a regime is working well, it ought to be possible for individual citizens in different countries to follow the progress of regime policies and to see how the policies chosen can be justified by reference to the evidence and principles upon which the regime is working.

I do not suppose that these principles of action provide a blueprint for the construction of democratically justifiable institutions at the international level. However, they are supposed to express what might be termed the virtue of democratic solidarity. This is not a form of unilateral altruism. Rather it requires an attempt at the inter-national level to provide a commitment to cooperation in the collective interest. Cooperation, given the circumstances of human societies, cannot be had without conflict. That is why we need the institutions of democracy to provide the good of the peaceful reconciliation of disputes. Who can deny that we need the functional equivalent at the international level?

Epilogue: The Democratic Reform of Democracy

The institutions of democracy have now become objects of policy choice. Japan and New Zealand changed their electoral systems in the 1990s. Countries in Europe have increasingly turned to referendums as ways of resolving problems, not least about the future pace and direction of European integration. In the US the close result of the presidential election in 2000 and the poor quality of electoral administration that it revealed has led to a search for improvements in practice. Political parties in many democracies have adopted procedures to make their candidate selection processes more open and representative in a statistical sense. High rates of international migration are raising questions about the conditions of membership in democratic societies and the requirements that ought to be imposed on individuals if they are to be permitted the rights of citizenship.

Within the UK the scale of constitutional change has been unprecedented in terms of its own history for the last two hundred years (King, 2001). Devolution has broken up one of the most politically centralized systems of authority in Europe. It has been accompanied by electoral reform at the level of the devolved institutions. The Human Rights Act has domesticated the European Convention on Human Rights, thus affording citizens more constitutional protection than they previously had. The Monetary Policy Committee of the Bank of England has been given operational responsibility for interest rate policy. Referendums have become a recognized, if not regular, feature of decision making. Systems of public consultation on matters to do with health and the environment in particular have become more open and innovative. House of Lords reform has been initiated if not completed.

It would, of course, be foolish to suppose that there have not been previous examples of the reform of political institutions. The Allied powers imposed liberal democratic constitutions on Germany and Japan. Decolonization in the mid-twentieth century produced an out-pouring of institutional and constitutional design, much of it based upon false premises. The British government required STV with multi-member constituencies on Irish independence as a way of protecting the Protestant minority (Hart, 1992). De Gaulle created the institutions of the Fifth French Republic as a reaction to the failures of the Fourth. The European Union, as it is now known, was created as a new form of political community in 1957.

Yet, despite these precedents, there is a sense in which the contem-porary situation provides novel and distinctive challenges. Unlike previous attempts to establish democratic institutions, we now have many more models of functioning democracies to consider. Until 1989, it was impossible to find more than some twenty-five countries that had long-standing democratic stability, and many of those were relatively small countries concentrated in northern and western Europe, or were former UK dominion countries. With the growth of democra-tization, we now not only have more countries to consider, but we also have a greater range of experience judged in cultural, economic and social terms.

Secondly, all political systems are confronted by a changing con-stellation of issue characteristics. As Gellner (1983, pp. 129–30) once noted, it is a striking feature of nationalism that it developed contrary to the predictions of both Marxism and liberalism, both of which fore-cast the withering away of national concerns. In the mid-twentieth century, national systems of government came to acquire responsibility for an unprecedentedly large number of policy concerns. Many of them effectively nationalized the policy sectors previously associated with local government, including environmental protection, health care and financial support; science and higher education acquired national significance, all this on top of new responsibilities to manage the economy. Whatever the causes of this nationalization, it is now clear that some issues, like many aspects of the environment, have now gone to the international level and local and regional governments are increasingly asserting their powers in economic development.

Thirdly, although there is still a struggle between left and right, it can no longer be identified in a straightforward way with the struggle between capital and labour. New forms of economic inequality have arisen, sometimes associated with changing family structures and sometimes with localized patterns of economic change. Concerns about the recognition of identities have proliferated. And political parties are finding it increasingly difficult to rely upon their traditional social bases of support.

However, there is one important feature of the current situation to which I would wish to draw attention: the choice of democratic institutions is now itself a democratic choice. The previous instances of institutional design – decolonization, the aftermath of war or domestic constitutional redesign – were elite projects. Citizens may have been given a role in their approval, as happened in the referendums on the Fifth Republic in France, but nobody supposes that these were more than the means of securing legitimacy for what has been decided elsewhere.

In a situation of the democratic choice of democratic institutions, it is tempting for democratic theorists to want to act as advisers and counsellors to their fellow citizens – and perhaps sometimes, in their wilder imaginations, the world at large. However, I do not think that the task of political theorists is to advocate specific institutional designs. They are, I think, better employed in seeking to identify the values that might be involved in choices that are made.

I have my own judgements of course, and they reflect the arguments pursued in this book. In my opinion, the ideal to which these arguments lead is what I have termed a representational system of government, in which there is inclusiveness of citizenship, broad representation of interests and opinions and acceptance of majoritarian (in the true sense of the term) devices to break deadlocks of disagreement. At a local level and through non-governmental organizations, active citizens in such a system would not only play their fair part in a scheme of political cooperation that was necessary to maintain the system in being, but would also themselves hold civic office and contribute to the common life. At a national level they would also scrutinize the acts and decisions of their representatives with a critical rationality to ensure that what was being done in their name was justifiable in the court of public opinion, both in their own country and abroad. They would seek occasions to express democratic solidarity with citizens in other countries.

I think this not so very far from the conception of democracy advanced by John Stuart Mill, but without the fancy franchise and the metaphysics about national character. If we couch this conclusion in terms of the comparative political science analysis that I have taken as the closest real-world embodiment of these normative principles, then the practices of some of the continental European democracies approximate most closely to this conception of political life. If I have these views, why do I not think that they form the basis for a set of practical recommendations of prescriptions?

In the first place, the models that I have laid out are static and deliberately oversimplified, even if we allow that some approximation to their principles is exemplified in some of the working democracies. The models are presented to clarify thought and meet the test of feasibility rather than inform a political programme. Although in distinguishing between representational government and Westminster systems I sought to draw upon a literature in comparative politics that has identified two powerfully discriminating variables (electoral laws and executive dominance on legislative committees) that divided countries into statistical clusters, the classification involved was nevertheless one which left many important features of political institutions out of account.

Secondly, to lay out an ideal, even one that is more fully described than the models that I have presented here, is not to furnish a guide to its implementation. Social and political systems are enormously complex, with inter-relations that are often difficult to fathom and replete with possibilities for unintended effects from human action. The history of the twentieth century is littered with intellectual projects whose implementation has caused countless misery to millions of people. Suitable modesty about our lack of understanding of the laws of the evolution of society, if there are any, should incline us to Popper's (1945a, pp. 158 9) 'piecemeal social engineering' rather than any more ambitious forms of politics. Even Rousseau saw that political ideals did not translate simply and directly into political prescriptions. His constitution for Poland is a representative scheme that has none of the elemental simplicity of the social contract.

Although I do not think it is possible to derive detailed institutional prescriptions from political theory, it is possible, in my opinion, to say something about how an understanding of political values facilitates a democratic dialogue on democracy. For example, it is, I think, a merit of the view of democracy presented here that it does not link democratic values to a strong, pre-political notion of identity. To speak of common interests is not to assume that there is one, and only one, way of politically segmenting humanity. Democratic institutions are primarily means with which we deal with our common problems. As the scale and character of those problems changes, so we should expect our conception of democracy to adjust. We cannot simply transpose our understanding of democracy from one level of political association to another. Even if the best form of democratic polity at

the level of the nation-state is the system of representational government, it does not follow that a democratic system of internationalized
governance should simply seek to replicate the institutions of the
nation-state. Our major common interests with others may now be
more highly segmented among the different layers of the complex
system of multi-level governance in which many now live.

Similarly, to my mind, it is a merit of an instrumental justification
for democracy that it does not link democratic values to particular
cultural traditions. Sir Ernest Barker was being over-optimistic when
he asserted that democracy was to be found in all forms of society in
which there was not the alien imposition of a cult of leadership.
The flight from responsibility is a common enough human response
to many situations, and trust in leaders then becomes all too easy.
However, in many societies in many different places at many different
times, the practices associated with the collective discussion and resolution of common problems have been adopted and have proved
successful. In this sense, there is nothing culturally specific about
democracy. To practise the ancient art of collective government under
conditions of equality and a recognition of fallibility is a challenge
for all societies.

References

Ackerman, B. A. (1980) *Social Justice in the Liberal State* (New Haven and London: Yale University Press).

Ackerman, B. (1991) *We the People 1. Foundations* (Cambridge, Mass.: Belknap Press of Harvard University Press).

Ackerman, B. (1998) *We the People 2. Transformations* (Cambridge, Mass.: Belknap Press of Harvard University Press).

Amy, D. (1987) *The Politics of Environmental Mediation* (New York: Columbia University Press).

Archibugi, Daniele (1995) 'From the United Nations to Cosmopolitan Democracy' in Daniele Archibugi and David Held (eds), *Cosmopolitan Democracy. An Agenda for a New World Order* (Cambridge: Polity Press), pp. 121–62.

Archibugi, Daniele and Held, David (1995) 'Editors' Introduction' in Daniele Archibugi and David Held (eds), *Cosmopolitan Democracy* (Cambridge: Polity Press), pp. 1–16.

Arendt, H. (1958) *The Human Condition* (Chicago: University of Chicago Press).

Aristotle, *The Nicomachean Ethics*, trans. H. Rackham (Cambridge, Mass. and London: Harvard University Press).

Aristotle, *The Politics*, trans. H. Rackham (Cambridge, Mass. and London: Harvard University Press).

Arrow, K. J. (1963) *Social Choice and Individual Values*, 2nd edn (New Haven: Yale University Press).

Atiyah, P. S. (1979) *The Rise and Fall of Freedom of Contract* (Oxford: Clarendon Press).

Austin, John (1832) *The Province of Jurisprudence Determine*, ed. Wilfred E. Rumble (Cambridge: Cambridge University Press).

Ayer, A. J. (1968) *The Origins of Pragmatism. Studies in the Philosophy of Charles Sanders Peirce and William James* (London and Basingstoke: Macmillan).

Bagehot, W. (1867) *The English Constitution*, ed. with introduction R. H. S. Crossman (London: Fontana/Collins, 1963).

Ball, T. (2006) 'Democracy', in A. Dobson and R. Eckersley (eds), *Political Theory and the Ecological Challenge* (Cambridge: Cambridge University Press), pp. 131–47.

Bambrough, R. (1956) 'Plato's Political Analogies', in P. Laslett (ed.), *Philosophy, Politics and Society* (Oxford: Basil Blackwell), pp. 98–115.

Barber, B. R. (1984) *Strong Democracy* (Berkeley: University of California Press).

Barker, E. (1951) *Essays on Government* (Oxford: Clarendon).

Barry, B. (1965) *Political Argument* (London: Routledge & Kegan Paul).

Barry, B. and Goodin, R. E. (eds) (1992) *Free Movement: Ethical Issues in the Transnational Migration of People and Money* (New York and London: Harvester Wheatsheaf).

254

Beetham, D. (1993) 'Liberal Democracy and the Limits of Democratization', in D. Held (ed.), *Prospects for Democracy* (Cambridge: Polity Press), pp. 55–73.

Beetham, D. (1999) *Democracy and Human Rights* (Cambridge: Polity Press).

Beitz, C. R. (1989) *Political Equality* (Princeton: Princeton University Press).

Bellamy, R. (1994) ' "Dethroning Politics": Liberalism, Constitutionalism and Democracy in the Thought of F. A. Hayek', *British Journal of Political Science* 24:4, pp. 419–41.

Bellamy, R. (1999) *Liberalism and Pluralism: Towards a Politics of Compromise* (London and New York: Routledge).

Bentham, J. (1780) *An Introduction to the Principles of Morals and Legislation*, ed. J. H. Burns and H. L. A. Hart (London: The Athlone Press, 1970).

Bentham, Jeremy (1782) *Of Laws in General* ed. H. L. A. Hart (London: The Athlone Press, 1970).

Berlin, I. (1969) *Four Essays on Liberty* (Oxford: Oxford University Press).

Bernstein, E. (1899) *Evolutionary Socialism*, trans. E. C. Harvey (New York: Schocken Books, 1961).

Bessette, J. M. (1994) *The Mild Voice of Reason: Deliberative Democracy and American National Government* (Chicago: University of Chicago Press).

Birch, A. H. (1972) *Representation* (London: Macmillan).

Black, D. (1958) *The Theory of Committees and Elections* (Cambridge: Cambridge University Press), rptd as Black (1998), *The Theory of Committees and Elections*, ed. I. McLean *et al.* (Boston, Dordrecht and London: Kluwer).

Blackburn, R. (1995) *The Electoral System in Britain* (Basingstoke: Macmillan).

Bohman, J. (1998) 'Survey Article: The Coming of Age of Deliberative Democracy', *Journal of Political Philosophy* 6:4, pp. 400–25.

Bohman, J. and Rehg, W. (eds) (1997) *Deliberative Democracy* (Cambridge, Mass.: MIT Press).

Bowler, S. and Donovan, T. (2000) *Demanding Choices: Opinion, Voting, and Direct Democracy* (Ann Arbor: University of Michigan Press).

Bowler, S., Donovan, T. and Tolbert, C. J. (1998) *Citizens as Legislators: Direct Democracy in the United States* (Columbus: Ohio State University Press).

Braithwaite, R. B. (1953) *Scientific Explanation* (Cambridge: Cambridge University Press).

Brennan, G. and Buchanan, J. M. (1985) *The Reason of Rules* (Cambridge: Cambridge University Press).

Bryce, J. (1888) *The American Commonwealth, volume 3* (London: Macmillan).

Buchanan, J. M. and Tullock, G. (1962) *The Calculus of Consent* (Ann Arbor: University of Michigan Press).

Budge, I. (1996) *The New Challenge of Direct Democracy* (Cambridge: Polity Press).

Budge, I., Klingemann, H.-D., Volkens, A., Bara, J. and Tanenbaum, E. (2001) *Mapping Policy Preferences: Estimates for Parties, Electors, and Governments 1945–1998* (Oxford: Oxford University Press).

Burke, Edmund (1774) 'Mr Burke's Speech to the Electors of Bristol', reprinted in *Burke on Empire, Liberty, and Reform*, ed. David Bromwich (New Haven and London: Yale University Press, 2000), pp. 50–7.

Burnheim, J. (1985) *Is Democracy Possible*? (Cambridge: Polity Press).

Butler, David and Butler, Gareth (1994) *British Political Facts* (Basingstoke: Macmillan, 7th edn.).

Calhoun, J. C. (1853) *A Disquisition on Government*, ed. C. Gordon Past (Indianapolis: Bobbs-Merrill, 1953).

Canovan, Margaret (2005) *The People* (Cambridge: Polity Press).

Caro, R. A. (2003) *The Years of Lyndon Johnson: Master of the Senate* (New York: Vintage Books).

Chan, J. and Miller, D. (1991) 'Elster on Self-Realization in Politics: A Critical Note', *Ethics*, 102:1, pp. 96–102.

Coase, R. H. (1974) 'The Lighthouse in Economics', *The Journal of Law and Economics* 17: 2, pp. 357–76; rptd in R. H. Coase, *The Firm, the Market and the Law* (Chicago: University of Chicago Press, 1988), ch. 7.

Cohen, J. (1989) 'Deliberation and Democratic Legitimacy', in A. Hamlin and P. Pettit (eds), *The Good Polity* (Oxford: Basil Blackwell), pp. 17–34.

Constant, Benjamin (1819) 'The Liberty of the Ancients Compared with That of the Moderns', in Benjamin Constant, *Political Writings*, translated and edited by Biancamaria Fontana (Cambridge: Cambridge University Press).

Cronin, T. E. (1989) *Direct Democracy: The Politics of Initiative, Referendum and Recall* (Cambridge, Mass.: Harvard University Press).

Crosland, C. A. R. (1956) *The Future of Socialism* (London: Jonathan Cape).

Crouch, C. (2004) *Post-Democracy* (Cambridge: Polity Press).

Dahl, Robert A. (1956) *A Preface to Democratic Theory* (Chicago: University of Chicago Press).

Dahl, Robert A. (1970) *After the Revolution?* (New Haven: Yale University Press).

Dahl, Robert A. (1989) *Democracy and Its Critics* (New Haven and London: Yale University Press).

Dahl, Robert A. (1998) *On Democracy* (New Haven and London: Yale University Press).

Dahl, Robert A. and Tufte, Edward R. (1972) *Size and Democracy* (Stanford: Stanford University Press).

Daniels, N. (1985) *Just Health Care* (Cambridge: Cambridge University Press).

Davie, G. (1963) *The Democratic Intellect* (Edinburgh: Edinburgh University Press).

Davies, Stella, Elizabeth, Susan, Hanley, Bec, New, Bill and Sang, Bob (1998) *Ordinary Wisdom: Reflection on an Experiment in Citizenship and Health* (London: King's Fund).

Diamond, L. and Plattner, M. F. (eds) (1996) *The Global Resurgence of Democracy*, 2nd edn (Baltimore and London: The Johns Hopkins University Press).

Dicey, A. V. (1915) *Introduction to the Study of the Law of the Constitution*, 8th edn (London: Macmillan).

Dobson, Andrew (1997) 'Representative Democracy and the Environment', in W. M. Lafferty and J. Meadowcroft (eds) *Democracy and the Environment: Problems and Prospects* (Cheltenham: Edward Elgar), pp. 124–39.

Downs, A. (1957) *An Economic Theory of Democracy* (New York: Harper and Row).

Dryzek, John S. (1996) 'Political and Ecological Communication', in F. Mathews (ed.), *Ecology and Democracy* (London: Frank Cass), pp. 13–30.

Dryzek, John S. (2000) *Deliberative Democracy and Beyond: Liberals, Critics, Contestations* (Oxford: Oxford University Press).

Dryzek, John S. (2001) 'Legitimacy and Economy in Deliberative Democracy', *Political Theory*, 29:5, pp. 651–69.

Duverger, M. (1964) *Political Parties*, trans. B. and R. North, 4th edn (London: Methuen).

Dworkin, R. (1985) *A Matter of Principle* (Oxford: Clarendon Press).

Dworkin, R. (1986) *Law's Empire* (London: Fontana).

Dworkin, R. (1996) *Freedom's Law* (Cambridge, Mass.: Harvard University Press).

Dworkin, Ronald (2000) *Sovereign Virtue: The Theory and Practice of Equality* (Cambridge, Mass.: Harvard University Press).

Eckersley, R. (2000) 'Deliberative Democracy, Ecological Representation and Risk', in M. Saward (ed.), *Democratic Innovation: Deliberation, Representation and Association* (London and New York: Routledge), pp. 117–32.

Elster, Jon (1983) *Sour Grapes: Studies in the Subversion of Rationality* (Cambridge: Cambridge University Press).

Elster, J. (1997) 'The Market and the Forum: Three Varieties of Political Theory', in J. Bohman and W. Rehg (eds) (1997) *Deliberative Democracy* (Cambridge, Mass.: MIT Press), pp. 3–33.

Elster, J. (ed.) (1998) *Deliberative Democracy* (Cambridge: Cambridge University Press).

Ely, J. H. (1981) *Democracy and Distrust* (Cambridge: Cambridge University Press).

Engels, Frederick (1892) *Socialism: Utopian and Scientific*, reprinted in *Marx/Engels Selected Works in One Volume* (London: Lawrence & Wishart), pp. 375–428.

Featherstone, K. (1994) 'Jean Monnet and the "Democratic Deficit" in the European Union', *Journal of Common Market Studies*, 32:2, pp. 149–70.

Federalist Papers (1787) ed. C. Rossiter (New York: New American Library, 1961).

Feinberg, J. (1970) 'The Nature and Value of Rights', *The Journal of Value Inquiry*, 4, pp. 243–57; rptd in J. Feinberg, *Rights, Justice and the Bounds of Liberty* (Princeton: Princeton University Press, 1980), pp. 143–55.

Feinberg, J. (1973) *Social Philosophy* (Englewood Cliffs, Prentice-Hall, Inc.).

Feinberg, J. (1984) *Harm to Others. The Moral Limits of the Criminal Law, volume 1* (New York and Oxford: Oxford University Press).

Finer, S. E. (1970) *Comparative Government* (Harmondsworth: Penguin).

Finley, M. I. (1985) *Democracy Ancient and Modern* (London: Hogarth Press, second edition).

Finnis, John (1980) *Natural Law and Natural Rights* (Oxford: Clarendon Press).

Fishkin, James S. (1991) *Democracy and Deliberation: New Directions for Democratic Reform* (New Haven and London: Yale University Press).

Fishkin, James S. (1995) *The Voice of the People: Public Opinion and Democracy* (New Haven and London: Yale University Press).

Fishkin, James S. and Laslett, Peter (eds) (2003) *Debating Deliberative Democracy* (Oxford: Blackwell).

Flora, Peter, Kuhnle, Stein and Urwin, Derek (eds) (1999) *State Formation, Nation-Building, and Mass Politics in Europe: The Theory of Stein Rokkan* (Oxford: Oxford University Press).

Føllesdal, Andreas (1998) 'Subsidiarity', *Journal of Political Philosophy* 6:2, pp. 190–218.

Freeman, M. (1996) 'Human Rights, Democracy and "Asian Values"', *The Pacific Review*, 9:3, pp. 352–66.

Fukuyama, F. (1989) 'The End of History?' *The National Interest*, 16, pp. 3–18.

Fukayama, F. (2006) *After the Neocons: America at the Crossroads* (London: Profile Books).

Gallie, W. B. (1955–66) 'Essentially Contested Concepts', *Proceedings of the Aristotelian Society*, 56, pp. 167–98.

Gamble, A. (1990) 'Theories of British Politics', *Political Studies*, 38:3, pp. 404–20.

Gellner, Ernest (1983) *Nations and Nationalism* (Oxford: Blackwell).

Golden, M. A. (2003) 'Electoral Connections: The Effects of the Personal Vote on Political Patronage, Bureaucracy and Legislation in Postwar Italy', *British Journal of Political Science*, 33:2, pp. 189–212.

Goodin, R. E. (1992) *Green Political Theory* (Cambridge: Polity Press).

Goodin, R. E. (1996) 'Inclusion and Exclusion' *Archives Européennes de Sociologie*, 37:2. pp. 343–71.

Goodin, R. E. (1996a) 'Enfranchising the Earth and Its Alternatives', *Political Studies*, 44:5, pp. 835–49.

Goodin, R. E. (2003) *Reflective Democracy* (Oxford: Oxford University Press).

Goodin, R. E. (2004) 'Representing Diversity', *British Journal of Political Science*, 34: 3, pp. 453–68.

Goodwin, Barbara (1978) *Social Science and Utopia. Nineteenth-Century Models of Social Harmony* (Sussex: The Harvester Press).

Goodwin, Barbara and Taylor, Keith (1982) *The Politics of Utopia* (London: Hutchinson).

Graham, K. (1986) *The Battle of Democracy* (Brighton: Wheatsheaf Books).

Grofman, B. and Lijphart, A. (eds) (1986) *Electoral Laws and Their Political Consequences* (New York: Agathon).

Gutmann, A. and Thompson, D. (1996) *Democracy and Disagreement* (Cambridge, Mass.: Harvard University Press).

Gutmann, A. and Thompson, D. (2004) *Why Deliberative Democracy?* (Princeton and Oxford: Princeton University Press).

Habermas, Jürgen (1985) *The Philosophical Discourse of Modernity*, translated by Frederick Lawrence (Cambridge: Polity Press).

Habermas, Jürgen (1996) *Between Facts and Norms*, translated by William Rehg(Cambridge: Polity Press).

Hacking, I. (1992) 'World-Making by Kind-Making: Child Abuse for Example', in M. Douglas and D. Hull (eds), *How Classification Works* (Edinburgh: Edinburgh University Press), pp. 180–238.

Halifax, Marquess of (1699) *The Character of a Trimmer*, in J. P. Kenyon (ed.), *Halifex: Complete Works* (Harmondworth: Penguin, 1969).

Hansen, Mogens Herman (1991) *The Athenian Democracy in the Age of Demosthenes. Structure, Principles, and Ideology* translated by J.A. Crook (London: Bristol Classics Press, 1999 edition).

Hardin, R. (1999) *Liberalism, Constitutionalism and Democracy* (Oxford: Oxford University Press).

Hargreaves Heap, Shaun, Hollis, Martin, Lyons, Bruce, Sugden, Robert and Weale, Albert (1992) *The Theory of Choice: A Critical Guide* (Oxford: Blackwell).

Hart, H. L. A. (1961) *The Concept of Law* (Oxford: Clarendon Press).

Hart, J. (1992) *Proportional Representation: Critics of the British Electoral System 1820–1945* (Oxford: Clarendon Press).

Hayek, F. A. (1973) *Law, Legislation and Liberty, Volume 1, Rules and Order* (London: Routledge).

Hayward, B. M. (1996) 'The Greening of Participatory Democracy', in F. Mathews (ed.), *Ecology and Democracy* (London: Frank Cass), pp. 215–36.

Hayward, J. (1996) 'Has European Unification by Stealth a Future?', in J. Hayward (ed.), *Elitism, Populism, and European Politics* (Oxford: Clarendon), pp. 252–7.

Hegel, G. W. F. (1807) *The Phenomenology of Mind*, trans. with introduction and notes J. B. Baillie (London: George Allen & Unwin Ltd, 1949).

Hegel, G. W. F. (1956 edn) *The Philosophy of History* (New York: Dover Publications).

Held, D. (1995) *Democracy and the Global Order* (Cambridge: Polity Press).

Held, D. (1996) *Models of Democracy*, 2nd edn (Cambridge: Polity Press).

Held, David (1998) 'Democracy and Globalization' in Daniele Archibugi, David Held and Martin Köhler (eds) *Re-Imagining Political Community. Studies in Cosmopolitan Democracy* (Cambridge: Polity Press), pp. 11–27.

Held, D., McGrew, A., Goldblatt, D. and Perraton, J. (1999) *Global Transformations. Politics, Economics and Culture* (Cambridge: Polity Press).

Hesse, M. (1982) 'Science and Objectivity', in J. B. Thompson and D. Held (eds), *Habermas. Critical Debates* (London and Basingstoke: Macmillan), pp. 98–115.

Hiebert, J. L. (2005) 'Interpreting A Bill of Rights: The Importance of Legislative Rights Review', *British Journal of Political Science*, 35:2, pp. 235–55.

Hirsch, F. (1977) *The Social Limits to Growth* (London and Henley: Routledge Kegan Paul).

Hobbes, T. (1651) *Leviathan*, ed. with introduction M. Oakeshott (Oxford: Basil Blackwell, n.d.).

Hohfeld, W. N. (1923) *Fundamental Legal Conceptions* (New Haven: Yale University Press).

Holmes, S. (1988) 'Gag Rules or the Politics of Omission', in J. Elster and R. Slagstad (eds), *Constitutionalism and Democracy* (Cambridge: Cambridge University Press).

Honoré, A. M. (1961) 'Ownership' in A.G. Guest (ed.), *Oxford Essays in Jurisprudence* (Oxford: Oxford University Press), pp. 107–47.

Hume, David (1739–40) *A Treatise of Human Nature*, edited by Ernest C. Mossner (Harmondsworth: Penguin, 1969).

Hume, David (1742) 'On the Independency of Parliament', in *Essays, Moral, Political, and Literary, Vol I*, ed. T. H. Green and T. H. Grose (London: Longmans, Green & Co., 1889 edn), pp. 117–22.

Huntington, Samuel P. (1991) *The Third Wave: Democratization in the Late Twentieth Century* (London: University of Oklahoma Press).

Hyland, J. L. (1995) *Democratic Theory: The Philosophical Foundations* (Manchester: Manchester University Press).

Jones, P. (1988) 'Intense Preferences, Strong Beliefs and Democratic Decision-Making', *Political Studies*, 36:1, pp. 7–29.

Jones, P. (1994) *Rights* (Basingstoke: Macmillan).

Kenny, A. (1975) *Will, Freedom and Power* (Oxford: Basil Blackwell).

King, A. (1997) *Running Scared* (New York: The Free Press).

King, A. (2001) *Does the United Kingdom Still Have a Constitution?* (London: Sweet & Maxwell).

Kitschelt, H. (1986) 'Political Opportunity Structures and Political Protest: Anti-Nuclear Movements in Four Democracies', *British Journal of Political Science*, 14:1, pp. 57–85.

Kjær, A. M. (2004) *Governance* (Cambridge: Polity Press).

Knei-Paz, B. (1978) *The Social and Political Thought of Leon Trotsky* (Oxford: Clarendon Press).

Lakoff, S. (1996) *Democracy: History, Theory, Practice* (Boulder: Westview Press).

Landman, T. (2005) 'The Political Science of Human Rights', *British Journal of Political Science*, 35:3, pp. 549–72.

Lane, D. (2005) *Berlusconi's Shadow: Crime, Justice and the Pursuit of Power* (London: Penguin Books).

Larmore, C. E. (1987) *Patterns of Moral Complexity* (Cambridge: Cambridge University Press).

Leftwich, A. (1983) *Redefining Politics* (London and New York: Methuen).

Lijphart, A. (1968) *The Politics of Accommodation: Pluralism and Democracy in the Netherlands* (Berkeley and Los Angeles: University of California Press).

Lijphart, A. (1977) *Democracy in Plural Societies* (New Haven and London: Yale University Press).

Lijphart, A. (1984) *Democracies: Patterns of Majoritarian and Consensus Government in Twenty-One Countries* (New Haven and London: Yale University Press).

Lijphart, A. (1994) *Electoral Systems and Party Systems* (Oxford: Oxford University Press).

Lijphart, A. (1997) 'Unequal Participation: Democracy's Unresolved Dilemma', *American Political Science Review*, 91:1, pp. 1–14.

Lijphart, A. (1999) *Patterns of Democracy: Government Forms and Performance in Thirty-Six Countries* (New Haven and London: Yale University Press).

Lipset, S. M. (1963) *Political Man* (London: Mercury Books).

Lively, Jack and John Rees, *Utilitarian Logic and Politics* (Oxford: Clarendon Press, 1978).

Locke, J. (1690) *Two Treatises of Government*, ed. P. Laslett (New York: Mentor, 1965).

Lucas, Caroline and Woodin, Mike (2000) *The Euro or A Sustainable Future for Britain?* (London: New Europe).

Lucas, J. R. (1966) *The Principles of Politics* (Oxford: Clarendon Press).

Lukes, S. (1982) 'Of Gods and Demons: Habermas and Practical Reason', in J. B. Thompson and D. Held (eds), *Habermas: Critical Debates* (London and Basingstoke: Macmillan), pp. 134–48.

Luskin, R. C., Fishkin, J. S. and Jowell, R. (2002) 'Considered Opinions: Deliberative Polling in Britain', *British Journal of Political Science*, 32:3, pp. 455–87.

Macaulay, T. B. (1829) 'Mill on Government', rptd in J. Lively and J. Rees, *Utilitarian Logic and Politics* (Oxford: Clarendon Press, 1978).

Macaulay, T. B. (1906) *The History of England from the Accession of James II* (London: J. M. Dent).

MacCormick, Neil (1989) 'Unrepentant Gradualism', in O. W. Edwards (ed.), *A Claim of Right for Scotland* (Edinburgh: Polygon), pp. 99–109.

MacCormick, Neil (1999) *Questioning Sovereignty. Law, State, and Nation in the European Commonwealth* (Oxford: Oxford University Press).

Macedo, Stephen (ed.) (1999) *Deliberative Politics: Essays on Democracy and Disagreement* (New York and Oxford: Oxford University Press).

Mackie, Gerry (2003) *Democracy Defended* (Cambridge: Cambridge University Press).

Macmillan, H. (1938) *The Middle Way* (London: Macmillan).

Macpherson, C. B. (1966) *The Real World of Democracy* (Oxford: Clarendon Press).

Macpherson, C. B. (1977) *The Life and Times of Liberal Democracy* (Oxford: Oxford University Press).

Madison, J. (1787) 'Federalist Paper No. 51', in *The Federalist Papers*, ed. with introduction C. Rossiter (New York: The New American Library Inc., 1961 edn).

Maier, C. S. (1992) 'Democracy since the French Revolution', in J. Dunn (ed.), *Democracy: The Unfinished Journey* (Oxford: Oxford University Press), pp. 125–53.

Manin, B. (1997) *The Principles of Representative Government* (Cambridge: Cambridge University Press).

Mansbridge, Jane J. (1980) *Beyond Adversary Democracy* (New York: Basic Books).

Mansbridge, J. (2003) 'Rethinking Representation', *American Political Science Review*, 97:4, pp. 515–28.

Mapel, D. R. (1990) 'Civil Association and the Idea of Contingency', *Political Theory*, 18:3, pp. 392–410.

Marx, Karl (1852) *The Eighteenth Brumaire of Louis Bonaparte*, reprinted in Karl Marx, *Surveys from Exile*, edited David Fernbach (Harmondsworth: Penguin, 1973).

May, K. O. (1952) 'A Set of Independent, Necessary and Sufficient Conditions for Simple Majority Decision', *Econometrica*, 20, pp. 680–4.

Mayhew, D. R. (2002) *Electoral Realignments: A Critique of an American Genre* (New Haven and London: Yale University Press).

McDonald, Michael D., Mendes, Silvia M. and Budge, Ian (2004) 'What Are Elections For? Conferring the Median Mandate', *British Journal of Political Science*, 34:1, pp.1–26.

McDonald, Michael D. and Budge, Ian (2005) *Elections, Parties, Democracy. Conferring the Median Mandate* (Oxford: Oxford University Press).

McLean, I. and Hewitt, F. (1994) *Condorcet: Foundations of Social Choice and Political Theory* (Aldershot: Edward Elgar).

McLean, I. (2006) 'The Dimensionality of Party Ideologies', in J. Bara and A. Weale (eds), *Democratic Politics and Party Competition Essays in Honour of Ian Budge* (London and New York: Routledge), pp. 127–42.

Medearis, J. (2005) 'Social Movements and Deliberative Democratic Theory', *British Journal of Political Science*, 35:1, pp. 53–75.

Menzel, P. T. (1983) *Medical Costs, Moral Choices: A Philosophy of Health Care Economics in America* (New Haven and London: Yale University Press).

Mill, James (1820) *Government*, in Terence Ball (ed.), *James Mill: Political Writings* (Cambridge: Cambridge University Press).

Mill, John Stuart. (1859) *On Liberty*, rptd in J. Gray (ed.), *John Stuart Mill On Liberty and Other Essays* (Oxford: Oxford University Press, 1991).

Mill, John Stuart (1861a) *Considerations on Representative Government*, rptd in J. Gray (ed.), *John Stuart Mill On Liberty and Other Essays* (Oxford: Oxford University Press, 1991).

Mill, John Stuart. (1861b) *Utilitarianism*, in J. Gray (ed.), *John Stuart Mill On Liberty and Other Essays* (Oxford: Oxford University Press, 1991).

Miller, D. (1983) 'The Competitive Model of Democracy', in G. Duncan (ed.), *Democratic Theory and Practice* (Cambridge: Cambridge University Press), pp. 133–55.

Mishler, W. and Sheehan, R. S. (1993) 'The Supreme Court as a Countermajoritarian Institution? The Impact of Public Opinion on Supreme Court Decisions', *American Political Science Review*, 87:1, pp. 87–101.

Moore, G. E. (1903) *Principia Ethica* (Cambridge: Cambridge University Press).

Moravcsik, A. (2003) 'In Defence of the "Democratic Deficit": Reassessing Legitimacy in the European Union', in J. H. H. Weiler, I. Begg and J. Peterson (eds), *Integration in an Expanding European Union: Reassessing the Fundamentals* (Oxford: Blackwell), pp. 77–97.

Mouffe, C. (2000) *The Democratic Paradox* (London: Verso).

Nagel, J. H. (1993) 'Populism, Heresthetics and Political Stability: Richard Seddon and the Art of Majority Rule', *British Journal of Political Science*, 23:2, pp. 139–74.

Nagel, J. H. (1998) 'Social Choice in a Pluritarian Democracy: The Politics of Market Liberalization in New Zealand', *British Journal of Political Science*, 28:2, pp. 225–70.

Nagel, J. H. (2006) Occam No, Archimedes Yes', in J. Bara and A. Weale (eds), *Democratic Politics and Party Competition: Essays in Honour of Ian Budge* (London and New York: Routledge), pp. 143–58.

Nagel, T. (1991) *Equality and Partiality* (New York and Oxford: Oxford University Press).

Norris, Pippa (ed.) (1999) *Critical Citizens: Global Support for Democratic Government* (Oxford: Oxford University Press).

Norris, P. and Lovenduski, J. (1993) '"If Only More Candidates Came Forward": Supply-Side Explanations of Candidate Selection in Britain', *British Journal of Political Science*, 23:3, pp. 373–408.

North, D. (1990) *Institutions, Institutional Change and Economic Performance* (Cambridge: Cambridge University Press).

Nozick, R. (1974) *Anarchy, the State and Utopia* (Oxford: Basil Blackwell).

Nozick, R. (1989) *The Examined Life: Philosophical Meditations* (New York: Simon & Schuster).

Nursey-Bray, P. (1983) 'Consensus and Community: The Theory of African One-Party Democracy', in G. Duncan (ed.), *Democratic Theory and Practice* (Cambridge: Cambridge University Press), pp. 96–111.

Oakeshott, M. (1975) *On Human Conduct* (Oxford: Clarendon Press).

O'Flynn, I. (2006) *Deliberative Democracy and Divided Societies* (Edinburgh: Edinburgh University Press).

O'Leary, K. (2007) *Saving Democracy: The Citizen Assembly in America* (Stanford: Stanford University Press).

Olson, Mancur (1982) *The Rise and Decline of Nations* (New Haven and London: Yale University Press).

Olson, Mancur (2000) *Power and Prosperity. Outgrowing Communist and Capitalist Dictatorships* (New York: Basic Books).

Ordeshook, P. C. (1986) *Game Theory and Political Theory* (Cambridge: Cambridge University Press).

Parry, G., Moyser, G. and Day, N. (1992) *Political Participation and Democracy in Britain* (Cambridge: Cambridge University Press).

Paterson, W. E. (1989) 'Environmental Politics', in G. Smith, W. E. Paterson and P. H. Merkl (eds), *Developments in West German Politics* (Basingstoke: Macmillan), pp. 267–88.

Peirce, C. S. (1934) 'The Fixation of Belief', in *Collected Papers of Charles Sanders Peirce volumes v and vi*, ed. C. Hartshorne and P. Weiss (Cambridge, Mass.: Harvard University Press), pp. 223–47.

Pennock, J. Roland (1979) *Democratic Political Theory* (Princeton: Princeton University Press).

Perelman, C. (1963) *The Idea of Justice and the Problem of Argument* (London: Routledge).

Phillips, A. (1993) *Democracy and Difference* (Cambridge: Polity Press).

Phillips, A. (1995) *The Politics of Presence* (Oxford: Clarendon Press).

Pitkin, H. F. (1967) *The Concept of Representation* (Berkeley: University of California Press).

Plamenatz, J. (1963) *Man and Society, volume 1* (London: Longman).

Plamenatz, J. P. (1968) *Consent, Freedom and Political Obligation*, 2nd edn (London: Oxford University Press).

Plant, Raymond (1973) *Hegel* (London: George Allen & Unwin).

Plato, *The Republic*, trans. F. M. Cornford (Oxford: Clarendon Press).

Popper, K. R. (1945a) *The Open Society and Its Enemies, volume 1 Plato* (London: Routledge & Kegan Paul).

Popper, K. R. (1945b) *The Open Society and Its Enemies, volume 2 Hegel and Marx* (London: Routledge & Kegan Paul).

Popper, K. R. (1972) *Objective Knowledge: An Evolutionary Approach* (Oxford: Clarendon Press).

Powell, Jr, G. Bingham (1982) *Contemporary Democracies. Participation, Stability, and Violence* (Cambridge, Mass.: Harvard University Press).

Powell Jr, G. Bingham (1989) 'Constitutional Design and Electoral Control', *Journal of Theoretical Politics*, 1:2, pp. 107–30.

Powell Jr, G. Bingham (2000) *Elections as Instruments of Democracy. Majoritarian and Proportional Visions* (New Haven and London: Yale University Press).

Pulzer, Peter G. J. (1975) *Political Representation and Elections in Britain,* 3rd edn (London: George Allen & Unwin).

Putnam, Robert D. (1988) 'Diplomacy and Domestic Politics: The Logic of Two-Level Games', *International Organization* 42:3, pp. 427–60.

Putnam, Robert D. (1993) *Making Democracy Work: Civic Traditions in Modern Italy* (Princeton: Princeton University Press).

Putnam, Robert D. (2000) *Bowling Alone: The Collapse and Revival of American Community* (New York: Simon and Schuster).

Rae, D. W. (1975) 'The Limits of Consensual Decision', *American Political Science Review*, 69, pp. 1270–94.

Rawls, J. (1996) *Political Liberalism* (New York: Columbia University Press).

Rawls, John (1999a) *A Theory of Justice* (Oxford: Oxford University Press).

Rawls, John (1999b) *The Law of Peoples* (Cambridge, Mass.: Harvard University Press).

Raz, J. (1986) *The Morality of Freedom* (Oxford: Clarendon Press).

Raz, Joseph (1990) *Practical Reason and Norms* (Princeton, New Jersey: Princeton University Press).

Reeve, A. (1986) *Property* (Basingstoke: Macmillan).

Richardson, H. S. (2002) *Democratic Autonomy: Public Reasoning about the Ends of Policy* (Oxford: Oxford University Press).

Riker, W. H. (1982) *Liberalism against Populism* (San Francisco: Freeman & Co.).

Riker, W. H. (1986) *The Art of Political Manipulation* (New Haven and London: Yale University Press).

Robertson, D. (2006) 'On the Dimensionality of Political Space and Its Inhabitants', in J. Bara and A. Weale (eds), *Democratic Politics and Party Competition: Essays in Honour of Ian Budge* (London and New York: Routledge), pp. 159–78.

Rogowski, R. (1981) 'Representation in Political Theory and Law', *Ethics*, 91:3, pp. 395–430.

Rorty, R. (1989) *Contingency, Irony, and Solidarity* (Cambridge: Cambridge University Press).

Rousseau, J. -J. (1762) *The Social Contract*, trans. G. D. H. Cole (London: J. M. Dent and Sons, 1973).

Royal Commission on Environmental Pollution (1998) *Twenty-First Report: Setting Environmental Standards*, Cm 4053 (London: The Stationery Office).

Rueschemeyer, D. Stephens, E. Huber and J. D. Stephens (1992) *Capitalist Development and Democracy* (Cambridge: Polity Press).

Runciman, W. G. (1969) *Social Science and Political Theory* (Cambridge: Cambridge University Press).

Salmon, W. C. (1973) *Logic* (Englewood Cliffs: Prentice-Hall).

Samuelson, P. A. (1954) 'The Pure Theory of Public Expenditure', *Review of Economics and Statistics*, 36, pp. 387–9.

Sanders, L. (1997) 'Against Deliberation', *Political Theory*, 25:3, pp. 347–76.

Saward, Michael (1998) *The Terms of Democracy* (Cambridge: Polity Press).

Scanlon, T. M. (1982) 'Contractualism and Utilitarianism', in A. Sen and B. Williams (eds), *Utilitarianism and Beyond* (Cambridge: Cambridge University Press), pp. 103–28.

Scharpf, F. W. (1988) 'The Joint-Decision Trap: Lessons from German Federalism and European Union', *Public Administration*, 66:3, pp. 229–78.

Scharpf, F. W. (1989) 'Decision Rules, Decision Styles, and Policy Choices', *Journal of Theoretical Politics*, 1, pp. 149–76.

Scharpf, F. W. (1999) *Governing in Europe: Effective and Democratic?* (Oxford: Oxford University Press).

Schattschneider, E. E. (1960) *The Semi-Sovereign People: A Realistic View of Democracy in America* (New York: Holt, Rinehart & Winston).

Schumpeter, J. A. (1954) *Capitalism, Socialism and Democracy* (London: Allen & Unwin, 1st edn, 1943).

Sen, Amartya K. (1970) *Collective Choice and Social Welfare* (San Francisco: Holden-Day, Inc.).

Sen, Amartya K. (1977) 'Rational Fools: A Critique of the Behavioural Foundations of Economic Theory', *Philosophy and Public Affairs*, 6, pp. 317–44; rptd in Amartya Sen, *Choice, Welfare and Measurement* (Oxford: Basil Blackwell, 1982), pp. 84–106.

Shepsle, K. A. (1979) 'Institutional Arrangements and Equilibrium in Multidimensional Voting Models', *American Journal of Political Science*, 23, pp. 27–59.

Shklar, J. N. (1976) *Freedom and Independence: A Study of the Political Ideas of Hegel's Phenomenology of Mind* (Cambridge: Cambridge University Press).

Sidgwick Henry (1891) *The Elements of Politics* (London: Macmillan).

Sidgwick, Henry (1901) *The Methods of Ethics*, 6th edn (London: Macmillan).

Simon, H. (1983) *Reason in Human Affairs* (Oxford: Basil Blackwell).

Skinner, Q. (1974) 'Some Problems in the Analysis of Political Thought and Action', *Political Theory*, 2:3, pp. 277–303; rptd in J. Tully (ed.), *Meaning and Context: Quentin Skinner and His Critics* (Cambridge: Polity Press), pp. 97–118.

Skinner, Q. (1978) *The Foundations of Modern Political Thought: The Age of Reformation* (Cambridge: Cambridge University Press).

Smith, A. (1776) *An Inquiry into the Nature and Causes of The Wealth of Nations, two volumes*, (Indianapolis: Liberty Classics).

Smith, R. M. (2003) *Stories of Peoplehood* (Cambridge: Cambridge University Press).

Steiner, J. (1971) 'The Principles of Majority and Proportionality', *British Journal of Political Science*, 1:1, pp. 63–70.

Steiner, Jürg, Bächtiger, André, Spörndli, Markus and Steenbergen, Marco R. (2004) *Deliberative Politics in Action* (Cambridge: Cambridge University Press).

Stimson, J. A., MacKuen, M. B. and Erikson, R. S. (1995) 'Dynamic Representation', *American Political Science Review*, 89:3, pp. 543–65.

Sunstein, C. R. (1988) 'Constitutions and Democracy: An Epilogue', in J. Elster and R. Slagstad (eds), *Constitutionalism and Democracy* (Cambridge: Cambridge University Press), pp. 327–56.

Sunstein, C. R. (1991) 'Preferences and Politics', *Philosophy and Public Affairs*, 20:1, pp. 3–34.

Taylor, M. (1976) *Anarchy and Cooperation* (London: John Wiley & Sons).

Thompson, D. F. (1970) *The Democratic Citizen* (Cambridge: Cambridge University Press).

Thucydides, [1954] *History of the Peloponnesian War*, trans. R. Warner, introduction M. I. Finley (Harmondsworth: Penguin).

Tocqueville, A. de (1835) *Democracy in America*, vol. 1, ed. P. Bradley (New York: Vintage Books, 1945).

Tribe, L. (1988) *American Constitutional Law*, 2nd edn (Mineola, NY: Foundation Press).

Urbinati, N. (2006) *Representative Democracy. Principles and Genealogy* (Chicago and London: University of Chicago Press).

Waldron, J. (1999a) *Law and Disagreement* (Oxford: Oxford University Press).

Waldron, J. (1999b) *The Dignity of Legislation* (Cambridge: Cambridge University Press).

Waltz, Kenneth N. (1979) *Theory of International Politics* (New York: McGraw-Hill Publishing Company).

Weale, Albert (1978) *Equality and Social Policy* (London: Routledge & Kegan Paul).

Weale, Albert (1992) *The New Politics of Pollution* (Manchester: Manchester University Press).

Weale, Albert (1998) 'From Contracts to Pluralism?', in P. J. Kelly (ed.), *Impartiality, Neutrality and Justice* (Edinburgh: Edinburgh University Press), pp. 9–34.

Weale, Albert (2001) 'Can We Democratize Decisions on Risk and the Environment?', *Government and Opposition*, 36:3, pp. 355–78.

Weale, Albert (2004) 'Contractarian Theory, Deliberative Democracy and General Agreement', in K. Dowding, R. E. Goodin and C. Pateman (eds), *Justice and Democracy. Essays for Brian Barry* (Cambridge: Cambridge University Press), pp. 79–96.

Weale, Albert (2005) *Democratic Citizenship and the European Union* (Manchester and New York: Manchester University Press).

Weber, M. (1947) *The Theory of Social and Economic Organization*, trans. A. M. Henderson and T. Parsons (New York: Oxford University Press).

Williams, B. (1973) 'A Critique of Utilitarianism', in J. J. C. Smart and B. Williams, *Utilitarianism For and Against* (Cambridge: Cambridge University Press), pp. 77–150.

Williams, Philip M. (1964) *Crisis and Compromise. Politics in the Fourth Republic* (London: Longman).

Wolff, R. P. (1970) *In Defense of Anarchism* (New York: Harper Colophon Books).

Woodward, L. (1962) *The Age of Reform 1815–1870* (Oxford: Clarendon Press).

Woolf, V. (1929) *A Room of One's Own* (Harmondsworth: Penguin, 1945).

Young, I. M. (1989) 'Polity and Group Difference: A Critique of the Ideal of Universal Citizenship', *Ethics*, 99:2, pp. 250–74.

Young, I. M. (2000) *Inclusion and Democracy* (Oxford: Oxford University Press).

Young, O. (1989) *International Cooperation: Building Regimes for Natural Resources and the Environment* (Ithaca, NY: Cornell University Press).

Index